Greatness is **NOW**HERE

First Edition: November 2021

Cover and interior design by Coverkitchen

Illustrations by Léopoldine Vittori

ISBN: 978 1 7378443 0 3

Published by MRT Books

www.melkartrouhana.com

Greatness is **NOW**HERE

Three Principles to Jazz up Your Culture, Pep up Your
People, and Spice up Your Customer Experience

Melkart Rouhana

Foreword by **Bob Kharazmi**, Senior Vice President,
U.S. Luxury Brands, Marriott International, Inc.

Afterword by **George Wills**, President & Managing Director,
Porsche Latin America, Inc.

MRT
BOOKS

Praise for *Greatness is NOWHERE*

"Audacious, insightful and thought-provoking, *Greatness is NOWHERE* is a must-read as it brilliantly and pragmatically shows, through real examples and experiences, the power of culture, leadership and the customer experience—and more so, how to accomplish it! The wisdom and tools featured in this book will enable you to create an organization of excellence."

– **Horst Schulze, Founder, Former President & COO**
of The Ritz-Carlton Hotel Company,
Founder & Former CEO of Capella Hotel Group

"A riveting read! Melkart's passion and extensive knowledge of the intricacies of organizational culture, exceptional service, and leadership are evident from cover to cover. *Greatness is NOWHERE* is brimming with practical golden nuggets, activities, and inspiring designs to create a healthy organizational culture leading to engaged employees and delighted customers."

– **Diana R. Oreck, NetJets Vice President,**
Service Representatives and Philanthropy,
Former Vice President, The Ritz-Carlton Leadership Center

"Should your organization be looking for the recipe to finally understand the connection between purposeful leadership and service excellence, Melkart has written a fabulous book to cook this tasteful meal. Spiced with humor and wit, this book is opening doors for finally convincing leadership in organizations and for individuals. A must read for all leadership fans."

– **Dr. Andreas Löhmer, MLitt, Director of Corporate**
Programs, Executive School of Management, Technology and Law
(ES-HSG), University of St. Gallen (HSG), Switzerland

"Melkart has masterfully harnessed his high-octane energy and passion in written form. If you have borne witness to Melkart in full flight, you will know that it is no easy task. I read it in one sitting—nowhere did my attention drop off!"

**– Shelley Perkins, Chief Talent & Culture Officer,
Rosewood Hotel Group**

"Melkart has found an impressive and inspirational way to articulate practical insights for achieving greatness that will transform the way organizations think about how they do business. Whether you're a CEO or an entrepreneur, you will be energized for more effective leadership if you embrace the principles advanced in this book."

**– Andre Bisasor, Founder & Chairman,
Negotiation & Leadership Conference at Harvard University;
Founding President, Harvard Negotiation Alumni Society;
President, Institute for Negotiation Leadership & Diplomacy**

"Melkart's *Greatness is NOWHERE* harnesses how leaders create purposeful workplaces in a stronger experiential economy. Through Melkart's wisdom and insights, you feel his enthusiasm for people discovering greatness in themselves and others. This actionable read is for those who wish to inspire the hearts, souls and minds of their teams."

– Kimberly Rath, MBA, Co-Founder & Co-Chair, Talent Plus

"In this sensational book, Melkart combines his exciting concepts and learnings in an easy-to-read and truly impactful way. The title says it all, and I find the book's message vital, especially as we come out of a global crisis that has impacted the world of hospitality. The principles in this book will guide your thinking on how to focus on recovery with a strong positive aim at enabling greatness!"

**– Marc Dardenne, Chief Operating Officer,
Accor Europe Luxury Brands**

"I thoroughly enjoyed reading the book and my head is now spinning with ideas, plans and activities. If a non-fiction book can be described as a "page turner," this is certainly that book. An invaluable leader's handbook—for reading in its entirety or dipping in and out of—for motivation, ideas, and practical tools and tips. It's aligned to a Masters dissertation in leadership, making the research and writings of academics applicable, drawing upon personal experiences and sharing hand-picked examples of successful company—while being written in such a way that a leader, at any level, will be educated, inspired, and given the tools and confidence to lead any team."

– Jacqueline Moyse, Vice President of Organizational Development, Mandarin Oriental Hotel Group

"Melkart's *Greatness is NOWHERE* is an eminently practical guide for every individual regardless of their role in their organization. It shares pragmatically the correlation between company culture, talent and people, and the customer journey/experience. This beautifully-written book is a masterpiece that qualifies as a real call for action to enable greatness and promote extraordinary achievements."

– Hagop Doghramadjian, Former Chief Experience Officer CEXO, Aldara Hospital and Medical Center —a partner of Henry Ford Health System

To the Tears of Beirut

You bowed in the blink of an eye.
A resilient city that refuses to die
Beirut, from the ashes
like a phoenix you will fly.

Beirut…
you are mine.

There are no limits here—
We are determined to enable greatness.

GREATNESS *is* NOW *here.*

Melkart Rouhana

Contents

PRINCIPLE 1

PRINCIPLE 2

Foreword

What is your definition of greatness?
Is greatness nowhere? Or is it now here?

When the Scottish novelist and historian John Buchan was asked about greatness, he answered, "The task of leadership is not to put greatness into humanity, but to elicit it, for the greatness is already there."[1] How true that is! Along my 40 years of leadership experience shaping the culture and the operational standards for The Ritz-Carlton, I came to this one conclusion:

Every human being is versed in greatness and leadership main purpose is to unveil the best in others.

Today's leaders and organizations must grasp that greatness is "now here" by promoting a winning culture, selecting the right people who fit the culture, and leading with the ideal of service. Question is, how do you make this happen? This question is explored in Melkart Rouhana's book, *Greatness is NOWHERE*, which is filled with treasurable tools, significant examples, inspirational stories, golden nuggets, and alluring illustrations.

When Melkart Rouhana asked me to write the foreword for *Greatness is NOWHERE*, I was honored and thrilled. Honored because as one of my colleagues for many years, together we cultivated and strengthened a culture of service excellence in many of The Ritz-Carlton Hotels around the world, long before Melkart successfully founded his organization, MRT Consultants. And thrilled because it's time to put Melkart's sauce—his philosophy and operational model—along with his unending passion, boundless devotion, and unshakeable drive in a book that will ultimately enrich every reader yearning for greatness.

In *Greatness is* NOWHERE, Melkart makes the case that to enable greatness in any organization, one must embrace three fundamental principles:

1. You can't be what your culture is not.
Culture is the hidden mark of distinction that shapes your business. There is no time like now to define the forces that determine the success of your organization.

2. You can't be what your people are not.
People are your most important resource. There is no time like now to reimagine the way you lead and treat them, shifting from *in*human resources to talent maximizers.

3. You can't be what your investment is not.
Your investment is your customer experience. There is no time like now to shift to the "experience" economy and deliberately design emotional experiences.

What I find most exciting about *Greatness is* NOWHERE is the "is **now**here" part of it. Melkart shows us how to embrace the "now here" mindset, find opportunities to move forward, and enable greatness in a rapidly changing world. Yes, leadership is a challenge, but Melkart reveals that leadership is also a choice.

A choice to inspire and promote a winning culture and accelerate your success in today's turbulent environment.

A choice to select the right people, uncover the cream of the crop, and translate talent to performance.

A choice to craft unique, emotional connections and experiences and win the hearts and souls of your customers.

Equipped with these choices, sustainable greatness can be achieved...

*Greatness is NOWHERE i*s a brilliant read for leaders with the nerve to take the plunge and deliver nothing less than excellence. This book is a reference you will refer to time and time again.

Let's face it. I don't know of any individual or organization that doesn't want to unleash greatness.... So roll up your sleeves, because this book shows you how to jazz up your culture, pep up your people, and spice up your customer experience.

Bob Kharazmi. Senior Vice President
U.S. Luxury Brands, Marriott International, Inc.

INTRODUCTION

The definition of genius is to make the complex simple.[2]

Albert Einstein

Greatness Defined

I once heard of a businessman who had a problem with the engine on his yacht. He hired many experts to fix the engine, but it was in vain. On one sunny day, he hired an engineer who went into action and examined the engine from top to bottom. After a thorough investigation, the engineer pulled out his rusty red toolbox, grabbed a hammer, and tapped on the engine three times. Suddenly, the engine lurched to life. The owner couldn't believe it! He was thrilled, until he received the engineer's bill: $50,000! "$50,000!" he proclaimed, "That's absurd! That engineer only used a hammer after all, and he just knocked on that engine three times, for crying out loud." He then asked the engineer to email him a detailed bill, which he later received with two items ticked:

- Using a hammer: $1.00
- Knowing where to tap: $49,999

This book is all about knowing where to tap and making the mind shift from greatness is nowhere to **greatness is now here.**

Greatness: The Voice of Our Human Spirit

Greatness is the ability to unleash
the best version of yourself,
your team, and your organization.

Ever since the dawn of civilization, greatness has been the voice of our human spirit. It is not an outcome, but a way of living. We are in a constant chase after meaning and progress. We seek to find the best possible version of everything, including ourselves, yearning to unleash our potential and make an impact.

Greatness is not exclusive to athletes or famous people who have left their footprints in our world. It concerns every one of us—you and me, people who choose to find meaning, the voice to lead a purpose-driven life, and the courage to make a meaningful contribution.

Can you imagine the impact you and your organization would have if you harness the power of greatness and tap into the highest reaches of potential, inspiration, and execution?

In the organizational context, I believe that greatness is not a philosophy or a strategy. It is a deliberate commitment to inspire engaged colleagues, fashion customer excitement, produce exponential results, and leave a distinct footprint in the world.

1. Inspire engaged colleagues

Great leaders and organizations craft and promote a winning culture; a core ideology that inspires them and their people to engage in what they do best every day. They don't merely hire; they select the right, talented, and passionate colleagues who have an inner fire to engage. They bring out the gold in them and empower them to experiment, collaborate, lead, and contribute their best selves to live out the organization's values and go above and beyond in service of the organization's core purpose.

2. Fashion customer excitement

Great leaders and organizations craft a deliberate customer experience and evoke intensely positive emotions, creating customers for life—customers who are intensely loyal even in the presence of other choices. Great leaders and organizations create moments that thrill and chill, resulting in brand advocates who will come back for more and refer others to the organization. They inflame their customers' passion for the brand and strengthen their emotional connection with the organization.

3. Produce exponential results

Great leaders and organizations continuously improve their game, reinvent themselves and their businesses, and measure performance relative to their potential. They stir newness and are fanatic about staying the course and making great things happen. Great leaders and organizations elevate the measures of success, maximize their potential relative to the opportunities presented in their industry, and drive sustainable performance.

4. Leave a distinctive footprint

Great leaders and organizations leave their footprints in the community they serve. They give back and leave a legacy for generations to come. They believe that greatness will never flourish without the act of giving, and therefore they strive to promote others' welfare, enrich their lives, and care about our world. Great leaders and organizations bring people together to contribute to something bigger than themselves, promote a positive change, and make a significant social impact.

Simplicity: The Way Forward

During my workshops[1], I group participants into teams of five and hand them each a blank piece of paper. I then share the following instructions:

"Imagine that you are on a deserted island. You can use nothing but the paper given to you. That's the only available resource. I will be counting to five, and when I reach five, a huge wave will cover your island for only one second. For that second, you can't be touching the floor. If you wish to, you can step onto the papers given to you and save your lives. Are you ready?"

Teams will jump into action by exhibiting a remarkable sense of teamwork, hopping onto their papers and holding on to one another to survive the round. As we progress through the activity, I then start taking the papers away from them, one paper at a time, making the task more challenging (more participants, fewer papers). The activity goes on until they are left with only one paper. You will be amazed by the creativity they then display. I have witnessed participants jumping on one another, sometimes tearing up the paper into tiny pieces just to ensure survival.

The activity doesn't end there, though. I then take away the last piece of paper, and you can certainly feel how worried they become. I repeat the same instructions one final time. "I will be counting to five, and when I reach five, a huge wave will cover your island for only one sec-

---

[1] I am the Chief Engagement Officer of MRT Consultants, which offers one-size-fits-one learning solutions to enable greatness (www.mrtconsultants.com).

ond. For that second, you can't be touching the floor. If you wish to, you can step onto the papers given to you and save your lives. Oops! You are out of paper! Are you ready?" It is then that the participants decide to JUMP together for that one second to win the challenge. The best part is that I always get the same "OH!" reaction.

This activity reinforces Einstein's definition of genius: "To make the complex simple."[2] As human beings, we have a tendency to complicate everything. Psychologically, it makes us feel better, busy, and important. The truth is, greatness is simple.

Join me on this journey to explore three vital principles, 15 Truths, and 20 pragmatic tools to jazz up your culture, pep up your people, and spice up your customer experience.

I believe that wisdom lives within. The Truths presented in this book represent the accumulation of knowledge and insights I have gained throughout the years, drawing on a wealth of thoughts, practices, and experiences of great organizations, executives, authors, researchers, and practitioners.

In this book, I share a roadmap that will guide you to find greatness and lead your people and organization to ultimately unleash their potential and, in the process, impact the future of our world. I deliberately wrote this book in an informal way. At times, I passionately express certain calls to action. This is done intentionally to make your reading experience feel conversational and inspire you to pass this message to those you lead and serve, whether in a formal meeting or just over a cup of coffee.

I structured each Truth presented in this book to be inspirational, digestible, practical, actionable, and most importantly, simple. At the end of each Truth, you will find a tool (or more) designed to translate the learning outcomes into actions. You don't have to read the book front to back, as each Truth is a stand-alone learning experience supported by a tool and an illustration for maximum retention and impact. Finally, this book is about you. Why? Because you transform great people and enable great execution to promote great organizations.

The call is for greatness.
You have a voice.
Choose the road to greatness.
Step up! The choice is yours.
Once again, it is that simple.

PRINCIPLE 1

You can't be
what your culture is not

*I came to see, in my time at IBM, that culture isn't just one aspect
of the game, it is the game. In the end, an organization
is nothing more than the collective capacity of its people to create value.*[3]

Louis V. Gerstner, Jr.

Defining culture

I am your reliable friend or nastiest enemy.
I am your supreme advantage or ultimate liability.
I am your operating system.

I inspire trust or unleash fear.
I determine your success or failure.
I shape the behavior in your organization.

I can lift you up or drag you down.
I can enable your talents or suppress them.
I am your organizational immune system.

Who am I?
I am your culture.

"Culture eats strategy for breakfast"[4] is a quote credited to one of the most influential thinkers on management, Peter Drucker. I personally believe that culture eats strategy not only for breakfast, but also for lunch and dinner. While any strategy, blueprint, or policy imposes the direction of a team or an organization, it is the culture that inspires and enables an environment for the strategy to thrive. Culture is that hidden factor that defines the success of the organization. It is "energy in motion,"[5] your competitive asset[6] that fosters strategic thinking[7] and promotes employee motivation,[8] commitment,[9] organizational citizenship behavior,[10] higher performance, innovation, and adaptability.[11] A great and vibrant culture leads to an organization's effectiveness,[12] greater average levels of ROI and net income growth,[13] and drives financial performance.[14] In their book *Change the Culture, Change the Game,* authors Roger Connors and Tom Smith write, "Either you will manage your culture, or it will manage you…. As you take accountability for your culture and manage it well, you will produce amazing results that will greatly benefit yourself, the people you work with, your entire organization, and, most important, your customers. Change the culture, and you will change the game!"[15]

Organizational culture is a system of a shared ideology—
a set of beliefs, values, assumptions, and norms that define
what is important and determines people's emotions,
thoughts, actions, and performance.

We Are Made to Fly

There was once a farmer who acquired two falcons. One of the falcons flew freely, soaring high up in the sky, while the other clung to the branch of a tree. Many experts tried to assist the farmer, but it was in vain. They tried every trick in the book, yet the second falcon wouldn't let go of the branch. Finally, the farmer took things into his own hands and succeeded. How? He cut the branch of the tree and set the bird free.

The people within your organization are made to fly. It is your job as a leader to promote a culture that enables them to find the best version of themselves and soar. Remember, culture is the hidden part of the iceberg that impacts everything that is visible. The truth is, every company has a culture. This culture could be deliberately crafted or the by-product of unconscious ways of thinking and acting. Where do you stand? You might need to craft a new culture or reassess your current culture and bring about cultural change if it's hindering your efforts to compete, thrive, and win. On the other hand, you might have a winning culture and all you need is to revisit it and connect people's emotions, thoughts, actions, and performance to its purpose and values. Wherever you stand, the truth is your culture defines your explicit and implicit patterns of success.

Let's play!
The following page shows the numbers 1 to 60 all jumbled up.

Round 1
Step 1. Glance at the number page for few seconds before proceeding to step two.

Step 2. You have one minute to touch the numbers sequentially from 1 to 60. After the minute is done, record how many numbers you were able to touch. Are you ready? Set your timer for 60 seconds and start the game. GO!

How did you do?
How many numbers did you manage to touch? Probably around 15, right? How did you feel about losing the challenge? Frustrated? Confused? Do you feel the same when you miss your organizational or personal goals? Knowing how many numbers you managed to touch, what would you do differently next time? Would you lower your goal?

Round 2
Step 1. On the next page, draw a line from A to B, C to D, E to F, and G to H. (Forming 9 quadrants)

Step 2. Did you notice a pattern? The numbers flow sequentially from one quadrant to another. For example, number 1 is in quadrant 1 (top left), 2 in quadrant 2, 3 in 3, 4 in 4, 5 in 5, 6 in 6, 7 in 7, 8 in 8, and 9 in 9. Now, 10 is in quadrant 1, 11 in quadrant 2 and so on.

Step 3. Set your timer for 60 seconds and run your finger, touching as many numbers as possible from 1 to 60 before the time is up. GO!

How did you do?

What did you achieve in round two?

You probably managed to touch at least 50 numbers. Congrats!

Patterns Matter

Finding the pattern empowered you to be more efficient and effective without jeopardizing your goal, right? That is the power of your organizational culture. It clearly specifies the patterns that shape the forces required to win in today's competitive, complex, and challenging environment. One of the most well-known theorists working with organizational culture, Edgar Schein, writes that culture "provide[s] group members with a way of giving meaning to their [people] daily lives, setting guidelines and rules for how to behave, and, most important, reducing and containing the anxiety of dealing with an unpredictable and uncertain environment."[16] These patterns allowed companies the likes of The Ritz-Carlton, Zappos, Walt Disney, Google, Apple, Netflix, Southwest Airlines, and others to compete, thrive, and win. In their book *Nuts! Southwest Airlines' Crazy Recipe for Business and Personal Success*, authors Kevin and Jackie Freiberg write that culture is "the glue that holds our organization together. It encompasses beliefs, norms, rituals, communication patterns, symbols, heroes, and reward structure. Culture is not about magic formulas and secret plans; it is a combination of a thousand things."[17] That is true, but let's take on this challenge and put it all in one magic formula.

Putting It All in One Formula

Culture is definitely not an exact science; it is that elusive and hidden mark of distinction that shapes everything you do. Through my many years of culture and talent consulting, enabling organizations to discover and refine their organizational culture, I found the following formula to be true and effective:

$$(\text{People} + \text{Investment}) \times \textbf{Mindset} =$$
$$\text{Organizational Greatness}$$

Your organizational culture is your mindset—that unique multiplier; a set of beliefs, values, patterns, and norms that define:

The way people see the organization.
The way people interpret things.
The way people think.
The way people connect.
The way people feel and behave.
The way people do business.
The way people integrate and deliver.

Who Am I?

Based on each of the following brief culture descriptions, can you guess the names of the organizations? *Check your answers.*[2]

1. (Hospitality) I empower my employees to move heaven and earth in order to WOW our guests. We believe that "We are Ladies and Gentlemen serving Ladies and Gentlemen," and everything we do is inspired by our credo and 12 service values. Who am I?

_____

2. (Online retailer) I inspire a core purpose "to live and deliver WOW." We call our employees "Zapponians." Our values guide all our actions, and we deliver happiness through our four Cs: commerce, customer service, company culture, and community. Who am I?

_____

3. (Media and entertainment) I enable magical experiences. Our employees, also known as cast members, master the art of storytelling and creative imagination. Happiness is at the heart of our culture, and it drives everything we do. Who am I?

_____

[2] 1. The Ritz-Carlton; 2. Zappos; 3. Disney; 4. Google

4. (Technology) I encourage people to work "when they like and how they like." We foster a work environment founded on fun, trust, and flexibility. Our unique and cool employee perks enable us to integrate all of life, and most importantly, encourage our people to shoot for the moon. Some refer to us as googlers. Who am I?

_____

It amazes me how few words can describe the character of a global organization. Remember, culture is that underlying force that drives everything. Like lenses in glasses that change the way you look at things, your culture shapes your organization and defines the way you do business and the business you do.

Five Truths to Jazz up Your Culture

In Principle 1, I present five Truths to jazz up your culture:

Truth #1: A purpose-driven culture is a culture worth living

The purpose of your organization is that inner compass that powers its passion and reason for existing. It is by far the one key ingredient for organizations to endure and thrive. In this Truth, I reveal the power of the core purpose and present a tool that will guide you to find your true north; the vital conditions for success, your organization's heartbeat, reason for being, and noble aim.

Truth #2: Every culture has a silver lining: The Attar Factor

Your organization's core values are your "Attar;" the essence that defines your identity and enables your organization to unleash its heavenly fragrance. This Truth explores the rock mindset and shares a silver lining exercise that will guide you to craft your values, the indispensable and permanent pillars that drive thoughts, behavior, performance, and results.

Truth #3: Make culture happen. For real. Every day!

For many, values are murky and elusive, and people don't know how to live them. This Truth presents a six-step habit-formation process to form winning habits and automate the translation of your values into actions—transforming your organization from a culture of saying to a culture of doing.

Truth #4: With oxytocin we charge

Significant organizational research is presenting accumulating proof of the considerable benefits of trust. This Truth provides a simple challenge (the oxytocin challenge) to inspire a culture of trust and show your people, in every way you lead, that they are at the heart of what you do.

Truth #5: This is the era of agility

Your organization is alive; it is a living organism longing to grow and flourish. New norms will continue to shape our business and new challenges to rewrite our world. This Truth shares five fundamentals of agile cultures and will guide you to uphold your core ideology while continuously adapting to complexity, ambiguity, and change.

I chose these five Truths because I have witnessed its powerful and practical impact on the organizations I consult and work with. If you choose to use the tools presented in this principle, you will be able to update, upgrade, and boost your operating system.

It is time to rethink—reimagine—redefine.

– TRUTH # 1 –

A purpose-driven culture is
a culture worth living

The Doors of Heaven

I was once presenting at a general manager conference in Burj Al Arab, UAE. At the end of my keynote, the doorman of the hotel who was assigned the task of opening and closing the ballroom door to ensure the attendees' seamless entrance and exit approached me.

"I overheard your keynote and I loved it, but I am just a doorman," he said. "I don't think I am that important. I just open and close doors."

I could see how unhappy he was.

"Do you have a house?" I asked.

"Well, yes, I do," he said.

"If I go knock on the door of that house right now, who will open the door?" I asked.

"My father," he whispered.

"Why?" I enquired.

"Well, because my father owns the house," he said.

"You see, when you open the doors of Burj Al Arab, it is not because you are a doorman, it is because you OWN the house," I proclaimed.

"Really?" he exclaimed.

"Yes," I replied. "Truth be told, you are more important than your general manager," I said.

"Really?" he exclaimed.

"Yes," I replied. "If your general manager doesn't show up to work, many might not even pay attention. But if you don't, the guests will feel it, your team will feel it, and results will be affected. In fact, you are more important than anyone else in this entire building," I said.

"Really?" he exclaimed.

"Yes," I replied. "You are the first and last impression of this entire hotel. You are a vital part of the guest experience. You are the beginning and the end," I passionately proclaimed.

I could certainly spot a twinkle in his eyes. He thanked me and left inspired, energized, and with a sense of purpose. That afternoon, while passing by the lobby, I saw him opening the doors of Burj Al Arab as if they were the doors of heaven.

A Barber with a Purpose

Another unique encounter that moved me took place during an evening walk in Singapore. I visited a very modest two-chair barbershop called The Western Salon, managed by a 60-plus year old barber. This gentleman was the most zealous, vigorous, and enchanting barber. He had such a fascination with hair, but most importantly he had a genuine approach, humble character, and engaging passion. He asked me about my family and work, and together we debated life's most interesting topics. I looked at this barber and thought to myself, "Maybe someone at his age would rather be anywhere in the world than cutting hair for $12 in a two-chair barber shop," so I couldn't help but ask him, "What is you secret to creating such amazing connections over cutting hair?"

"I am not cutting hair," he said. "I beautify people."

He went on to passionately describe that it is never about cutting hair; it is about making people happy, building relationships, and touching lives, one person at a time. This barber's purpose empowers him to sing his song and be his best self, every day.

When you find your purpose,
you will show up constantly as
the best version of yourself to uplift those
you serve, lead, and love.

The One Key Ingredient to Endure and Thrive

Your organization's core purpose is by far the one key ingredient for it to endure and thrive. This is not your vision, mission, or values, but it incorporates the essence of these labels to describe in few words the organization's heartbeat, reason for being, and noble aim. The truth is, your purpose powers your **Reason** (forming effective judgment about what and how you do what you do) and **Passion** (powering why you do what you do).

21

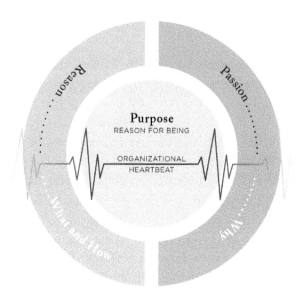

Figure 1. The Integration of What and How (Reason) With Why (Passion)

As my fellow Lebanese philosopher Gibran Khalil Gibran says in his book *The Prophet*, "Your reason and your passion are the rudder and the sails of your seafaring soul. If either your sails or your rudder be broken, you can but toss and drift, or else be held at a standstill in mid-seas."[18] Sustaining your true identity as well as stimulating progress requires you to be guided by a purpose. It is that same purpose that will integrate your reason (what and how) with your passion (why) to guide your organizational drive and impact.

True North

During my workshops, I ask participants to close their eyes and point north with their right hands. Once done, I ask them to open their eyes and look around the room. In addition to the confusion and laughter generated by hands pointing in all directions, they then realize how vital it is to be aligned and have a clear purpose to bring into line with their talents, resources, and energy.

In 2004, a group of my colleagues and I were escorted to visit the construction site of Burj Khalifa in Dubai, UAE. I saw hundreds of workers engaged in what looked like building a fence. I approached one of the builders and asked him what he was doing, and he said clearly, "I am building a wall." I then asked the person next to him, engaged in exactly the same activity, the same question, but this person looked at me with a sense of pride and said, "I am building the tallest tower in the entire world." You see, the first worker was only focused on the "what and how" part of the job (**Reason**, as in building a wall), while the other integrated the what and how with the "why" of the job (**Passion,** as in building the tallest tower in the entire world). This is one of the major reasons why some companies or individuals fail while others compete, grow, and multiply. The problem is that most companies around the globe know "what and how" they do what they do, but few make that integration with "why" they do what they do in order to unlock their core purpose.

Purpose = Reason + Passion

The Eternal Shape of Success

It is time to find your true north—your purpose, the vital condition of success. Your purpose is your legacy and impact— that inner compass that enables you to reorient your actions when needed and ensure you remain grounded and true to who you really are. It is the idea of *who* you are as a company and *why* you exist.[19] Working for a greater objective, a noble goal, ignites people's passion, motivation, and energy.[20] It shapes your long-term choices, calibrates your actions, feelings, and thinking, enables emotional self-mastery, and drives you to be and live your best.[21]

The EY Beacon Institute and *Harvard Business Review* conducted research that revealed that organizations with a strong sense of purpose promote employee satisfaction, loyalty, and engagement, are able to transform and innovate better, achieve sustainable growth, and deliver higher-quality products and services.[22] Jim Collins and Jerry Porras, authors of *Built to Last,* did a great job over a six-year research period to show the positive impact of a core purpose on organizations' capabilities to win and ensure sustainable performance. The authors revealed that visionary companies are not centered around great ideas or charismatic leadership, but are first and foremost driven by a core ideology, inspired by a purpose to enable ideas, leadership, progress, and enduring success.[23] In his book *Excellence Wins*, the legend and leader in the service world, and cofounder of The Ritz-Carlton Hotel Company Horst Schulze writes, "The most important thing a new employee can learn is not how to tighten a bolt or log into the network or find the first-aid kit on the wall. It is rather to grasp who we are, what our dreams are, and why we exist as an organization."[24] He adds, "If you don't believe people have a bedrock yearning for purpose and relationship, then you may turn into something very dark—an exploiter of people…people quickly come to distrust you…they begin to shrivel on the inside, or else they run away to a healthier environment."[25]

One of the most inspiring characterizations of purpose comes from theologian Theodore Thornton Munger in his 1880 book *On the Threshold*, in which he states, "A purpose is the eternal condition of success. Nothing will take its place. Talent will not; nothing is more common than unsuccessful men of talent. Genius will not; unrewarded genius is a proverb; the 'mute, inglorious Milton' is not a poetic creation. The chance of events, the 'push of circumstances,' will not. The natural unfolding of faculties will not. Education will not.… There is no road to success but through a clear, strong purpose. Purpose underlies character, culture, position—attainment of whatever sort."[26]

The Journey

To enable greatness, you have to clearly integrate the reason (what and how) with passion (why), and then weave that purpose into the DNA of your people's jobs. For example, you are not in the business of cooking meals, selling cars, or nursing patients. That's the functional part of the job. Instead, you are in the business of inspiring senses, selling memories, and saving lives. It is a totally different mindset that will transform the way you cook, sell cars, or take care of your patients.

Starbucks is not in the business of selling coffee; they are in the business of "inspiring and nurturing the human spirit—one person, one cup, and one neighborhood at a time."

Uber is not in the business of transportation; they are in the business of "setting the world in motion."

Google is not in the business of selling Internet-related services and products; they are in the business of "organizing the world's information and making it universally accessible and useful."

Microsoft is not in the business of selling computer products, software, and related services; they are in the business of "empowering every person and every organization on the planet to achieve more."

Nike is not in the business of selling sports footwear, apparel, equipment, accessories, and services; they are in the business of "bringing inspiration and innovation to every athlete in the world."

The Ritz-Carlton is not in the business of managing luxury hotels; they are in the business of "inspiring life's most meaningful journeys."

Nordstrom is not in the business of selling clothing, shoes, and accessories; they are in the business of "being relevant in the customers' lives and to form lifelong relationships."

Kellogg's is not in the business of manufacturing food; they are in the business of "nourishing families so they can flourish and thrive."

The beauty of the core purpose lies in the fact that you can translate it to every position within your organization. During our workshops, I ask participants to define the "what" of their jobs (Reason) and then identify the "Why" (Passion). I can't sufficiently describe the internal drive participants exhibit when they integrate reason with passion to craft their purpose. Think of it; imagine you work as a hotel's doorman, opening and closing doors all day long. That's depressing isn't it? Unless you think of it differently.

Crafting Your Purpose

Step 1. Define the "what" (Reason)
Start by defining what you do (the what*)*. The organization's "what" revolves around the products you sell and services you offer. Your people's "what" is represented by their job titles or roles.

Step 2. Define the "why" (Passion)
Now that you have defined the what, think of the rationale for why you do what you do (the why, you noble goal). Find and write down all your answers, as long as it revolves around your noble goal or the contribution you make.

Step 3. Connect the dots
Find the patterns in your answers and blend it into a holistic six- to eight-word statement; the core purpose. Ensure that the statement fits the criteria below.

P	*Purposeful*	Highlights the most important reason for being and embodies all dimensions of your business.
U	*Uplifting*	Connects with the hearts and heads of your people.
R	*Relevant*	Aligns with what you believe and stand for; your ideology.
P	*Persuasive*	Convincing, authentic, genuine, and concise (six to eight words).
O	*Outward focus*	Focused on those you lead and serve.
S	*Stimulative*	Inspires progress and stretches aspirations.
E	*Enduring*	Permanent and timeless source of guidance.

At the end of this Truth, you will find two worksheets. The first will guide you to craft the purpose of your organization, and the second will guide your people to find purpose in their own specific jobs and devise a few vital actions to bring that purpose to life.

For example, a luxury resort I worked with considers their "what" (Step 1/Reason) as renting beach villas and selling tailor-made hospitality products and services. When I asked "why" (Step 2/Passion), the team came up with answers such as:

- To help guests disconnect with the world and connect with what really matters.

- To build strong relationships and gain truly loyal guests who will come back again for more memories.

- To enable others to live unique moments and discover the true meaning of life.

- To deliver unique experiences that last a lifetime.

- To inspire guests with enriched experiences.

We debated those statements, blended them, and ultimately the organization crafted the core purpose (Step 3) as *"Inspiring lives and creating endless memories."* Following the launch of the ideology, the colleagues used the second worksheet to craft their own job's purpose and in the process identified three winning habits to bring their job purpose to life and contribute to the success of the organization.

I recently coached an executive who identified his role as a hotel manager, a great citizen, and a proud father (Step 1/Reason). When I asked why (Step 2/Passion), he shared the below:

- To love my son deeply and be a vital part of his life.

- To be remembered as someone who instills the right principles in others.

• To define my professional success through the growth of those I work with.

• To influence my community and leave a productive mark in the world.

• To enjoy the moment, keep moving forward in a positive fashion, and become the best person I can be.

Together we blended those statements, and ultimately, he crafted his core purpose (Step 3) as *"To be a positive force in the lives of others."* He then identified five winning habits to bring his purpose to life.

Final Note: Stimulating Progress

What is your purpose? Once you discover the answer to this question, you and your organization will never stop stimulating change and progress as long as there is reason and passion left in our world. Gibran Khalil Gibran said it best: "Among the hills, when you sit in the cool shade of the white poplars, sharing the peace and serenity of distant fields and meadows—then let your heart say in silence, 'God rests in reason.' And when the storm comes, and the mighty wind shakes the forest, and thunder and lightning proclaim the majesty of the sky—then let your heart say in awe, 'God moves in passion.' And since you are a breath in God's sphere, and a leaf in God's forest, you too should rest in reason and move in passion."[18]

Don't fall into complacency in today's fast-paced world.
There is more to your organization than making money.
There is more to your job than a title.
Yes! God rests in reason.
Yes! God moves in passion.
Whatever your occupation, title, or status might be, walk, lead, and serve with purpose.
Purpose…NOW, more than ever.

Tool # 1: Organizational Purpose Worksheet

Instructions: Use this worksheet to craft the purpose of the organization. Ensure that the final statement fits the shared criteria (refer to the fundamentals of a core purpose above).

Step 1. Define the "what" (Reason)
Define what your organization offers. The "what" revolves around the products you sell and services you offer.

Step 2. Define the "why" (Passion)
Jot down the rationale for why you do what you do (the why); your noble goal.

Patterns:
Find the patterns from the reasons you jotted down in Step 2.

Step 3. Connect the dots (Purpose)
Blend your answers/patterns into a holistic six- to eight-word statement.

Tool # 2: Job Purpose Worksheet

Instructions: Use this worksheet to guide your team members to find the purpose of their job. First, define the main function of the job (job title, job role) then explore the "purpose" (six- to eight-word statement). Finally, determine three to five winning habits to bring the purpose to life.

FUNCTION	PURPOSE
List the **Function** of your job (What you do?)	List the **Purpose** of your job (Why do you do what you do?)

CONTRIBUTION
(List the few vital winning **habits** to translate the purpose into action?)

SUCCESS

"WORKING FOR A GREATER OBJECTIVE"

"THE DOORS OF HEAVEN"

N
W   E
S

Jibram Khalil Gibram

"I AM BUILDING THE TALLEST TOWER IN THE ENTIRE WORLD"

PURPOSE

What?

How?

Why?

PASSION

REASON

- TRUTH # 2 -

Every culture has a silver lining:
The Attar Factor

Indispensable and Permanent Pillars

Along with the purpose, your values are your organization's indispensable and permanent pillars. They represent the set of enduring guiding principles that guide your people's actions, decisions, and behaviors.

Your values embody your ideology and define what you represent and stand for. It is the glue that holds organizations and teams together as the organization grows, decentralizes, diversifies, and globalizes. In short, they represent your organization's deepest and most powerful motivators.

Values represent the organizational beliefs;
the norms that guide the choices,
decisions, and behavior of an individual,
team, and the entire organization.

In their book *Managing by Values*, Ken Blanchard and Michael O'Connor claim, "No longer is values-based organizational behavior an interesting philosophical choice—it is a requisite for survival."[27] Values are the glue that unites people within an organization[28] and the basic structure that supports it, the bedrock of any culture and the essence of its philosophy to achieve success.[29] In his article "The Living Company," Arie de Geus examines long-lived companies that evolved successfully to find that they have common characteristics including a sense of community bound by clearly stated values.[30] A common attribute of excellent companies,[31] values shape the organization's strategy and long-term success.[32] They represent the soul of the organization[33] and enable it to achieve its goals and generate positive results.[34] In his book *Discovering the Soul of Service*, distinguished professor of marketing at Texas A&M Leonardo Berry writes that values "are the ideals, principles, and philosophy at the center of the enterprise. They are protected and revered. They reveal the company's heart and soul."[35]

A Business to ROCK

"They are like a man building a house, who dug down deep and laid the foundation on rock. When a flood came, the torrent struck that house but could not shake it, because it was well built."[36] – Luke 6:48

Identifying the values that underpin your business is pivotal for lasting success. Your values represent the **rock** upon which everything in your organization rests. It is the groundwork for anything. Without it, you are building your organization on **sand,** and great will be the fall.

Values drive thoughts
Thoughts drive behavior
Behaviors drive performance
Performance drives results

Your values are your rock, and it is the strength of that foundation that determines the longevity and success of your organization. They promote your ethical practices and code of conduct and are the mortar of your organizational structure. They are your solid and dependable anchors that enable the organization to be grounded, endure, and prosper. Founded on timeless principles, these values become the organizational lighthouse against which your organization and people can set their direction and navigate this vast global economy in calm or challenging times.

Put your principle-centered values at the heart of your ideology to build a strong brand from within. Let it be the force that drives every decision you make, every process you create, every norm and practice you design, every product and service you provide, and every goal you inspire. Get rid of the sand mindset where values are just a plaque on the wall, and embrace the rock mindset where values are a way of life. The question is, is your business sitting on sand or on solid rock?

CONTRAST

SAND	ROCK
A plaque on the wall	A way of life
Rigid	Agile
"Need to know" rules	"Need to play" guidelines
About "If, If, If"	About "Why, Why, Why"
Manage change	Spur change
Transactional	Transformational
Focusing on products	Inspiring solutions
Driving services	Enabling experiences
Quantifiable	Qualitative
Vertical cooperation	Horizontal collaboration
Built on facts	Charged with emotions
Copy/paste trap	One size fits one

Because…they

Because they value *care*,[37] the video conferencing technology company **Zoom** empowers a "happiness crew" to focus on the well-being of its people, gives back generously to the community, and focuses on "delivering happiness" for all stakeholders.

Because they value *courage and customer obsession*,[38] the business and financial software company **Intuit** is laser focused on their customers, fosters innovation at every corner, and champions those who dare to dream.

Because they value *collaboration and innovation*,[39] the international media provider **Spotify** breaks the traditional structure and embodies "squads, tribes, and guilds" to allow people to connect, come together, innovate, have fun, and feel part of a greater whole.

Because they value *fun, learning, and imagination*,[40] the toy production company **LEGO** designs their offices more like a studio and a play space, welcomes children to the workplace for co-creation events, and operates a no-manual workplace where employees are encouraged to express their individuality and be free, bold, and different.

Because they value *curiosity and inclusion*,[41] the media-services provider and production company **Netflix** values people over process, inspires team members to step forward and organize their working hours, seek alternate perspectives, collaborate, and take smart risks.

> *As leaders, it is imperative to build*
> *your company on values.*
> *If not, you are playing a game that you will never win.*

Formulating Your Values

Finding your core values is a journey of discovery. I will not share every detail of this journey, so before you embark on completing the exercise below, you have to make sure that the journey is inclusive and solicit the feedback of your team—all those onboard—through focus groups, surveys, and brainstorming sessions. The inclusion of people in the discovery of the culture will generate significant heartfelt commitment, enthusiasm, and contribution. Remember, this is not a wordsmith exercise, and surely not about what you think your values are. It is a discovery journey inspired by the past, present, and future of the organization. After you consolidate the outcomes of your focus groups and surveys, invite your key executive team and teams' representatives to embark on discovering your values through the silver lining exercise. Here's how it works.

The Silver Lining Exercise

At the end of this Truth, you'll find a worksheet that will guide you to discover and craft your values. Here's another way to look at it.

1. Take a blank sheet of paper, and in the middle, draw a horizontal line representing the past (left), present (center), and future (right) of your organization (or your personal life should you decide to discover your own personal values).

2. Identify five events or key major milestones in the life of the organization—two in the past, two in the present (previous or current year), and one in the future (or any combination as long as you honor the past, celebrate the present, and anticipate the future). Those milestones might be positive (e.g., founding the company, winning an award, leading the market, etc.) or undesirable (e.g., losing to competition, facing a crisis, failed product or service, etc.). Now, for each positive event, answer the following question: "What value was observed that made this event so effective, successful, and fulfilling?" For each undesirable event, answer the following question: "What value was not observed (missing) that made this event so ineffective, unsuccessful, and unfulfilling?" And for the future milestone, answer the following question: "What value do you need to make this event so effective, successful, and fulfilling?" Don't settle for the first finding! Keep digging until each revealed value describes the root of the milestone.

3. Test your values against the following criteria:

- *Authentic*: Representing an extension of your own consistently held and established beliefs.
- *Foundational:* Does not change with circumstances, even if the world around you changes.
- *Principle-centered:* Founded on universal principles that transcend time and space.
- *Inspirational and timeless.*

4. Don't just settle for the words as revealed by the silver lining exercise or words that could be found on every value list such as teamwork, innovation, integrity etc. Reword the values to make them yours. Make them digestible, unique, relevant, and memorable.

5. Translate each value into three commitments; a set of behavioral statements highlighting the outcomes or results rather than steps or the "how to" to promote individuality and ensure the team march to the beat of the same drum. Below is an example from a hospitality organization I partnered with to craft their core ideology.

Value 1: **Take Charge**	
Commitment 1: We start with I; I start with yes.	The ability to own and hold yourself and others accountable; embrace a positive attitude; be assertive and proactive in thoughts and actions; work hard but smart; demonstrate confidence; be zesty and optimistic.
Commitment 2: I make things happen. Period.	The ability to make smart decisions; empower yourself and others; break down a task and act; be disciplined and focused; follow up and follow through; meet deadlines; translate ideas into actions; work systematically and persevere with passion.
Commitment 3: I shift from anticipation to action.	The ability to anticipate others' spoken and unspoken needs and wishes; read others and situations; deliver proactive service; hunt for preferences; listen to others and identify patterns; show passion for serving others; personalize the guest experience.

The Attar Factor

You might be wondering why I encourage having five values at most. When shopping for perfume, you most probably have come across these terms: Eau de Toilette (EDT) and Eau de Parfum (EDP). The difference between these terms is all about the perfume concentration and durability—how it sits on your skin. While shopping for perfume in the Middle Eastern and Far Eastern countries, I was introduced to a far more powerful perfume concentration, Attar—an Arabic word meaning scent—which is the pure fragrance of oil without any additives. Attars are distillates of flowers, herbs, spices, and other natural materials and are so strong that a drop or two is enough to last for more than 15 hours. No wonder that Attars are usually sold in small, jeweled decanters and in some cultures are considered the most cherished and treasured of material possessions. Like Attar, your values ought to be extracted by the distillation of your four to five past, present, and future milestones. A process through which you will identify only four to five most **treasured core values** that truly lay the foundation of your current and future success.

Putting It All Together: Silver Lining

Let's give your Attar a name! Once you extract your four or five values, connect those values to form your organization's silver lining. Inspired by the idiom "every cloud has a silver lining,"[42] *Merriam-Webster* defines silver lining as "a consoling or hopeful prospect."[43] In our philosophy, it represents the hope your values bring to the work environment and your business overall.

When you face obstacles, and you will, your organization can always evoke your silver lining and win. For example, an organization I worked with extracted their values as **C**urious, **A**uthentic, **R**esourceful and **E**ngaged. The silver lining—their Attar name—was obvious in this case and represented by the acronym CARE. This silver lining became the center of everything they do—care for their associates, care for their stakeholders, and care for the environment. It changed the rules of the game and inspired the way they do business and the business they do. Your silver lining might also be the name of your organization. For example, an organization I worked with extracted their values as **Z**est for magic, **A**lways Go Wild, **Y**ou Decide, and **A**bsolute Harmony. Their silver lining was represented by the acronym ZAYA (Zaya Nurai Island Resort).

What Smells Perfectly on Others Might Not Work for You!

Have you ever bought a perfume because it smelled perfect on a friend or someone you met to surprisingly find out that it didn't smell the same on you? We have all been there, and most probably have multiple perfumes lying unused in our dressing rooms. There are many reasons for this, but it's mainly because your body chemistry, hormones, diet, and medications affect how different perfumes react on your skin and smell. What does that mean?

> • I have witnessed many organizations approaching the value discovery journey from a copy/paste perspective. That is a huge mistake. Taking someone else's formula and imposing it on your organization won't serve the purpose.

> • The power of your Attar will be amplified when you align your systems and strategies to your values. Integrate your values in your selection, orientation, appraisal, communication, recognition systems, and strategies. That's how you win.

Final Note: A Journey of Discovery

Identifying your values is a journey of discovery and most probably the most rewarding journey you will ever embark on. You owe it to your people, your customers, and the community you serve. Embark on this journey, and once you discover your signature Attar, you will define your identity and enable your organization to unleash its heavenly fragrance.

Tool # 3: Silver Lining Worksheet

Instructions: Identify four to five events—key major milestones in the life of the organization honoring the past, celebrating the present, and anticipating the future. For each positive event, answer the following question: "What value was observed that made this event so effective, successful, and fulfilling?" For each undesirable event, answer the following question: "What value was not observed (missing) that made this event so ineffective, unsuccessful, and unfulfilling?" And for the future milestone, answer the following question: "What value do you need to make this event so effective, successful, and fulfilling?"

Milestones
Milestone 1: Value 1:
Milestone 2: Value 2:
Milestone 3: Value 3:

Milestone 4:

Value 4:

Milestone 5:

Value 5:

Silver Lining

Reword your values, make them yours, and craft your silver lining:

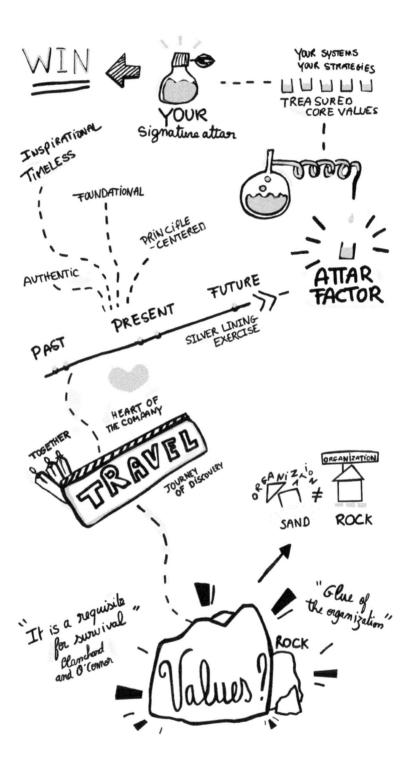

− TRUTH # 3 −

Make culture happen.
For real. Every day!

Winning Habits

For many, culture is just a plaque on the wall or an icing on the cake. Posters of the organization's purpose and values permeate the hallways, but the culture is still murky and elusive, and people don't know how to live it. In Truth #2, I discussed that organizations should be clear about their values, but most importantly, they should define how those values are translated into action within the organization. If not, then organizations will certainly not fully integrate and witness the true power of values on operation and performance. Catherine Dalton, Professor of Business at Indiana University, writes, "In too many organizations, values are rhetoric that graces the company's website or the halls of corporate headquarters, but do not form a solid foundation that guides employee behavior."[44] How can you then bring the values to life and make it tangible and understandable? By building a series of winning habits at every level throughout the organization.

Bestselling author Robert Ringer states in his book *Million Dollar Habits*, "The world is saturated with intelligent, highly educated, extraordinary skilled people who experience frustration because of their lack of success...." He adds, "Success is a matter of understanding and religiously practicing specific, simple habits that always lead to success."[45] What distinguishes successful organizations from others is that they rigorously practice winning habits that get the values off the wall and into the culture.

Habits express your values and determine who you are. In simple terms, there is no secret sauce for an enduring and successful culture other than tying your habits to your values to serve the core purpose of the organization.

Forming winning habits will automate the translation of your values into actions, transforming your organization from a culture of saying to a culture of doing.

What's Holding You Back?

Years ago, I saw a picture of an elephant farm and noticed that those huge elephants were connected to each other by a thin rope tied to their front lower legs. Confused and intrigued, I wanted to understand why these elephants couldn't just break away from these ropes. Well, when the elephants were small, the ropes served the purpose of keeping them from running away. As the elephants grew up, the rope mindset grew up with them too, and therefore, they never tried to break away. Aren't we and our organizations sometimes like these elephants? Paralyzed because of a misleading belief, a negative mindset, an old way of doing things. The truth is we are in control, and we can break free by building habits that can free us from what's holding us back and enable us to bring our organizational purpose and values to life. Remember, what's holding you back might be very minute and insignificant. Let's play!

Wherever you are, find someone to do this experiment with:

1. Have them sit down in a chair with both feet flat on the floor and both hands on their knees.

2. Place one of your fingers in the middle of their forehead and press lightly.

3. With both feet flat on the floor and both hands on their knees, ask the participant to stand up.

Sounds easy, right? Amazingly, they won't be able to!

I run this experiment in my workshops to reinforce that self-inflicted or external obstacles (like this very light press on the forehead) can sometimes paralyze us and hold us back from success. In reality, no matter what the circumstances are, you are in control of your actions.

Leaders are required to close the gap between "who we are" and "what we want to be" as an organization, transform the culture into powerful, winning habits that will ultimately empower people to work and play by values and accordingly shape the organization.

From Abstract to Concrete

In Will Durant's book *The Story of Philosophy*, the author captures in his own words an Aristotelian philosophy, "We are what we repeatedly do. Excellence, then, is not an act, but a habit."[46] In fact, 40 percent of our everyday actions are the byproduct of habits.[47] Therefore, influencing and inspiring day-in and day-out habits will ultimately transform hundreds if not thousands of interactions and decisions. Those winning habits will inspire supreme confidence in your people, vitalize your values, bring you closer to your purpose, and ultimately put your team and organization on the big stage. In simple terms, if you want to breathe life into your culture, identify winning habits for each of your values. Practice those habits, integrate them into your systems, and celebrate them until you reach a plateau of automaticity and it becomes part of your DNA.

When **The Ritz-Carlton** wanted to inspire a culture of WOW, they steered their people to hunt for guests' preferences, likes, and routines. They made this hunt a habit supported by tools and a reward system in order to craft personalized, unique, and memorable stories for every guest.

When **Starbucks** wanted to cultivate a culture that serves a twist of joy alongside a cup of coffee, they made willpower a habit in their employees' lives. They introduced role-playing, practicing how to serve, dealing with unhappy customers so that employees can regulate their emotions, developing self-discipline, and being able to automatically deliver positive vibes and happiness with every serving.

When **Nordstrom** wanted to create a culture of empowerment, they led with an inverted pyramid mindset where employees were put at the top of the organizational hierarchy. They encouraged them to openly speak with their leaders, voice their thoughts, and soar because there is only one rule, "Use good judgment in all situations."

When **Disney** wanted to promote a culture of magic, they empowered their employees to kneel down and strike up a conversation with every kid, use themed nicknames such as prince and princess, and charm their precious little guests.

When the **Virgin Group** wanted to cultivate a culture of smart disruptions and changing business for good, they stirred people to explore new ideas, find innovative solutions, and challenge the status quo.

When **Apple** wanted to empower a culture of focus and perfection, they inspired people to excel and engage in lots of trial and error guided by the philosophy that "There are a thousand no's for every yes."

Building Habits: Not an Event, a Journey

Maybe one of the most fantastic pieces of information about neuroscience that I ever came across is brain plasticity. In simple terms, every one of us has enormous capacity to learn new things. So, let's eliminate the negative self-talk; "I can't learn it; I can't make it; I am too old to learn that; I can't do it; I can't change, etc." Our capacity as human beings to learn, achieve, change, and succeed is literally limitless.

The journey of transforming your organization from a culture of saying to a culture of doing starts by looking at each value and focusing on what you want to become (see *The Change*, below). Figure 2 highlights the six-step habit formation journey that will guide you to make culture happen, for real, every day.

Our capacity as human beings is literally limitless. Period!

Figure 2. Habit Formation Journey

At the end of this Truth, I will summarize this journey in a worksheet to enable the process of reflection and change.

Step 1: The Change—*Focus on What You Want to Become*

In my teenage years, I constantly struggled with obesity. God is my witness; I tried every trick in the book focusing on everything I should stop eating, but I always failed. I might have lost few pounds but gained it all back. It was only when I discovered these two facts that I managed to change the game:

Fact #1: Your brain sees in pictures.

Your brain sees words as pictures rather than a group of letters. For example, if I ask you, "What did you do on your last birthday?" you won't see words scrolling in the back of your mind, you will see pictures of that particular day.

Fact #2: Your brain (specifically the unconscious part of it) cannot filter out negative pictures.

Why do you think your people always do what you ask them not to do? Here it is. If I tell you, "Whatever you think about, DO NOT think of a bicycle." Well, you will immediately think of one, right? During those years struggling with obesity, I started every day by focusing on what not to eat, and that's why I always failed. When I focused on what I wanted to become (I am eating healthy; I live a healthy lifestyle, etc.) I lost 110 pounds. To identify what you want to become, focus on one value at time and ask your team:

> *What is the one thing that we need to embrace so we can promote our value _____ (state the value)?"*

Remember, The Change should be a key driver to enhance a specific organizational value, clearly understood, aligned with your purpose, and with a great likelihood of positive impact at every level of the organization.

First, focus on what you want to become.

Step 2: Emotions

Have you wondered why you remember certain memories over others? The answer is simple—because those memories were charged with powerful emotions, your brain's fertilizers. When charging The Change with positive emotions, you will commit to that change and find the desire and drive to learn and work hard towards what you want to become. Ask your team:

How would you feel if we achieve what we want to become?

Step 3: Core Habits

Core habits are small changes or habits that people or organizations introduce into their routines to translate the values to life. Pulitzer-prize winning journalist and author Charles Duhigg refers to these habits as "keystone habits" in his book *The Power of Habit*. Like the domino effect, these "keystone habits can influence how people work, eat, play, live, spend, and communicate. Keystone habits start a process that, over time, transforms everything."[48] Work with your team and identify one or two core habits in order to support The Change. You can build one or two habits for each of your values. Once identified, you have to practice those habits systematically for 66 repetitions (days) to reach automaticity.[49] It is also imperative to set up weekly checkup meetings to revisit those habits, adjust your actions if needed, see how everyone is progressing, and ensure full commitment. Ask your team:

What is a specific habit that we need to develop in order to support The Change (identified in step 1)?"

Step 4: Habit Uplifter

Building a support system is vital to enable positive change. Your people will establish accountability by partnering with one another and working with a coach—The Habit Uplifter. Your next step is to identify a Habit Uplifter for each habit. The Habit Uplifter's mission is to generate momentum, encourage, and facilitate the cultivation of the new habit.

Step 5: Reward

Often, people quit or fall short of their habits. To finish strong and solidify the habit, you should insert enjoyment and gratification into the process of change. Celebrate small wins with your team by injecting the habit formation journey with a relevant reward that intensifies the craving, the triggering force behind every habit, which therefore reinforces the habit. Discuss and agree on the nature of the reward with your team—some organizations I've worked with developed a reward points system, others rewarded their teams daily with praise, extra attention, learning and development, etc.

What is a relevant reward that will encourage us
to make things happen?

Step 6: Integration

Like anything in life, molding a culture requires concentration and effort at first. To be successful you have to integrate these habits in every system within the organization, from selection, orientation, communication, appraisal and reward, to strategy.

Once integrated, these habits will then
form part of the game plan.

Powerful Thoughts

1. **Nurture a desire for renewal: It's a survival must.** Have the eagerness and drive to reinvent yourself. Otherwise, you will end up on the bench.

2. **Redefine habits: All bets are off.** Don't turn this habit formation journey into a copy/paste exercise. Redefine yourself and the way you make things happen.

3. **Blame no one: Put yourself in the driver's seat.** Stop the blaming game, and should you wish change, start small. Build one winning habit at a time and soar.

4. **Don't fire people: Fire bad habits.** Instead of firing people, fire them up by rewiring their habits. Possibilities are born from winning habits.

5. **Laugh off your failures: It's a noble journey.** Stay strong, reward outstanding failures, and keep focusing on those winning habits. Dust yourself off when needed and get on the ride again. PS: it never ends.

Tool # 4: Habit Worksheet

Instructions: Below are the steps required to make your culture real through the power of building winning habits. The journey starts by identifying the required change and crafting winning habits to promote your values and purpose accordingly.

Step 1. The Change: What is the one thing that we need to embrace so we can promote our value ---------- (state the value)?

Step 2. Emotions: How would you feel if we achieve The Change?

Step 3. Keystone Habit: What is a specific habit that we need to develop in order to support The Change?

Step 4. Habit Uplifter: Who is the Habit Uplifter that will generate momentum, encourage, and facilitate the cultivation of this new habit?

Step 5. Reward: What is a relevant reward that will encourage us to make things happen?

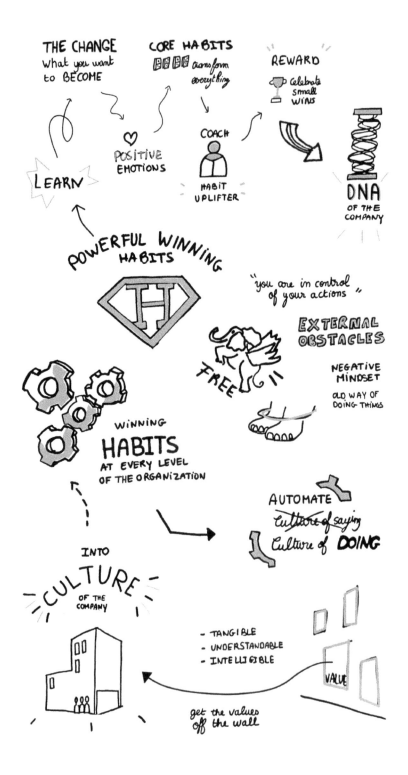

- TRUTH # 4 -

With oxytocin we charge

The Power of Trust

Everything in your culture should be rooted in trust. Neuroeconomist Paul J. Zak reports that "compared with people at low-trust companies, people at high-trust companies report 74% less stress, 106% more energy at work, 50% higher productivity, 13% fewer sick days, 76% more engagement, 29% more satisfaction with their lives, and 40% less burnout."[50] Significant organizational research presents accumulating proof of the considerable benefits of trust. Stephen R. Covey, one of the world's leading authorities on trust, shares in his book *The Speed of Trust* that trust is the one hidden variable that significantly improves personal and professional success.[51] He asserts that high-trust organizations maximize speed (high-trust dividends such as increased value, accelerated growth, enhanced innovation, loyalty, collaboration, and execution) and lower cost (low-trust taxes such as eliminating bureaucracy, redundancy, politics, turnover, and fraud). Many scholars have reinforced that trust generates higher perceived organizational support, lowers turnover intention, and causes higher commitment.[52] It positively impacts sales performance,[53] satisfaction,[54] organizational citizenship behaviors,[55] and organizational climate,[56] among other forms of workplace behavior. Its absence, on the other hand, is the one real threat to your personal and organizational growth.

Now, being responsible for creating a workplace of trust isn't about creating a line item in the budget. It is about forging a core ideology, a culture that inspires people to bond, be involved in the planning of the work that affects them, bring their passion to work, make decisions, be open, have fun, connect and care, learn, grow, and most importantly, do what they do best every day.

Oxytocin

In 2014, my wife Nancy got pregnant, and due to some complications, our doctor recommended early delivery. On the day of the delivery, the nurse injected Nancy with a dose of oxytocin. Intrigued by the name, I learned that oxytocin stimulates powerful contractions that helps with the delivery. I also came to know that oxytocin is found to be the highest in maternal behavior but also in relationships, social bonding, and acts of kindness. Oxytocin is associated with human trustworthiness.[57] It affects interpersonal interactions, causing a substantial increase in trust among humans.[58] It is also reported that oxytocin affects other virtues such as generosity and sacrifice.[59] Many scholars have investigated oxytocin and its implications on organizational behavior, hence its reputation as the love hormone, liquid trust, or the moral molecule. That being said, it is fair to state, from a business perspective, that a leader's most integral mission is to inject the culture with a dose of oxytocin. That's how Fortune 500 companies changed the way they operate and function. Their high-trust cultures are bolstered by a unique dose of camaraderie, pride, and joy. They inspire their people to connect, make meaningful contributions, and achieve higher performance.

The Oxytocin Challenge

Creating a culture of trust is a journey with multiple implications. For the sake of simplicity and immediate impact, I will suggest a pragmatic challenge to boost trust within your culture.

High-Trust Culture: Oxytocin Challenge (Part 1)

1. In your next team meeting, introduce oxytocin and its potential impact on your team and organization.

2. With you team, think of ways to inject oxytocin in your culture, i.e., find a term, an action, or expression for each letter of the word oxytocin.

3. Design your unique acronym poster and integrate it into your culture. This acronym should highlight the patterns required to capture the spirit of trust in the workplace.

4. Inspire trust!

The Spin

Having led this activity all over the globe at team bonding events and leadership workshops, I have collated some of the best findings below.

O for Optimize

Inspire achievable, specific but challenging goals that are aligned with the organization's core purpose. This will take your team to a new level of commitment and performance. Have faith in your people and limit running your business on SOPs. If an SOP doesn't stretch your people, throw it in the garbage and start writing again.

Additional actions:
- Encourage risk taking and deliver results.
- Provide stretched assignments and goals.
- Support shared learning and cross-functional collaboration.

X for X-Out the Negativity

Negative attitudes, thoughts, and emotions create a work environment where people live and work well below their abilities within an endless stream of disapproval, discouragement, and disengagement. X-out that negativity with a machete if you have to.

Additional actions:
- Be accountable for your choices and actions.
- Clear the path, overcome challenges, remove obstacles, and bring hope.
- Cut out negative thoughts and embrace change.

Y for Yay! Fun at Work

Great organizations consistently earn higher marks for fun. A workplace filled with fun and warmth enables your people to work harder, smarter, and faster. Infuse the spirit of play into your workplace. Share moments of enjoyment, make your people excited about their jobs, uplift their spirits, and bring smiles to their day.

Additional actions:
- Introduce fun-boosting rituals.
- Connect people with their passions.
- Give people the space to play at work.

T for Togetherness

It's not a cliché. Teamwork is and will remain vital to enable trust and promote organizational citizenship. Great leaders and organizations deliberately build relationships and develop a spirit of collaboration and comradeship. Project a sense of being in it together, inspire loyalty, and turn a team of all stars into an all-star team.

Additional actions:
- Build bonds and enthuse strong relationships.
- Capitalize on the strengths of others.
- Allow your people to have a voice, and encourage healthy conflicts.

O for Openness

When you lead, you should arm yourself with candor and ongoing communication. Organizational transparency promotes trust and stimulates efficiency and effectiveness. Share the direction of your organization, your goals, strategies, and tactics. Clarify expectations and let people know where "we" stand. Lead courageously; that's the way to go.

Additional actions:
- Be honest and demonstrate integrity.
- Talk straight. Be transparent in your communication.
- Demonstrate authenticity, inside and out.

C for Care

Your people don't care about what you know or say unless they see *through actions* how much you genuinely care. Focus on your people's needs and emotions. Demonstrate real care for your people and keep your commitments at all costs. Respect and celebrate diversity. Create a culture that promotes meaningful associations and connections.

Additional actions:
- Be a servant leader and show kindness.
- Be sensitive to the emotions of others and act accordingly.
- Show loyalty and stand with your people.

I for Independence

Empower your people; give them the authority to make decisions, the means to be resourceful, and the voice to fight their battles. Involve your people in the planning and designing of their work and projects. Bottom line: they will amaze you!

Additional actions:
- Celebrate diversity and encourage autonomy.
- Unleash the individuality of your people.
- Encourage responsibility and reward self-sufficiency.

N for Nurture

Your people should be given the opportunity to learn, grow, and most importantly, be recognized. When it comes to leadership, be a gardener, not a mechanic. Provide the nourishment of focused learning (personally and professionally) as well as tangible, candid, and personalized feedback and recognition. Remember, all plants need food, water, and sunlight to thrive, but different plants require different amounts of each.

Additional actions:
- Give and celebrate credit where it is due.
- Create a learning culture.
- Coach and mentor your people.

The Taproot: e.Oxytocin

In today's high-tech world we live in, I added one additional ingredient to the formula to reinforce the importance of disconnecting to connect with what really matters: people. The "e" in e.oxytocin stands for Empathy. Empathy is the taproot ingredient upon which the other eight elements of oxytocin are founded. It is there to remind us that managers manage numbers, while leaders lead people. Empathy is the ability to listen, recognize, and respond to people's feelings, thoughts, and emotions. It is key to build genuine connections, promote collaboration, and develop long-lasting and trusting relationships.

Trust ROI

The question that many leaders would then ask is "What is trust return on investment?" What follows is a great story from the novelist Paulo Coelho about a disciple at the monastery of Piedra who asked an abbot if prayers get humanity close to God. The abbot replied by asking, "All those prayers you pray, will they make the sun rise tomorrow?"

"Of course not! The sun rises because it obeys a universal law!" the disciple replied.

The abbot then said, "So that is the answer to your question. God is near to us, regardless of the prayers we say."

The disciple then concluded that all prayers are useless.

The abbot replied, "No. If you don't get up early, you will never be able to see the sun rise. If you don't pray, even though God is always near, you will never be able to notice His presence."[60]

This story is the answer for those of us doubting the power of trust in business. Yes, this word is not featured in our balance sheets or profit and loss statements, but it is not until you embrace actions of trust that you will clearly witness its unique impact on every aspect of your business.

An Executive Steward with a Story to Tell

When I was the director of human resources at The Ritz-Carlton, Sharm el Sheikh, Egypt, I met Ahmed Tharwat, an executive steward with an interesting story. After meeting the love of his life, Ahmed asked her father's permission to marry his daughter. The father, who wasn't knowledgeable about the hospitality industry and believing that an executive steward wasn't the right fit for the family, rejected the marriage proposal. A few days later, Ahmed shared his frustration with his general manager, who promised to assist.

"How could the GM help me?" Ahmed thought. "He is a busy leader, and he is not even an Egyptian. How can he understand how complicated this matter is? I thought he was trying to empathize and show that he cares. That's all!"[61]

After three days, Ahmed was the talk of the town. An article featuring his leadership legacy and impact on his team and the resort was on the front pages of four major Egyptian newspapers and two Middle East magazines. The GM's injection of oxytocin changed Ahmed's life. Equipped with these newspapers and magazines, Ahmed visited Dina's father again, and the rest is history. Ahmed got married, and he currently has two gorgeous kids, Haya and Amer. He's been working for The Ritz-Carlton Hotel Company for the last 21 years.

"I will never work somewhere else. That day, I didn't only marry Dina, but I also married my company. This act of loyalty and genuine care inspired a new level of trust. I am forever hooked," Ahmed proudly proclaimed.[62]

That story exemplifies the power of injecting oxytocin, one relationship at a time. Some argue that leading in today's world of rising technology, where leaders spend most of their energy investing in machines and systems, you can't win them all. They believe that technology (represented by machines and systems) and oxytocin (represented by people) do not always match. But remember that although oil and vinegar don't mix, they work together beautifully to create a divine taste. As leaders, we are invited to inspire the hearts and nurture the souls of those we lead. Again, we are in the business of leading people, and relationships are governed by trust.

Oxytocin Challenge (Part 2)

How are you injecting your culture with a dose of e.oxytocin? That is the ultimate test. How do you show your people, in every way you lead, that they are at the heart of what you do?

Let's start this journey together with the oxytocin challenge highlighted in this Truth's worksheet:

1. Launch the challenge in your organization.

2. Everyone should complete all the actions within 30 days.

3. Add your own "actions" in the three empty squares to adapt this challenge to your culture.

4. Enjoy the ride, have fun, and inspire trust.

Tool # 5: Oxytocin Challenge

Instructions: Complete the Oxytocin Challenge (Part 1) and then launch this 30-day challenge. Enjoy the ride and inspire trust. Check off each day as you and your team progress through the challenge.

☐ **Day 1:** Build one "habit" to connect better with others.	☐ **Day 2:** Go the day without complaining.	☐ **Day 3:** Use "can" and "yes." Avoid "but," "no," and "can't."
☐ **Day 4:** Be a cheerleader. Greet and smile at everyone you meet.	☐ **Day 5:** Recognize three colleagues for doing something special.	☐ **Day 6:** Give 10 "high fives" for colleagues going the extra mile.
☐ **Day 7:** Build one new relationship at work.	☐ **Day 8:** Fix a broken relationship at work.	☐ **Day 9:** Write a personal note to thank a colleague.
☐ **Day 10:** Learn something new.	☐ **Day 11:** Teach a colleague something new.	☐ **Day 12:** Go the day without excuses or blame.
☐ **Day 13:** Volunteer to mentor a colleague.	☐ **Day 14:** Do one random act of kindness.	☐ **Day 15:** Embrace a colleague with a genuine hug.
☐ **Day 16:** Encourage and uplift a colleague.	☐ **Day 17:** Offer assistance to a colleague or department.	☐ **Day 18:** Share one idea to promote trust at work.

☐ **Day 19:** Have coffee with someone you don't normally socialize with.	☐ **Day 20:** Offer to stay late or come early to assist a colleague.	☐ **Day 21:** Forgive a colleague.
☐ **Day 22:** Tell each of your colleagues what you appreciate about them.	☐ **Day 23:** Tell your immediate supervisor(s) what you appreciate about them.	☐ **Day 24:** Share one idea to promote a happy/fun work environment.
☐ **Day 25:** Be straightforward. Let people know where you stand.	☐ **Day 26:** Approach each discussion with the goal to learn something.	☐ **Day 27:** Seek feedback on how to improve.
☐ **Day 28:**	☐ **Day 29:**	☐ **Day 30:**

- TRUTH # 5 -

This is the era of agility

Survive and Thrive

Our business landscape is morphing into something totally new.
The game and the rules are constantly changing, and the pace of change
will continue to accelerate. By reflecting on the past, we know for a
fact that agility is the one organizational capability required to survive
and thrive in a world where turbulent market conditions and external
factors can turn your business upside down overnight. In this rapidly
changing and disruptive economy, new norms, expectations, and challenges continue to transform and revolutionize our landscape. To survive and thrive, organizations need to promote an agile culture by continuously anticipating change, rethinking their strategies, reinventing
their processes, reimagining their hierarchy, leveraging their resources,
enabling speed, and maximizing impact.

Did You Know?

- 52 percent of Fortune 500 companies closed for business since
2000 and three-quarters will be replaced by 2027.[63]

- Nine out of 10 startup businesses fail.[64]

- 92 percent of executives believe that agility is critical to business success, while only 27 percent consider themselves agile.[65]

- Almost 30 percent of executives admit that their organizations
are at a competitive disadvantage because they lack agility.[66]

- 15 percent of executive possess the critical attribute of agility.[67]

- 43 percent of HR professionals believe that their organization
is equipped to "quickly turn challenges into opportunities." And
only 31 percent have a strategy to enable leaders to become agile.[68]

• Based on a survey of 506 global senior executives, 50 percent reported that their current culture is one of the biggest road-blocks to higher levels of agility.[65]

• 85 percent of 2030's jobs are yet to be invented.[69]

If you believe your organization is immune, think twice.
Agility is not a luxury; it is a necessity!
Your choice: Agility or fragility?

A Living Organism

Your organization is alive; it is a living organism longing to grow and thrive. This comparison is not surprising. Organizations share certain characteristics with living organisms. They work on maintaining a stable internal environment while yearning to identify patterns, act on them, grow, and reproduce. It is then reasonable to state that for organizations to endure, thrive, and flourish, they need to uphold their ideology to drive internal stability but also empower a flexible, ingenious, and resilient culture to lead the change and play to win.

An "agile culture" is not a luxury, it is a necessity.
It is the power to uphold your core ideology and continuously
adapt to complexity, ambiguity, and change.

Research done by Michael Bazigos, Aaron De Smet, and Chris Gagnon involving two million respondents at over 1,000 companies showed that agile organizations have a 70 percent chance of being in the top quartile of organizational health. The authors note that their analysis suggests that "speed and stability are significant catalysts for organizational health and performance."[70] In their "Achieving Greater Agility" report, *Forbes Insights*, on behalf of the Project Management Institute, reported an interview with Felix Hieronymi, the corporate project leader for agile transformation for Bosch in 2017, in which he stated, "There is a cultural change behind agility.... You cannot become agile without changing your behavior and your mindset. It is not about transforming the company and then claiming success or victory. It is about bringing the company to a state in which it is regularly learning and adapting."[65]

It is undeniable that agility is a core differentiator and critical for your success. Agile companies outperform lean companies in performance measures such as sales turnover, market share, and customer loyalty.[71] Research conducted at MIT states that agile firms grow revenue 37 percent faster and generate 30 percent higher profits compared to non-agile companies.[66] Another study shows that agile firms are more than twice as likely than the average organization to achieve top-quartile financial performance.[72] This is why one of the most decisive tasks of leadership is to explore these two questions:

1. How do we continuously uphold the core ideology and inspire stability?

2. How do we infuse our culture with agility in order to anticipate, adjust and respond to the changes we face and make the shift from survive to thrive?

Leaders as "Culture Musicians"

During one of my trips to Morocco, I embarked on a culture transformational journey at Mazagan Beach and Golf Resort. I worked with the managing director Max Zanardi and his team to inspire a winning culture and enable the colleagues to embrace it and translate it into actions that could be taken every day. The secret recipe? Agility.

"Leaders are culture musicians," Max said. "We sometimes play classical music (follow a traditional approach) while other times we play jazz (we improvise) or rock and roll (go bold and wild)."[73]

This analogy is very true. Leadership and music are both very powerful forces in our ever-changing world. They both transcend space and time and allow us to connect with one another and the world around us. Just like musicians, leaders should play what inspires the world so they can clear the clutter and pursue answers on how to make things happen, lead the change, and deliver. Being a musician is about being *stable but also adaptive*, as change without a sense of stability could lead to chaos. It is when you integrate stability (guided by your core ideology) with adaptability (guided by continuous agility, innovation, and progress) that you will be able to navigate change.

"You adapt, you adjust, and you win their hearts," Max said. "You lead the train, there is no question about that. And the speed becomes irrelevant if you don't effectively pull the wagons behind you. Once those wagons and passengers are on board, your job is to lead through the chaos of crossroads and tunnels to ensure you are on the right track, heading toward your new destination."[74]

The Bat and the Weasels

The fable of the bat and the weasels intrigued me for years. It shares the story of a bat that was caught by a weasel who loved eating birds. The bat begged for his life.

"I am not a bird, Mr. Weasel. I am a bat, can't you see?"

"So you are," said the weasel, and he set him free.

A few weeks later, the bat was caught again by another weasel who loved eating bats. The bat again begged for his life.

"I am not a bat Mr. Weasel. I am a bird, can't you see?"

"So you are," said the weasel, and he, too, set the bat free.

This fable reminds me of how vital agility is to enable winning. When it comes to your culture, you can't live by the book! Freedom is of the essence, and it is vital for your people, once they understand and embrace your purpose and values, to be quick and nimble, adapt to the wind of change, and consequently transform ambiguity into winning stories.

How can you infuse your culture with agility to ensure both stability and dynamism? How can you inspire your people to be flexible and volatile, freely collaborate, and address the change in their own unique ways?

The Five Fundamentals of Agile Cultures

1. Embrace a Four-Eyed Paradigm

Being agile will only pay dividends if founded on internal stability. Have you heard of four-eyed fish? They have two parts to each eye. These fish live at the water's surface, and their eyes are divided in two different parts separated by a band of tissue. They can look above the water and at the same time look below to simultaneously scan two different environments. Similar to these four-eyed fish, organizations need to a) look down to absorb their strengths from their ideology and drive internal stability; and at the same time b) look up to seize opportunities by scanning the environment and empowering a flexible, ingenious, and resilient culture.

2. Be Like Water

Would you stand still knowing that a car is coming your way? Strictness and rigidity wouldn't save you from being crushed. Stamp out strictness and be like water. Fluid, formless, shapeless, adaptive, renewable, etc. Like water, change with the change and take the shape of your new environment with rapid decision-making and execution. As Bruce Lee said, "Now you put water into a cup, it becomes the cup. You put water into a bottle, it becomes the bottle. You put it in a teapot, it becomes the teapot. Water can flow or it can crash. Be water, my friend."[75] The Ritz-Carlton Hotel Company embraced that philosophy in 2006 when they made the transformation from the 20 Basics to the 12 Service Values to stay relevant and deliver on their service commitment to their guests. Unlike the 20 Basics, which constrain the Ladies and Gentlemen (employees) by telling them what to do, the 12 Service Values represent a declaration of a trust in the power of the people to deliver the "why" in their own unique ways depending on the different situations they face. It is an invitation to be adaptive over prescriptive, inclusive over restrictive, and dynamic over passive.

3. Play with a Full Deck

Think of how many changes your team and organization faced recently. The constant state of change requires us to give up conservative management and traditional hierarchy for less restrictive structures and empowered multidisciplinary teams working in alignment, accountability, and absolute coordination. Organizations like Netflix, Apple, Spotify, Google, GE, ING, and Zappos eliminated the pain of bureaucracy by building nimble teams, assigning accountability, and celebrating cross pollination and cross collaboration. They devised a transparent environment where the free flow of information optimized learning, amplified experimentation, promoted autonomy, and accelerated execution. In a nutshell, agile organizations play with a full deck to leverage diversity and amplify innovation, speed, and impact.

4. Put People Over Processes

In late 2000, John W. Rowe, M.D., was appointed Aetna's fourth CEO in five years to lead the culture clash after the merger with U.S. Healthcare. John didn't reinforce a culture shift; instead he solicited the feedback of the team at all levels and introduced minute but effective behavioral changes that revitalized the culture of Aetna—New Aetna. Once heard and appreciated, your people will ride the wave of change and become your champions. We all agree that our people are more important than any process. But we sometimes lean toward processes because it allows us to be in control. Putting processes over people is a recipe for failure. It inhibits creativity and leads to a shortage of inspiration and a deficit in relationships, sense of belonging, and synergy. Agile cultures position processes at the service of people. Investigate and simplify your processes, make information easy to use in order to promote engagement, autonomy, experimentation, and the adoption of fast-fail strategies. That is not enough, though. Agile organizations select (hire) an agile workforce, those with entrepreneurial skills, and inject their talents with the agile skills required to work differently, like situational awareness, mental toughness, critical thinking, change management, customer centricity, questioning and active listening, empowerment, accountability, sharing feedback, and ownership. Injecting your talent with these skills will build stronger professionals who are able to steer the organization in the right direction.

5. Devote to Ceaseless Progression

The transformation has no final destination. It is not as obvious as moving from point A to point B. Point B is constantly changing, and therefore you can't rest just because you've achieved what you wanted to. The ultimate test is to survive your own success, and therefore, the more successful you are, the more devoted you should be to change, progress, and grow. Our business world is full of examples of companies such as Kodak, Blockbuster, Motorola, Myspace, Nokia, and others who rested on their laurels and consequently failed. Why? Resting once you reach success generates complacency. The way to the top requires organizations to regularly scan its environment, embrace emerging technologies, and explore possible future changes facing the organization and its stakeholders. Change should not be triggered only during tough times, and leading an agile culture requires continuous progress and modification. It is a call to gather intelligence and accordingly re-innovate, be flexible, be vigorous, and unceasingly repackage your business.

Putting It All Together

Weaving agility through your organization should be holistic and depends on the following five factors. These factors are also highlighted in this Truth's worksheet, which will serve as a starting point and guide you to find answers and formulate actions that will put you on the path to agility.

> • **Culture:** Do you have a shared purpose? How do your values inspire a stable and dynamic culture? What are the wining habits you and the team need in order to embrace a four-eyed paradigm?

- **Processes:** How can you stamp out strictness and rigidity? What processes and tools do you need to introduce, change, or simplify to sense change, be like water, and respond effectively to business needs—be adaptive over prescriptive, inclusive over restrictive, and dynamic over passive?

- **Structure:** Are you playing with a full deck supported by a clear, flat structure and accountable roles? How can you ensure informational transparency, promote autonomy, and encourage experimentation? How can you replace the traditional hierarchy with a boundaryless structure and drive cross-functional collaboration?

- **People:** Do you have a talent-management system that attracts, retains, and develops talents ready to face the future? Do you put people over processes? What are the agile skills you and your team need in order to steer the organization in the right direction? How do you infuse these skills in your people?

- **Technology:** Are you devoted to ceaseless progression? How do you introduce next-generation tools and productivity-enhancing technologies to address ambiguity with flexibility and speed?

Final Note: The Way Forward

To endure, thrive, and flourish, organizations need to build an agile culture by a) upholding their ideology to drive internal stability, and b) empowering a flexible, ingenious, and resilient culture that shifts and adapts as circumstances, conditions, and expectations change. Weaving agility through your organization depends on factors such as your current culture, processes, structure, people, and technology. The Agility Worksheet presented at the end of this Truth will guide you to leverage those factors and infuse your culture with agility to ensure both stability and dynamism. That is the way to be in the game and play to win.

Embrace a four-eyed paradigm
Be like water
Play with a full deck
Put people over processes
Devote to ceaseless progression

During our event in Morocco, Max Zanardi told his leaders, "When you run that train, be ready to change direction and adjust the course, respond to fluctuating conditions, and lead the passengers, all the passengers, towards the right destination. And the key is, be flexible, volatile, and keep moving forward." That is so true. I urge you not only to embrace but invite change, anticipate, adapt, act, and in the process, remember the words of Oklahoma's favorite son, Will Rogers: "Even if you're on the right track, you'll get run over if you just sit there."[76]

Tool # 6: Agility Worksheet

Instructions: Weaving agility through your organization depends on factors such as your current culture, processes, structure, people, and technology. This worksheet will serve as a starting point and guide you to formulate actions that will put you on the path to agility.

1. Culture: Do we have a shared purpose? How do our values inspire a stable and dynamic culture? What are the wining habits we need in order to embrace a four-eyed paradigm?
Action(s):
2. Processes: How can we stamp out strictness and rigidity? What processes and tools do we need to introduce, change, or simplify to sense change, be like water, and respond effectively to business needs—be adaptive over prescriptive, inclusive over restrictive, and dynamic over passive?
Action(s):

3. Structure: Are we playing with a full deck supported by a clear, flat structure and accountable roles? How can we ensure informational transparency, promote autonomy, and encourage experimentation? How can we replace the traditional hierarchy with a boundaryless structure and drive cross-functional collaboration?

Action(s):

4. People: Do we have a talent-management system that attracts, retains, and develops talents ready to face the future? Do we put people over processes? What are the agile skills we need in order steer the organization in the right direction? How do we infuse these skills in our people?

Action(s):

5. Technology: Are we devoted to ceaseless progression? How do we introduce next-generation tools and productivity-enhancing technologies to address ambiguity with flexibility and speed?

Action(s):

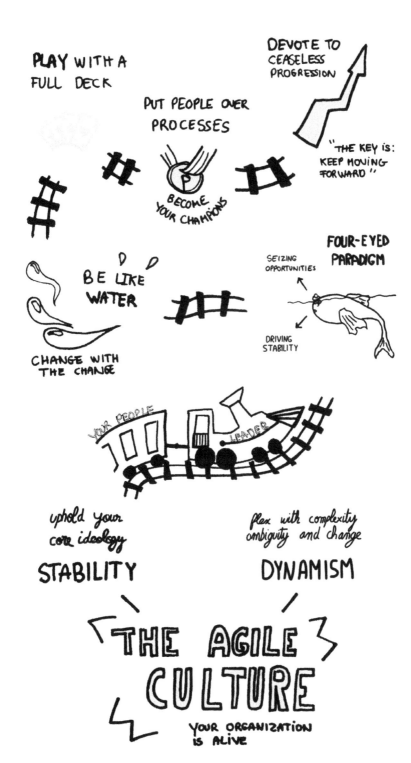

SUMMARY
PRINCIPLE 1

Organizational culture is a system of shared ideology—a set of beliefs, values, assumptions, and norms that define what is important and determine your people emotions, thoughts, actions, and performance. It is the force that defines the success of your organization; the hidden mark of distinction that shapes everything you are. It is your unique multiplier that defines:

- The way people see the organization.
- The way people interpret things.
- The way people think and behave.
- The way people do business, integrate, and deliver.

Truth #1: A purpose-driven culture is a culture worth living

Greatness is NOwhere Mindset: There is no need for a purpose beyond profit.
Greatness is NOWhere Mindset: There is no reason for being without a purpose.
Toolset: Organizational Purpose Worksheet (p. 29)   Job Purpose Worksheet (p. 30)

Truth #2: Every culture has a silver lining: The Attar Factor

Greatness is NOwhere Mindset: Values are just a plaque on the wall.
Greatness is NOWhere Mindset: Values are your deepest and most powerful motivators.
Toolset: Silver Lining Worksheet (p. 42)

Truth #3: Make culture happen. For real. Every day!

Greatness is NOwhere Mindset: Success is an act.
Greatness is NOWhere Mindset: Enduring success is a winning habit.
Toolset: Habit Worksheet (p. 56)

Truth #4: With oxytocin we charge

Greatness is NOwhere Mindset: We get things done because of fear.
Greatness is NOWhere Mindset: We get things done because of trust.
Toolset: Oxytocin Challenge (p. 70)

Truth #5: This is the era of agility

Greatness is NOwhere Mindset: Agility is a luxury.
Greatness is NOWhere Mindset: Agility is a necessity.
Toolset: Agility Worksheet (p. 85)

Golden Nuggets

Organizational greatness is the ability to produce exponential results, inspire engaged colleagues, fashion customer excitement, and leave a distinctive footprint.

Like lenses in glasses that change the way you look at things, your culture shapes your organization and defines the way you do business and the business you do.

Your core purpose powers your reason (forming effective judgments about what and how you do what you do) and passion (why you do what you do).

Values drive thoughts; thoughts drive behavior; behavior drives performance; performance drives results. Case closed.

Once you discover your signature Attar, you will define your identity and enable your organization to unleash its heavenly fragrance.

Instead of firing people, fire them up by rewiring their habits. Possibilities are born from winning habits.

Nurture a desire for renewal: it is a survival must. Have the eagerness and drive to reinvent yourself. Otherwise, you will end up on the bench.

One of your most integral roles as a leader is to inject your culture with a dose of oxytocin. It can significantly change the way you do business and leads your people and the organization to connect, make meaningful contributions, and achieve higher performance.

In the midst of this dynamic and ever-changing environment, agility should be at the heart of your culture —it is not a luxury; it is a necessity.

Build an agile culture by a) upholding your ideology to drive internal stability, and b) empowering a flexible, ingenious, and resilient culture to shift and adapt as circumstances, conditions, and expectations change.

Laugh off your failures: it is a wonderful journey. Stay strong and reward outstanding failures. Dust yourself off when needed and get on the ride again. PS: it never ends.

PRINCIPLE 2

You can't be
what your people are not

A company is known by the people it keeps.[77]

Anonymous

Once you craft and inspire a powerful winning culture, a system of a shared ideology, it is then time to start sifting people and getting the right performers on stage—performers powered by the right frame of mind and free to experiment, collaborate, lead, and deliver.

I once heard a story about a sculptor who spent his days chiseling a rock at the bottom of a mountain. One day, while passing by the emperor's palace, he was reflecting upon the emperor's supreme command and power.

"I am nothing! I am just a sculptor. How great and powerful that emperor must be. I wish I could be that emperor," he thought.

Someone must have heard his wish, and he suddenly became the mighty emperor. He found himself lying in a golden chair, with people paying him tribute and soldiers surrounding his thrown. As he was waving to the crowd, the sun hit his eyes. He was amazed by its power.

"I am nothing! I am just an emperor. How great and powerful the sun must be. I wish I could be that sun so I can make a difference," he proclaimed.

Once again, his wish was heard, and he became the sun. Roaming the skies, warming the planet, the oceans, and the atmosphere, until a cloud drifted between him and the earth. He was amazed by the cloud's power.

"I am nothing! I am just the sun. How great and powerful that cloud must be. I wish I could be that cloud so I can make a difference," he stated.

His wish was once again answered, and he became a cloud. Floating in the air, giving rain, preventing droughts, and cooling the planet until, the cloud hit a mountain. And here we go again.

"I am nothing! I am just a cloud. How great and powerful that mountain must be. I wish I could be that mountain so I can make a difference," he moaned.

Yes! He became that mountain. Feeling more powerful than anything on earth.

"Now, it is time to make a difference," he declared.

As he stood there enjoying the thrill of the moment, he heard an annoying sound. It felt like the mountain was losing some of its structure.

"What's happening? Who is more powerful than I am?" he wondered. He looked down to see a sculptor pounding a chisel into his surface with a hammer. With mixed emotions, he made his final appeal, wishing to be the man he used to be.

This story is the foundation of Principle 2. You and I exist to make a difference, regardless of our position, status, or job title. We are all influential in our own way, and we all have our own pace and place. Like most people, we are sometimes faced with a variety of personal and professional obstacles. At times we simply think of success as having more power, more possessions, better titles, prestige, and more authority. I invite you to challenge this concept of success prescribed by our culture, the media, our peers, and society, and deliberately develop your personal definition of success. It is that definition that will eventually drive you. Whatever your position, vision, mission, or motive in reading this book, you will only reach your full potential and enable organizational greatness when you harness your personal power and that of your people and gain a clear understanding of the true meaning of success.

Side Note: What Is Success?

Along my journey of coaching and leadership, I've met many individuals who sought to become someone else or were constantly comparing their lives to others. That is a monumental success trap; a journey in which you lose your uniqueness and personal viability. We constantly pursue power, prestige, and titles; yet how many stories have you heard of powerful people with broken families, prestigious organizations with crumbling reputations, or prominent executives and celebrities with ruined lives? As Dr. Ron Jenson says in his book *Achieving Authentic Success*, "You are a whole person. You have emotional, mental, physical, spiritual, and relational sides to your being.... You must be winning in all vital areas to be successful."[78] He goes on to introduce the Seven F's of our lives:

Family – Firm (career) – Fitness – Faith –
Friendships – Finances – Fun

I, too, firmly believe that success should incorporate the whole person, integrating all Seven F's, be congruent with one's core ideology, and most importantly, be measured by the lives you touch and your contribution to someone else's world.

From *In*human Resources to Talent Maximizers

We live in a new world of business where the nature of human resources (HR) is going through a major shift. And the only way forward is to reimagine the way we treat and lead our people. I have been a director of HR and always believed that human resources should sit at the helm of any executive table. After all, it is the age of talent, and people are the bedrock upon which every organization stands. The problem is, HR people are always viewed as the organization's "admins" and "mechanics" who hire, fire, safeguard regulations, and sometimes monitor productivity.

With this mindset, we will go nowhere.
That is an epic failure of the imagination.
Time to redefine.
Sit at the executive table.
Recommend talent solutions.
Inspire contribution. Case closed.

Let's play! The crossword below will challenge you to find words that describe the old "*in*human resources" mindset versus the required change to embrace the new, reimagined "talent maximizers" mindset. The words you will find either describes the world we need to let go of or depicts the mindset to embrace.

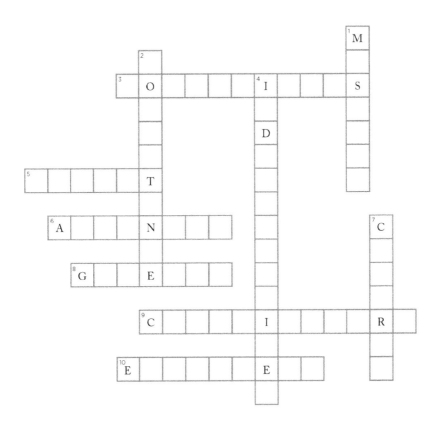

Clues: *The world to let go of (moving from)*
3. A word describing people when treated as things
7. The act of being the go-to person
8. Lacking individuality and personalization
2. Possession of a required skill, knowledge, or capacity
10. People employed for wages or salary

Clues: *The mindset to embrace (moving toward)*
9. Those who supply effort toward a cause
6. A self-governing approach
4. Shaping something to suit the individual
1. The action of mastering a subject or skill
5. Enduring natural ability; you know it when you see it

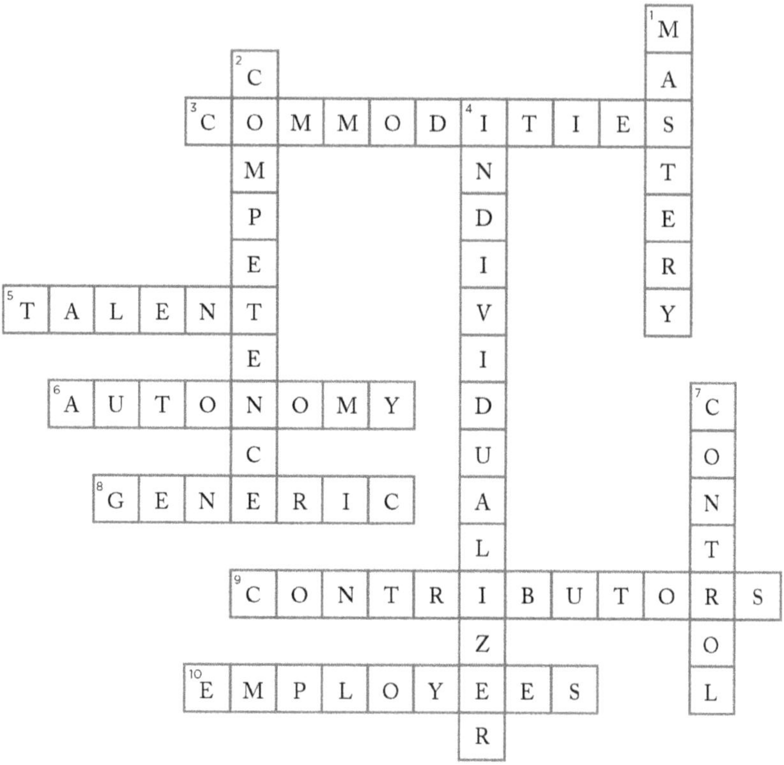

Answers: *The world to let go of (moving from)*
3. Commodities: Treating people like goods and materials—moved around, changed, and replaced at any time.
7. Control: Controlling people to achieve a set of goals.
8. Generic: Approaching and treating employees the same; a "one size fits all" management approach.
2. Competence: Striving for everyone to be able to deliver; the age of competence.
10. Employees: Managing relationships with contracts; a transactional approach.

Answers: *The mindset to embrace (moving toward)*
9. Contributors: Treating people like partners and empowered business stakeholders.
6. Autonomy: Empowering people and releasing their highest talents to achieve results.
4. Individualized: Building relationships and treating employees uniquely and individually; a "one size fits one" leadership approach.
1. Mastery: Grasping abilities and increasing performance fluency, collaboration, agility, and performance; the age of mastery.
5. Talent: Affirming and unleashing people's value and potential; a transformational approach.

Remember, you can't be what your people are not. To win and become the best in your business, it is vital to surround yourself with talented, passionate, and engaged employees who go above and beyond, bring your organizational values to life, and serve its purpose.

Five Truths to Pep up Your People

In Principle 2, I present five Truths to pep up your people:

Truth #6: Talent alone is not enough

Your talents are the cards you were dealt, but it is how you play your hand that translates talent to performance. This Truth will guide you to inject talent with its vital allies, deliberate practice and inner drive to achieve "near perfect" performance.

Truth #7: Rethink leadership: All bets are off!

Today's pace of change is relentless. The world as we know it is shifting, and at some point, it is vague as hell. This Truth repackages and redefines leadership. This new definition does not eliminate any of what you know about leadership, but in fact augments it.

Truth #8: Autonomy is the ruling currency

Winning in today's competitive battleground requires leaders to shift from a *me*-centered paradigm (control paradigm) to a *we*-centered paradigm (release paradigm). This Truth makes the case that autonomy is critical for personal growth, vital for societal prosperity, and pivotal for organizational success. This Truth also presents the "Nine is Mine" autonomy kit to inspire you to navigate the world of autonomy.

Truth #9: Bring out the gold: A to Z

Leadership is a balancing act between focusing inward (self-awareness, self-control, and cultivating your personal operating system) and focusing outward (zero in on uplifting and leading others). This Truth shares 26 action statements with the aim to inspire you to approach leadership with the "Alchemist" mindset—finding your inner gold and bringing out the gold in others.

Truth #10: Energy: The supreme power

An impalpable power lies at the core of your organization. This invisible force makes your culture, and everything for that matter, work. This Truth reveals the power of organizational energy and will inspire you to orchestrate energy through the power of play, fun, and focus.

I challenge you to see how these Truths and the respective tools can be applied. Work with your team to translate the learning outcomes into actions to enable great teams, great execution, and great results. Remember what Henry Ford once said: "You can take my factories, burn up my buildings, but give me my people, and I'll build the business right back again."[79]

- TRUTH # 6 -

Talent alone is not enough

Talent: The Word

I love the sound of it: Talent.

The English writer and philosopher Aldous Huxley once said, "There is no substitute for talent. Industry and all its virtues are of no avail."[80] Talent is powerful, positive, and vibrant. It is associated with words like gift, flair, genius, ingenuity, special aptitude, knack, forte, and brilliance, and is defined as the natural endowments of a person.[81] When you think of the word talent, you think of people such as Leonardo da Vinci, William Shakespeare, Ludwig van Beethoven, Anna Pavlova, John Lennon, Andrew Carnegie, Andrea Bocelli, Gerhard Richter, Steve Jobs, Meryl Streep, Michael Jordan, J. K. Rowling, etc.; people who exhibited true distinction and enriched our world.

Make no mistake, the word talent is not limited to world-class performers and superstars but is also true in the same way and to the same degree of people in any kind of industry and organization.

We all have innate abilities. You might find it difficult to accept this, but you and I can acquire greatness in any field. Many scholars and researchers argue that talent is overrated, while others are on the quest to find more answers.[82] But one thing remains true. We all possess amazing potential and more abilities than we can imagine, and anyone can achieve mastery and exceptional performance in any area of life.

I define talent as your abilities and potential that, if invested in, would yield near perfect performance.

You've got to love the world of talent.
Talent creates brands that inspire.
Talent resides everywhere.
The matter is settled.

BUT… Talent Alone Is Not Enough

If your talents are the cards you were dealt, how you play your hand is what translates talent to performance. Talent—your abilities and potential—will only yield ideal perfect execution if partnered with its vital allies—deliberate practice and inner drive.

Figure 3. Reimagine Talent

Ally #1: Deliberate Practice

In his book *Talent is Overrated*, Geoff Colvin refers to amazing performers such as Tiger Woods and Mozart and presents evidence showing that the secret to outstanding success is deliberate practice. The author says, "Deliberate practice is hard. It hurts. But it works. More of it equals better performance. Tons of it equals great performance."[83] Injecting your talent with deliberate practice will lead to change and mastery. As Michael Fullan states in his book *Change Leader*, "The best source of learning is day-to-day practice because it is the only experience that can engage and reshape the brain."[84] In their book *Peak: Secrets From the New Science of Expertise*, psychologist K. Anders Ericsson and science writer Robert Pool make the case that talent is crucial for success but also emphasizes that "expert performers develop their extraordinary abilities through years and years of dedicated practice."[85] For example, in their pioneering study, psychologists Herbert Simon and William Chase observed that attaining the level of an international chess master (grandmaster) requires a decade of intense preparation.[86] These findings were supported by other studies involving athletes, authors, artists, composers, and educators.

The evidence is overwhelming:
Maximizing performance requires a deliberate effort to improve.

Question #1: How much deliberate effort do we need to achieve world-class mastery?

In the praised book *Outliers: The Story of Success,* Malcolm Gladwell writes about some of the most successful people, such as Bill Gates and the Beatles, to show that the concept of a "self-made man" is a myth and that innate abilities only matter to a point. Extensive practice, up to 10,000 hours, enables true mastery.[87] Before reaching mastery, Michael Jordan practiced for five to six hours a day; the Beatles performed for eight hours a day, seven days a week; Bill Gates practically lived in a computer lab for five years; Mozart endured 10 years of deliberate practice before he produced his greatest compositions. Now, don't be discouraged by these numbers. You are capable of mastering any ability if you train in the correct way. Ericsson and Pool studied the top performers in many fields to find out that it's about focus and intensity, not duration.[85] In one of his articles, author Michael Simmons describes a pattern he identified in the lives of some of the top business leaders such as Bill Gates, Elon Musk, Warren Buffett, and Oprah Winfrey; these leaders engaged in deliberate practice for one hour a day.[88] My rule of thumb: it is not about how much you practice but *how* you practice—the quality of the practice. Practice smarter, not harder!

Question #2: What is deliberate practice?

Deliberate practice is not just practice. Much of the practice we are involved in is mere repetition or is governed by autopilot. Deliberate practice is about engaging systematically in an activity to achieve well-defined improvement goals through intense focus, continuous experimentation, and smart repetition. In other terms, it is a purposeful, focused, and systematic repetition. The journey should be supported by an expert coach and powered by a structured, precise, informative, constructive, and active feedback mechanism with a combination of coaching, observations, surveys, self-rating, and 360-degree evaluations, for the purpose of improving proficiency of the practice.

Question #3: How can you apply deliberate practice in the business world?

The idea of practicing in business sounds overwhelming. However, companies such as Toyota, Apple, Porsche, GE, and Marriott strive to invest in, stretch, and grow people, inject practice and reflection into the day-to-day operation, design rich feedback mechanisms through mentoring and coaching, etc. We all strive to improve the way we operate. The key is to transform your normal business tasks and activities into continuous learning and improvement practices—forecasting, solving problems, leading effective meetings, strategizing, speaking in public, providing a superior service, negotiating and closing deals, designing marketing plans, etc. Can you imagine the impact on your business if you and your organization engage in deliberate practice and slightly improve every day? Jump out of your comfort zone, make it a habit to practice new skills, find a mentor, ask for feedback, reflect on how to improve, and win. In this Truth, I share a roadmap and a worksheet that will guide you to put deliberate practice to work.

Ally #2: Inner Drive

Deliberate practice is a highly intensive and demanding activity. The continuous act of smart repetition towards achieving a progressive goal, accompanied by intensive constructive feedback and self-criticism, will take its toll on you. This is why you have to be equipped with a deep feeling of determination to move forward and finish strong. It is fair to say that your inner drive is your lifeblood, and it will eventually determine your success or failure. Much of the research supports the power of inner drive to endure the pressure and power the passion required along the journey to greater performance. The question is, how do you manage your inner drive? Investigating decades of scientific research on motivation, Daniel Pink's book *Drive* offers evidence that intrinsic motivation is ignited if and when people are given the freedom to choose (autonomy), supported by a larger sense of meaning (purpose) and an inner urge to achieve perfection (mastery).[20] As leaders, it is our calling to ignite the fire within us and those we lead to drive momentum and ensure effective, deliberate practice. Many organizations are reaping the fruits of this powerful drive. They are inspiring a sense of purpose (refer to Truth #1), promoting mastery through continuous learning and building winning habits (refer to Truth #4), and stimulating autonomy (subject of Truth #8) to generate results. As Frederick Herzberg, the American psychologist wrote in his most notable article "One More Time: How Do You Motivate Employees?", "If I kick my dog (from the front or the back), he will move. And when I want him to move again, what must I do? I must kick him again. Similarly, I can charge a person's battery, and then recharge it, and recharge it again. But it is only when one has a generator of one's own that we can talk about motivation. One then needs no outside stimulation. One *wants* to do it."[89]

Below are a few more tips to cultivate your inner drive:

1. Visualize success and stretch your capabilities: Picture the outcome and envision yourself achieving it. Put that picture in your everyday life, stretch your capabilities, work hard, focus your attention on the task at hand, and link your actions to the next step and ultimately your greater purpose. In his book *Flow*, psychologist Mihaly Csikszentmihalyi's investigations of optimal experience reveals that, "The best moments usually occur when a person's body and mind is stretched to the limits in a voluntary effort to accomplish something difficult and worthwhile."[90]

2. Trust yourself and practice optimism: Nurture hope and optimism by toasting your worth and potential, tracking your achievements, and leveraging the power of incremental progress. Celebrate yourself; you deserve it.

3. Chase utter joy: Sometimes practice isn't fun, so find the sense of joy it brings to you. Despite the hard work, the journey should be internally fulfilling, interesting, and enjoyable. If it is not, that might not be your calling. You should find happiness in what you do. True happiness is ignited when you fully engage your talents and inner joy.

4. Find your inspiration: Take a ride in nature, clear your mind with meditation, or listen to music. Surround yourself with what inspires you and disconnect to refocus.

5. Embrace patience: Patience is the art of intelligent growth. It will give you the gifts of time, reflection, and preparation and fuel your endurance and persistence. Patience is a virtue.

Talent Maximizer Worksheet (TMW)

The worksheet at the end of this Truth will guide you to unlock your own, and your people's potential. Let's explore!

Step 1: Talent

A: Goal: Define the capability or potential that you seek to unleash.
E.g., improve my public speaking skills.

B: Targets: Identify measurable, well-defined steps aligned with the capability or potential that you seek to master. Think of this as breaking down your goal into specific targets and defining the phases of improvement or clarifying the milestones to achieve.
E.g., focus on building a story board. Then storytelling. Then enunciation, posture, and gestures. Then the whole routine, etc.

Step 2: Deliberate Practice

A: Coach: Identify a coach for effective collaboration, accountability, and guidance. If you don't have the opportunity to work directly with a coach, identify a peer, a mentor, or some form of self-assessment.
E.g., coach XYZ.

B: Duration: State the number of practice hours that you are planning to complete.
E.g., two hours per day.

C: Resources: Identify the required resources for practice.
E.g., checklist, video camera, games, exercises, books, space for practice, technology, etc.

D: Plan: Craft a detailed plan and find a block of time in your day for deliberate practice *(concentration zone:* mostly when your energy is at its highest). Keep track of your practices and try new learning and practice methods. Think of stretched actions to take and push yourself out of your comfort zone.
E.g., 9:00 to 11:00 a.m. Speak at forums, debate clubs, meetings; read and summarize public speaking books; listen to and analyze speeches; model the best speakers; learn through case studies; practice in front of a mirror, etc.

E: Measurement and feedback: Monitor progress by defining the measurement system and developing mechanisms for structured, precise, constructive, and immediate feedback. Engage in self-reflection, solicit feedback from your coach, and learn from the process. Modify previous skills. Think of how you could do better. Prioritize and address the areas to improve systematically, one area at a time.
E.g., analyze your speech using a checklist and log your progress (time, content, pace, clarity, hand gestures, posture, breathing, etc.).

Step 3: Inner Drive

A: Progress: Define the progress milestone(s) and celebrate the tiniest improvements.
E.g., building a story board. Then storytelling. Then enunciation, pace, posture, and gestures. Then the whole routine, etc.

B: Recovery: Your deliberate practice requires deliberate rest. Identify a handful of rituals to recover, recharge, avoid mental weariness, and continuously ignite your inner drive during and after the practice.
E.g., do something mindless and recharge your batteries (visualization, a walk in nature, listening to music, a quick break, etc.)

No Finish Line

There is no denying that deliberate practice seems like a challenge, or even a struggle. I love to see it as an exceptional race; not a sprint but a marathon that requires consistent planning, preparation, discipline, hard work, and consistency. A journey in which you discover and unleash the greatness in you and in those you lead and serve. You and I are not immune to adversities, so be determined, and despite all odds, never ever quit and keep chasing that finish line. The following quote attributed to David Goggins, considered by many to be one of the world's best ultra-endurance athletes, says it all: "When I cross the finish line of a big race, I see that people are ecstatic, but I'm thinking about what I'm going to do tomorrow. It is as if my journey is everlasting, and there is no finish line."[91]

Talent Springs From the Most Unexpected Places

The ripple effect of September 11, 2001 struck the hospitality industry hard on several counts. There was an instantaneous impact. People were scared, guests moved out of hotels, traveling became difficult, and hotel occupancy hit record lows. It was during these turbulent times that Rainer J. Bürkle was assigned the task of leading the newly opened Ritz-Carlton, Istanbul. Managing the crisis, Rainer had to make some tough decisions to ensure sustainable performance. In the midst of this emotional journey, he was approached by one of his leaders suggesting he hire a shoeshine valet in the lobby named Halis. Despite the fact that the shoeshine valet was from a traditional shoe shining family who had built a reputation for quality service, Rainer immediately rejected the idea. "We are in the middle of a crisis," he thought.[92] Any general manager could have done the same. What Rainer wasn't prepared for was the persistence of his leader and the unconventional approach of Halis, who pleaded for a chance and insisted that he would not want any money until the business was back on track.

"All I want is to be part of this family and have a corner in the lobby," Halis said.

A few weeks later and to Rainer's surprise, he noticed that guests were fully engaged with Halis; he was at the heart of the guest experience.

"He polished those shoes like Michelangelo painted," Rainer exclaimed. "He became the focal point in the arrival area of the hotel, greeting guests, anticipating needs, and making every guest feel wanted and at home. Soon enough, Halis became part of the team, and played his role to save our hotel."

Fifteen years later, one of the videos in The Ritz-Carlton digital marketing video series depicts this same shoeshiner, Halis, sharing details of the role he played within The Ritz-Carlton, Istanbul to create one-of-a-kind experiences and enliven The Ritz-Carlton mystique. This story exemplifies the role your talented people play in making your company thrive. Sometimes we tend to unintentionally suppress those talents and lead by assumptions. "The experience undoubtedly changed my approach and perception of certain situations we normally feel so sure about," Rainer exclaimed.

Final Note: How Do You Play Your Hand?

Remember how I started this Truth? Your talents are the cards you were dealt, but it is how you play your hand that translates talent to near perfect performance. My final, thought-provoking question is:

How do you nurture the talent of your people so they can perform like Halis did, polishing every shoe like Michelangelo painted?

And what better way to end this Truth than with the words of the Irish poet, Brendan F. Behan: "If you have a talent, use it in every which way possible. Don't hoard it. Don't dole it out like a miser. Spend it lavishly, like a millionaire intent on going broke."[93]

Tool # 7: Talent Maximizer Worksheet (TMW)

Instructions: Start by defining the capability or potential that you seek to unleash. Then work your way through the worksheet to unlock your and your people's potential.

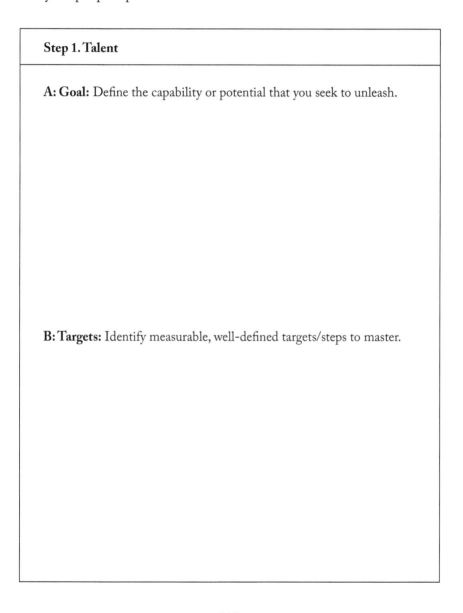

Step 1. Talent

A: Goal: Define the capability or potential that you seek to unleash.

B: Targets: Identify measurable, well-defined targets/steps to master.

Step 2. Deliberate Practice

A: Coach: Identify a coach for effective collaboration, accountability, and guidance.

B: Duration: State the number of practice hours that you are planning to complete.

C: Resources: Identify the required resources for practice.

D: Plan: Craft a detailed plan and find a block of time in your day for deliberate practice.

E: Measurement and feedback: Monitor progress. Reflect and learn from the process. Modify previous skills. Think of how you could do better. Prioritize and address the areas to improve.

Step 3. Inner Drive

A: Progress: Define the progress milestone(s) and celebrate the tiniest improvements.

B: Recovery: Identify rituals to recover, recharge, avoid mental weariness, and continuously feed your motivation.

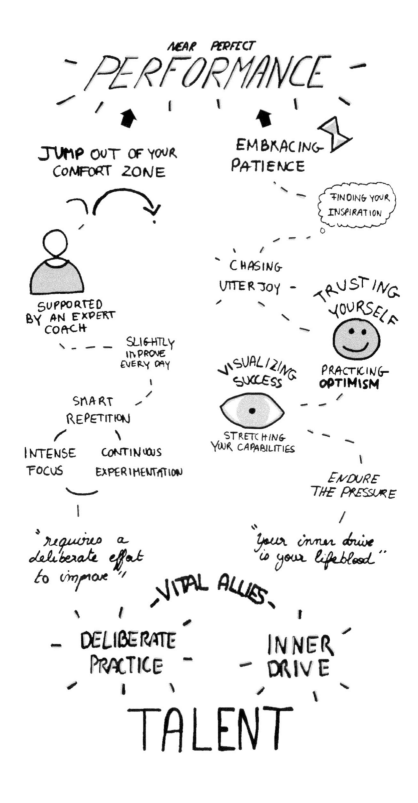

- TRUTH # 7 -

Rethink leadership:
All bets are off!

All Bets Are Off!

As leaders, we exist to serve, develop, and grow others. Our leadership success is not only measured by financial results, it is also measured by our ability to grow talents that are capable of driving sustainable performance at every level. Many definitions of leadership exist, some vague, others downright puzzling; however, the various definitions highlight leadership's role as positively affecting people, teams, and organizations. The most-cited leadership scholar in the world, Bernard Morris Bass, saw leadership as an act and an art and defined it "as the focus of group processes, as a personality attribute, as the art of inducing compliance, as an exercise of influence, as a form of persuasion, as a power relation, as an instrument in the attainment of goals, as an effect of interaction, as a differentiated role, and as the initiation of structure."[94] In his *Handbook of Leadership*, Ralph M. Stogdill concludes that "there are almost as many definitions of leadership as there are persons who have attempted to define the concept."[95] And finally, the leadership guru Warren Bennis, in his 1989 book *On Becoming a Leader,* summed it up by comparing leadership to beauty, stating that while it may be difficult to define leadership, "you know it when you see it."[96]

You Know It When You See It…

Leaders symbolize a source of power, bravery, and strength from which their people acquire their self-esteem, self-confidence, and enthusiasm. Leaders project a purpose to which others can aspire, shifting their awareness, needs, and wants toward higher-order ideals. Leaders foster innovation, taking risks and seizing opportunities to change the status quo for the better. Leaders acknowledge differences, coach, mentor, and provide individualized support. Leaders empower and foster delegation, authority, and decision-making, and integrate their people into their work process, enhancing organizational contribution and commitment.

It is true—you absolutely know it when you see it!

The Oath of Leadership

Today's pace of change is relentless. The world as we know it is changing constantly. Today's leaders are facing new challenges of huge proportions. Consider these 10 forces that are changing our world:

1. Working with socially conscious leaders and organizations will be the norm.

2. Personalized employee experiences will pervade headlines.

3. The days of lifetime employment is over.

4. For the first time, five generations are working together.

5. People are not looking for work, they are looking for meaning.

6. What leaders know and do can rapidly become obsolete.

7. Thinking out of the box is the music of yesterday; leaders need to smash the box.

8. Disruptive trends are always "on the way."

9. The technology parade just started; AI, automation, and robotics will continue to reshape our world.

10. Inflation of customers' expectations! You have seen nothing yet.

These 10 forces and others make one think about what the true essence of leadership in today's vigorous world is. After much contemplation, intensive research, and debates with executives from all around the globe, I came to the conclusion that:

Leadership is an oath to enrich the lives of others—
a one-size-fits-one choice to enable greatness.

This new notion does not eliminate any of what you know about leadership, but in fact augments it. Let's dig into this statement.

A: One Size Fits One

Many blogs, articles, and books discuss analogies between gardening and leadership. These powerful concepts provide fresh ways of seeing, understanding, and shaping our world of leadership and organizational growth. In these discussions, leaders are compared to gardeners whose purpose is to get the right plants (right people), provide the right environment (culture), and nurture the plants to grow and bear fruit (results). Adding to this analogy, I would love to share some insights from a recent gardening experience I had. A short time ago, I made a decision to refurbish my backyard and bought several flowers of all shapes and sizes. Despite my efforts to nurture these plants, I realized a few months later that many plants had started to wilt, developed yellow and brown leaves, and their growth was stunted. I hired a gardener to assist me on this quest to realize one simple truth: *It's all in the pot.* I learned that if the pot is too small, the soil dries quickly, which can lead to growth issues or the plant rooting to the pot. Being proactive, I then bought ultra-large pots so I wouldn't have to move the plants again in the future. I also learned that doing so can hinder the plants' progress. The water takes longer to dry out in ultra-large pots, making the plant more susceptible to root rot, which could ultimately kill the plant. The perfect pot size really depends on the plant's diameter, and you should only increase the diameter of the pot by two to three inches at a time. By finding the right pot, my plants grew over 40 percent larger.

The lessons here are critical.

1. Leadership is not a one dimensional, one-size-fits-all approach.

People, like plants, are different. You should not treat everyone the same. Some people will thrive in their current pot, while others require a larger one (higher authority, focused mentoring, individualized coaching, stretched goals, increased job scope, specialized assignment, responsibilities outside of their job function, etc.) The question is, beyond their names and job titles, how much do you know your people, their likes and dislikes, passion and aspirations, learning styles, obstacles and fears? Your people are valuable and worth knowing, and therefore it is crucial to embrace a one-size-fits-one approach whereby you genuinely know them and lead them accordingly.

2. There is no such thing as "the best leadership style."

Remember, plants grow in different containers. Labeling yourself with a single leadership style is the ultimate trap. The truth is, every style might be a great choice. It is your ability to adapt your leadership style to different people that matters. This refers to coaching, mentoring, advising, supporting, and providing individualized support.

3. Going too big too fast can be detrimental.

Like plants, people are unique and tend to grow depending on their distinctive environment, so take the time to properly nurture them. I am always inspired by the story of the man who was watching a butterfly struggling to get out of the chrysalis (aka cocoon). He finally decided to assist the butterfly and cut open the cocoon, only to find that his action disrupted the natural growth process required to strengthen the butterfly's muscles for it to be able to fly. The very first truth you must accept is the fact that you can't build six-pack abs overnight. As a leader, discuss your people's interests and career goals, then foster a gradual, ongoing development roadmap together.

In a world where everyone is unique, there is nothing more liberating and uplifting than crafting one-size-fits-one choices that will ultimately enable greatness.

B: Choice

In September of 2014, I was invited to meet Darrell Schaeffer at a gorgeous boutique hotel in Souq Waqif, Doha, Qatar. He wanted to hire my company to craft the core ideology and service DNA of his organization. I knew Darrell from when he was the general manager of The Ritz-Carlton, Doha back in 2000 when I started my career at The Ritz-Carlton Hotel Company.

At the beginning of the meeting, I shared with him the following story.

1999: The Beginning

Back in 1999, my father convinced his employer to grant him his end-of-service benefits 10 years in advance of his retirement, freeing him up financially. He was determined to support my plan to travel to Switzerland and embark on my postgraduate education. I was too young back then to fully appreciate the extent of my father's sacrifice. Today, I can't grasp the depth of his love enough. The journey was indeed transformational on all levels, and toward the end of it, I grabbed the opportunity to join The Ritz-Carlton, Doha in the capacity of an income auditor. Truth be told, finance wasn't my cup of tea, but I saw this job as a stepping-stone to grow from within and become the learning and development professional I always aspired to be.

Note: As you continue reading this story, bear in mind that I am sharing it with Darrell over a cup of coffee in 2014.

August 2001: When Reality Strikes

A few months after joining the pre-opening team, I realized that I was way off the path to my dream. My transfer request to the HR department was rejected. Remember, the hotel wasn't open yet, and honestly, why on earth would you consider someone in finance to move into HR in the first place? So, despite my high degree of optimism, I doubted the choice I made and became heavy hearted, to say the least. With the kind of salary I was earning, I couldn't even save enough money to fly back to Lebanon and visit the family. Every time my father called, I was embarrassed to share my status. "With all the money he invested in me, he must think I am a manager by now," I thought.

January 8, 2002: The Daily Lineup

During the pre-opening period, the 600 Ladies and Gentlemen (as the employees are called) would come together to attend the daily lineup. The purpose of this daily forum was to inspire the team, promote the organization's culture, and keep us all posted on the status of the hotel's opening. It was also an open forum lead by Darrell where anyone could share ideas, thoughts, challenges, and opportunities. Speaking of opportunities, I saw this lineup as the perfect break to showcase my leadership and public speaking skills and enable everyone—especially the HR team—to acknowledge that hidden talent in the finance division (yes, me!). So, I volunteered to facilitate the lineup, and on that 8th of January, I literally rocked the house! It was fifteen minutes of pure inspiration. "Now, the HR team will come looking for me," I thought! But nothing happened, and two weeks later, I got another transfer rejected. That was the tipping point.

January 23, 2002: The Walk That Changed My Life

I remember that day vividly. Lying on my bed, my tears covering a piece of paper entitled, "Resignation." The day after, I gathered my strength and started my journey towards the HR department to hand in my resignation. A long, grey corridor separated the executive offices from the stairs that led to HR. While walking down the corridor, I saw Darrell approaching from the other side. I was in a desperate mood. I looked down at the grey carpet and moved at steady pace, trying to blend with the wall. When he got close, he stopped me, shook my hand, and said, "Hey, Melkart. Your speech a few weeks ago was stunning. You will grow to become an amazing trainer! Hang in there, buddy." Those few words ignited that fire within, and instead of going down the stairs, I recall stopping by the restrooms at the end of that corridor, tearing up my resignation letter, wearing my smile again, and refocusing on my dream. That was the walk that changed my life. In the next six years, I grew to become the corporate director of global learning at The Ritz-Carlton Hotel Company.

The Essence of Leadership

That's not the end of the story, though. Here's the golden nugget! Back to the 2014 meeting at Souq Waqif. After sharing my story with Darrell, he gazed at me with a sense of peculiarity and proclaimed, "Melkart, truth be told, I have no recollection whatsoever of that incident; our chat in the corridor." What a stunning lesson that is, isn't it? That is the essence of leadership. It is that CHOICE you make to enrich and transform people's lives, sometimes without even noticing that you did it…. Do you realize how transformational the impact of your choices—an act of kindness, a handshake, a smile or few words—can be on the lives of those you lead? Every day you are faced with hundreds of choices whereby you can ignite the talent and passion of others. Every choice is an opportunity to fashion transformation. Seize those moments because your greatness is defined by the lives you touch. The following quote by the German theologian and philosopher Albert Schweitzer encapsulates the message of this Truth: "In everyone's life, at some time, our inner fire goes out. It is then burst into flame by an encounter…. We should all be thankful for those people who rekindle the inner spirit."[97] Yes, leadership is an oath to enrich the lives of others—a one-size-fits-one choice to enable greatness.

C: Enabling Greatness

May 2016, Angola, Africa.

My trip to Angola was one experience that changed my perception of life in many ways. I was on a mission to enable greatness with a special group of architects and engineers who played a significant role in rebuilding the country after almost 27 years of civil war that ended in 2002. Even though I was born and raised in Lebanon during the civil war, witnessing the poverty in Angola was a choking experience. Now, bear in mind that Angola isn't on the list of the top poorest countries in the world. In fact, it is one of the most resource-rich countries in Africa. I visited the capital Luanda that year, and I can confirm that the government worked hard in recent years to build roads, schools, bridges, and hospitals, but this city significantly contrasts these signs of development, where some people face very harsh conditions. So there I was, facilitating leadership workshops and coaching architects and engineers on how to maximize their personal impact and promote authentic leadership, while outside that fancy training venue, people were living in poverty. A truth I couldn't successfully grasp until I met Bachir.

Bachir Zeidan, aka The Architect, took me on a ride to explore the city a few days after my arrival. We first visited the city center, which includes the Presidential Palace, the Palace of Justice, the Defense Ministry, the Ministry of Justice and Human Rights, the Episcopal Palace, and the premises of the former National Assembly headquarters. The latest addition was the state-of-the-art National Assembly Building, covering an area of 72,000 square meters and consisting of 11 tons of steel, 70,000 cubic meters of concrete, and 370 tons of metal. With 500 kilometers of low-tension electric wire surrounding the building, this project cost amounted to millions of Euros. Yet a few miles down the road, I saw people living in unacceptable conditions. You can't even withstand the smell permeating some streets. I couldn't help but feel discouraged by what I had seen, and I wondered how someone like my friend, The Architect, could embrace this reality and continue to push forward, executing a vision despite the truth of the present. Hearing my frustration, Bachir shared some leadership lessons that enabled him to strive and leave his mark throughout the years. I learned more about greatness from my friend The Architect than he learned from me that day. He made me believe in the words of Norman Foster, that "as an architect, you design for the present with an awareness of the past for a future which is essentially unknown."[98] Bachir added his own twist, "You have to forge ahead and make things better. We change lives one brick at a time," he said. "After all, we are all architects."[99]

I found his mindset very powerful and worth spreading:

> **A**gility in the face of unexpected obstacles
> **R**esilience and mental fortitude
> **C**ollaborative mindset
> **H**uman—everything goes back to H
> **I**ntercultural aptitude
> **T**eam and technology! Leverage both to win
> **E**motional intelligence
> **C**ritical thinking
> **T**olerance of change and uncertainty

Agility in the face of unexpected obstacles
Describes the leadership ability to swim in rapid, unpredictable white-water. Making the right choices and embracing the continuous process of learning and adapting at every turn.

Resilience and mental fortitude
Describes the leadership ability to deal with setbacks, stressors, and pressure. Being in control of your emotions, making and keeping promises, seeing challenges as opportunities, and having the inner strength to stand your ground.

Collaborative mindset
Describes the leadership ability to inspire trust and focus on "we" instead

of "me." Optimizing the collective brainpower of the entire organization, promoting diversity, and stimulating balanced contributions.

Human—everything goes back to H!
Describes the leadership ability to be authentic and celebrate the greatness in others. Radiating hope, optimism, and genuine care. Integrating the H into every policy, system, and structure, and humanizing the workplace.

Intercultural aptitude
Describes the leadership ability to build bridges, lead, and manage people of all cultures. Connecting the different kind of dots, understanding and valuing differences, and making the necessary changes to maximize the dynamics of teams.

Team and technology. Leverage both to win!
Describes the leadership ability to leverage technology. Taking advantage of the digital revolution, investigating emerging technologies, and mastering social media to rally people around the purpose and create raving fans.

Emotional intelligence
Describes the leadership ability to recognize, assess, and manage emotions. Being smart with emotions, understanding how emotions drive behavior, and setting the tone through self-awareness, self-management and relationship management.

Critical thinking
Describes the leadership ability to question the norms and examine assumptions. Considering different alternatives and diverse angles, exploring and analyzing potential risks and opportunities, and building powerful judgmental skills.

Tolerance of change and uncertainty
Describes the leadership ability to realign rigorously. Focusing on

agility, changing perspectives if and when needed, handling ambiguity, and most importantly, applying mid-course corrections to achieve the mission.

Final note: It's All About You:

Yes! Leadership is about enriching the lives of others—a one-size-fits-one choice to enable greatness. It is indeed true what one of the most influential architects of the 20th century, Louis Khan said, "Architecture is the reaching out for the truth."[100] I firmly believe that we are all architects in our own unique ways. We use different types of "bricks" to enable greatness, that's all. Your brick might be a word in a poem, a note in a symphony, or an idea for a project....

At the end of this Truth, I share a simple tool, "It's All About You" (IAAY), that you can practice with your team. It is designed to elicit unique information about your people in order to make effective choices and enable greatness. The questions in this tool are the outcomes of an activity I've led all over the globe, where I asked employees to answer the following question: "What would you like your leader to learn about you in order to make effective choices and enable greatness?"

Enable greatness, everywhere.
Start building.
Build a relationship, a team, an organization.
The key to greatness is to start building.
Pick up your own brick and make a difference.

And never forget the most valuable lesson of all:
Even a brick wants to be something.

Tool # 8: It's All About You Worksheet (IAAY)

Instructions: Share Part I with your employees and allow them ample time to complete it and share their findings.[3] In Part II, use the information (Part I) to craft one-size-fits-one leadership choices that ultimately unleash the greatness of each team member.

Part I: It's All About You!

What is your purpose? Why do you do what you do?	How do you prefer to work?	What are your unique talents and strengths?	What is it that you are really passionate about?
What would you like to learn?	How do you learn best?	What are your short-term aspirations?	What are your long-term aspirations?
How can I support you in your role?	How can I make your job more fulfilling?	What projects would you like to work on?	What do you enjoy doing most in your job?

---

[3] Make your own set of questions and repeat this exercise quarterly to identify new patterns, track progress, and craft your choices.

What obstacles do you currently face at work? Where are you stuck?	How can you create the most value in your role?	If you were the leader of this team, what would you do differently?	How can you integrate your life (all 7 Fs)?
How would you like to be recognized?	What is your favorite gift? Snack? Book? Hobby?	How often should we get together to discuss how things are going?	How can I be a better leader for you?

Part II: Based on the information above, list your one-size-fits-one leadership choices (personalized coaching, support, learning, etc.) to unleash the greatness of *(name of the team member)*.

- TRUTH #8 -

Autonomy is
the ruling currency

Yes, Freedom Matters

Freedom is a basic human need, a fundamental human interest, a precious right, and the power all of us seek. Freedom enables us to be ourselves, express our voice, and be who we really want to be. Freedom is simply important because its absence is detrimental to the very reason of our existence.

It is the bedrock of human development.
It is vital for societal prosperity.
It is crucial to mobilize energy.
It is pivotal for organizational growth.

Freedom and choice are essential for leadership. Instead of controlling or being controlled, you grasp the truth that everyone has the power to make their own choices. As leaders, we have a moral obligation to inspire freedom in those we lead, create a culture of liberty, and enable our people to use their freedom congruously in their pursuit to find the best versions of themselves. Nelson Mandela stated that fact clearly in his speech at the Chief Albert Luthuli Centenary Celebration on 25 April 1998, "Real leaders must be ready to sacrifice all for the freedom of their people."[101] I said it earlier; leadership is a choice.

Expanding that choice will always be a focus point for humanity.
Freedom of speech and freedom of expression.
Freedom to live and freedom to succeed.
Freedom of information and freedom of association.
Freedom to act and freedom to create…Freedom of CHOICE!

The American revolutionary and one of the founding fathers of the United States, Patrick Henry, said in his famous speech on March 23, 1775, "Almighty God! I know not what course others may take; but as for me, give me liberty or give me death!"[102]

Freedom is a basic psychological human need.
Freedom is vital for optimal wellness and performance.
Yes, freedom matters, and freedom works.
As leaders, it is time to work for freedom.

The Heaviest Burden in Your Team Might Be YOU

I am sure you don't like the sound of this statement, but before you scrap this section, hear me out. Do you catch yourself or others within your organization saying the following?

My way or the highway. Because I said so. Follow my orders. We tried this before. What does the policy state? It is the policy. Follow the way things are done around here. Did you check with me? Ask before you do it. Worry about your job and let me worry about mine. Wait until you are told to do so. Did you have my approval? I am the final authority. I am in control. It should be done by the book. I am the go-to person. I run the organization. You disobeyed me.

These statements usually come from those who constantly seek control, hovering over and checking up on everything. It is a ME-centered paradigm, and the damaging facts are troubling. Harry Chambers' cites a survey in his book *My Way or the Highway* that showed that 79 percent of respondents had experienced micromanagement and 69 percent of them said they considered changing jobs because of micromanagement. 36 percent actually changed jobs, 71 percent said being micromanaged interfered with their job performance, and 85 percent said their morale was negatively impacted.[103] The impact of a controlling leadership paradigm is detrimental. Micromanagement disempowers, demotivates, and disengages staff, leading to low morale;[104] it hurts productivity[105] and sparks fear and defensive silence, hence inhibiting creative performance.[106] It inhibits the growth and development of employees[103] and the organization alike. Another study from the Indiana University Kelley School of Business found that those in high-stress jobs with little control are associated with "a 15.4 percent increase in the likelihood of death."[107]

ME-Centered Paradigm: It's About CONTROL

Controlling managers are efficient and can achieve results, but they need to endlessly motivate and manage others and be part of crafting every solution and solving every problem. They might take credit and the opportunity from others to shine and ultimately set others and the organization up for failure. The outcome of this ME-centered paradigm is feckless, sparks distrust and fear in others,[108] and leads to negative total motivation scores.[109] When people don't have freedom, they revert to the automatic, built-in 3F mechanism: Fight, Flight, or Freeze.

Fight: Reaching out for assistance and help from inside or mostly outside the organization.

Flight: Leaving to find another job or finding satisfaction off the job.

Freeze: Staying put but totally disengaged.

WE-Centered Paradigm: It's About AUTONOMY

Every great leader knows when to let go. In today's dynamics, the leader's job is to free the passion of their people, engage their raw potential, capacities and talents, mobilize their energy, and elevate them to design and own their job. The leaders give up control but remain available to coach, clear the path, and provide feedback. The outcome of this WE-centered paradigm is significant on employee satisfaction, morale, creativity, involvement, performance, and motivation, among others. When people have freedom, they transform the automatic, built-in 3F mechanism into Focus, Foresee, and Fascinate.

Focus: Channeling talents, capacity, and energy to achieve the organization's purpose.

Foresee: Predicting the future, anticipating the change, and imagining the possibilities.

Fascinate: Leaving their personal marks in their organization and the world.

For *crying out loud*, it is time to shift from a
ME-centered paradigm to a WE-centered paradigm.

ME-Centered Paradigm (Control)
Success through the self-projection of the leader
Constantly checking up on others
Controlling people
Top-down, hierarchical structure
People follow rules
Controlled motivation
Profit centered
Believe in results
Fixed mindset
Fight, Flight, Freeze

WE-Centered Paradigm (Autonomy)
Success through the realization and growth of your people
Running alongside, coaching, and supporting others
Releasing people
Decentralized, flat structure
People have a voice
Autonomous motivation
People centered
Believe in results through people
Growth mindset
Focus, Foresee, Fascinate

Empowerment Is Not Enough

"We do empower our people," they tell me.
"Empowerment alone is not enough," I say.

Many organizations and executives I work with lead with a mix of empowerment and autonomy. Empowerment is most probably the most used word but also the most misused concept. Empowerment has to do with giving people the power to make decisions and is defined as "the state of being empowered to do something: the power, right, or authority to do something."[110] Let's make it clear: this definition of empowerment is not enough and is incomplete unless embodied with personal risk, self-determination, trust, and initiative.[111] On the other hand, autonomy has to do with the freedom of choice to pursue something. In other words, giving your people the choice on:

What to do (task and desired results)
When to do it (time)
How to do it (guidelines and technique)
Whom to do it with (partnership and accountability)
What's next (consequences)

Autonomy: The Antidote

Today's workforces are on a quest for autonomy, which fuels their energy and inner drive to achieve and grow. Autonomy over the what, when, and how. Autonomy over purpose, function, and tasks. In the sixth most cited psychiatry and psychology article of its decade, "Self-determination theory and the facilitation of intrinsic motivation, social development, and well-being," Richard Ryan and Edward L. Deci examine intrinsic and extrinsic motivation. They cofounded the Center for Self-Determination Theory (CSDT), highlighting competence, autonomy, and social relations as the three main intrinsic needs involved in self-determination, "which when satisfied yield enhanced self-motivation and mental health, and when thwarted lead to diminished motivation and well-being."[112] The two leading theorists of human motivation also found that "threats, deadlines, directives, pressured evaluations, and imposed goals diminish intrinsic motivation because, like tangible rewards, they conduce toward an external perceived locus of causality. In contrast, choice, acknowledgment of feelings, and opportunities for self-direction were found to enhance intrinsic motivation because they allow people a greater feeling of autonomy."[112] And it is intrinsic motivation powered by autonomy, competence, and relatedness (aka autonomous motivation) that ignites responsibility, creativity, openness to learning, positivity, engagement, and the ability to better oneself.[113]

In a meta-analytic review published in 2018 drawing from a database of 754 correlations across 72 studies, Gary Slemp and his coauthors found that Leader Autonomy Support (aka LAS) correlated strongly and positively with internalization of work motivation, well-being, work engagement, positive job attitudes, and desired job behaviors.[114] Regardless of the industry you are in, autonomy is your new superpower. As leaders, we have to create an environment where people are partners instead of workers; shifting their mindset from "having to" to "wanting to" make a difference, creating the conditions for them to motivate themselves, and fueling their passion to contribute their choice in the service of the organization's purpose. In his book *Drive*, Daniel Pink argues that autonomy, mastery, and purpose are the three factors that drive intrinsic motivation. Think of autonomy as the ability to drive your own car, mastery as the ability to drive it well, and purpose as the ability to drive it in a journey that matters.

In his book, Pink highlights research at Cornell University that "studied 320 small businesses, half of which granted workers autonomy, the other half relying on top-down direction. The businesses that offered autonomy grew at four times the rate of the control-oriented firms and had one-third the turnover."[20] Finally, in his book *The 8th Habit*, Stephen Covey shares a fundamental paradigm: people are whole and have infinite potential. He invited leaders to magnify this potential, engage in inspiring others to find their voice, and move beyond the command-and-control industrial age software. He concludes, "We have the hardwired power to rewrite that software and this power inspires us to lead (empower) people, who have the power of choice, and manage things, which do not."[115]

Autonomy is the antidote.
It is a we-centered paradigm.
Done and dusted.

There Is a Lot at Stake

And so, you might think, "In my organization, there is a lot at stake." Well, if David Marquet did it, so can you. David Marquet is a former U.S. submarine commander who took command of the nuclear-powered attack submarine USS Santa Fe (SSN-763), the worst-performing submarine in the fleet. In his book, *Turn the Ship Around*, Marquet shares how he turned the submarine from the worst to the best performing submarine, an organization with little room for error, by treating his followers as leaders, inspiring autonomy, and pushing the authority to the officers and crew.[116] Captain Marquet inspired absolute ownership where people became part of the command chain. His winning mindset, which he refers to as the Leader-Leader Model, is founded on the assumption that organizations become effective when everyone thinks and acts like a leader.

Nine is Mine

In many organizations, autonomy is believed to be a core message in every means of communication, but they remain unable to translate autonomy from a "noun" to a "verb." "Nine is Mine" is part of our lingo at MRT Consultants to fortify the absolute power we all have over how work should be done. And in this spirit, here are nine untraditional autonomy practices to get you onboard.

1. Permitted Bootlegging

Companies like Toshiba, Nespresso, and Merck allow their employees the freedom to do their own research and development (R&D) on anything they choose to work on. This practice has enabled new technologies and the development of new products.

The fruits of autonomy: Toshiba (first mass-market laptop T1100); Nespresso (Nespresso capsules); Merck (LCD displays).

2. 20 Percent Factor/ShipIt Days

In some organizations, autonomy is a way of work, such as 3M where 3Mers can spend 15 percent of their time working on their own projects; Google, where Googlers can spend 20 percent (or one day per week) of their time generating and experimenting with new ideas; and Atlassian, allowing Atlassians to work in teams for 24 hours of unlimited innovation every quarter (aka ShipIt days) conceiving, designing, and "shipping" new ideas and solutions. This ability to control their own schedule and time works for them and enables them to explore their curiosity and passion and chase mastery.

The fruits of autonomy: 3M (Post-it Notes, Scotch Tape); Google (Gmail, Google News, Google Talk, Google Translate); Atlassian (Jira Service Desk, and significant product improvements).

3. ROWE (Results-Only-Work-Environment)

Best Buy introduced ROWE for their headquarters-based people where colleagues don't have a specific work schedule. They have total autonomy over their time and when to show up to work, as long as they deliver results. Though Best Buy ended this practice, this strategy has been adopted by many companies such as Meddius, GAP, Yum! Brands, Reserve Advisors Inc., SpinWeb, Dixie Iron Works, and Brighton Bancorp.

The fruits of autonomy: Better relationships, high loyalty, more focus and energy. Higher productivity and lower turnover.[117]

4. $2,000 Per Guest Per Day

At The Ritz-Carlton, every Lady and Gentleman is allowed to use up to $2,000 per guest per day with complete discretion and autonomy, moving heaven and earth to create exceptional memories for their guest. There are no rules here, as long as the actions are ethically, legally, and morally correct and ultimately bring The Ritz-Carlton mystique to life. This philosophy is at the heart of their employee promise, communicated, encouraged, and celebrated daily through their lineups.

The fruits of autonomy: The legendary reputation of The Ritz-Carlton and two-time winner of the Malcolm Baldrige National Quality Award from the United States Department of Commerce.

5. Homeshoring

Zappos allow call center employees to work from home, removed them from physical monitoring, and encouraged them to bring their individuality to any conversation. Backed by customer-centric policies and a freedom-centered workplace, these employees are also enabled to make decisions, as long as it is aligned to their purpose "to live and deliver WOW." This practice has also been adopted fully or partially by many companies, including JetBlue.

The fruits of autonomy: WorldBlu named Zappos a 2019 Freedom-Centered Workplace. Zappos is also celebrated as one of the best companies for customer service in the United States.

6. C&D (Connect and Develop)

At P&G, employees are free to explore and source 50 percent of their innovation from outside the organization; no source of ideas is off-limits. Some see this paradigm shift as a model for innovation, but it is also a call for focused autonomy, where P&G employees, backed up with a list of needs, move from the traditional R&D to focused C&D (connect as in partnerships and collaboration; and develop as in sourcing technologies, packages, and products).[118]

The fruits of autonomy: Olay Regenerist, Swiffer Dusters, the Crest SpinBrush, and Mr. Clean Magic Eraser.

7. Tribe Model

Spotify has an unusual and unique organizational infrastructure; a combination of squads, tribes, chapters, and guilds to drive alignment, autonomy, and accountability.[119] In a nutshell, employees are aligned around the top priorities and product strategies, then organized into agile teams called squads within a tribe. These teams are self-organized, cross functional, and have the freedom to decide on what to build, how to build it, and with whom to work.

The fruits of autonomy: Winner of 2018,[120] 2019,[121] and 2020[122] best streaming service.

8. Holacracy

Many organizations such as Zappos, Emesa, Impact Hub, Swisscom, and Medium moved from the traditional top-down pyramid structure to a flat structure in which the power is distributed among units that are autonomous and self-reliant. In such a system, roles replace job descriptions and are organized into self-governed circles with clear goals and accountabilities. People within circles also have the autonomy and power to make decisions on how to achieve the goals.

The fruits of autonomy: Increased agility, efficiency, transparency, innovation, and accountability. [123]

9. Let My People Go Surfing

Patagonia promotes freedom for people to take time away from the office to do whatever they feel like doing. Known as "let my people go surfing time" (flextime policy), employees have a flexible work schedule as long as the work gets done. They are encouraged to leave the office to attend outdoor activities, pursue an education, or be with their kids. In his book, *Let My People Go Surfing*, Patagonia's founder Yvon Chouinard writes, "Work had to be enjoyable on a daily basis…. We needed to be surrounded by friends who could dress whatever way they wanted, even barefoot. We needed to have flex time to surf the waves when they were good, or ski the powder after a big snowstorm, or stay home and take care of a sick child."[124]

The fruits of autonomy: Intense energy, engagement, well-being, and the ability for colleagues to test and fall in love with Patagonia's outdoor products.

Making the Transition

Transitioning into an autonomous work environment requires a purposeful practice. Every practice I shared above has its own pros and cons. I encourage you to fine-tune and repackage those practices or invent your own while ensuring you create a self-governing state without sacrificing accountability, inspiring change without sacrificing the benefits of stability, and promoting organized chaos without sacrificing alignment. The transition from a controlling environment to an autonomous environment should be done one step at a time. Use the reflections in this Truth's worksheet, The Autonomy Toolkit, to reflect on how you can improve autonomy in your organization. Consider the following:

1. Energize the why: Ensure alignment is driven by lucid and quantifiable goals and expectations and inject a sense of why to shift awareness, needs, and wants towards a common purpose.

2. Provide the means: People feel free when they have the resources to make things happen. Give your people the tools, resources, and relevant details (what, who, when, and how) they need to have the power and ability to make effective choices.

3. Clear the path: See things from your people's point of view. Inspire your people to greater heights by building a culture of trust, removing obstacles, clearing the path, and being a source of guidance at the right time, in the right way.

4. Promote accountability: Explicitly embed a cadence of accountability to promote transparency and absolute commitment. People should understand the expectations and clearly define the measurements of success as well as the repercussions of failing them.

5. Get out of your people's way: Let go by creating an environment for your people to stretch, collaborate, experiment, fail forward, unleash their individuality, and bring their very best.

Final Note: Set Your People Free

As leaders, it is time to shift from "me" to "we," from "control" to "release." Like the great Philippine eagles—one of the rarest and most powerful birds in the world—which are left by their parents to build the courage and take their first flight, set your people free so they can progress and blossom. Let's remind ourselves that the ultimate goal of freedom is serving others and enabling them to serve our world. I wrap this Truth up with the words of the 31st president of the United States, Herbert Hoover, "Freedom is the open window through which pours the sunlight of the human spirit and human dignity."[125]

Tool # 9: Nine is Mine Autonomy Kit

Instructions: This kit highlights books, articles, statements, and practices. Explore it as you navigate the world of autonomy.

ME-Centered Paradigm (Control)
1. Why We Do What We Do: The Dynamics of Personal Autonomy by Edward L. Deci and Richard Flaste *2. The 8ᵗʰ Habit: From Effectiveness to Greatness* by Stephen R. Covey *3. Drive: The Surprising Truth About What Motivates Us* by Daniel H. Pink *4. Turn the Ship Around! How to Create Leadership at Every Level* by L. David Marquet *5. Holacracy: The New Management System for a Rapidly Changing World* by Brian J. Robertson *6. Carrots and Sticks: Unlock the Power of Incentives to Get Things Done* by Ian Ayres *7. Primed to Perform: How to Build the Highest Performing Cultures Through the Science of Total Motivation* by Neel Doshi and Lindsay McGregor *8. Self-Determination Theory and the Facilitation of Intrinsic Motivation, Social Development, and Well-being* by Richard M. Ryan and Edward L. Deci *9. The Road to Empowerment: Seven Questions Every Leader Should Answer* by Robert Quinn and Gretchen Spreitzer

---

Nine Questions to Inspire Autonomy

1. What's your perspective? What do you recommend?

2. How are things going? How do you like to work?

3. What can we improve? How can we improve?

4. How can we overcome the barriers that prevent you from achieving your job?

5. What do you intend to accomplish? Why?

6. What would you like to focus on?

7. What if you take the risk?

8. I trust you! You take care of it.

9. What can you do in these circumstances? Use your best judgment.

Nine Autonomy Practices

1. "Permitted" bootlegging

2. 20 Percent Factor/ShipIt days

3. ROWE (Results-Only-Work-Environment)

4. $2,000 per guest per day

5. Homeshoring

6. C&D (Connect and Develop)

---

7. Tribe Model

8. Holacracy

9. Let my people go surfing

Nine Reflections

1. How do you and the team feel about the current level of autonomy? Is the work environment governed by pressure (deadlines, surveillance, evaluations, etc.) or decision-making, power, and choice?

2. To what extent does the team have a sense of choice over what to do (task and desired results), when to do it (time), how to do it (guidelines and technique), whom to do it with (partnership and accountability), and what's next (consequences)?

3. How much do we engage in healthy conflicts and debates?

4. Do we share information, discuss experiences, support cooperation, and acknowledge emotions?

5. How much clarity does the team have about the purpose, strategic direction, and goals? How much are they involved in setting this direction?

6. What are the internal and external forces that hinder autonomy at work? How can it be eliminated?

7. How can we support autonomous motivation? Do we share knowledge and develop others to promote autonomy?

8. Are we a ME-centered or a WE-centered team/organization? How can we inspire a WE-centered paradigm?

9. Would any of the nine autonomy practices work for our team or organization? If yes, which one and how can it be fine-tuned and repackaged? If none, why not?

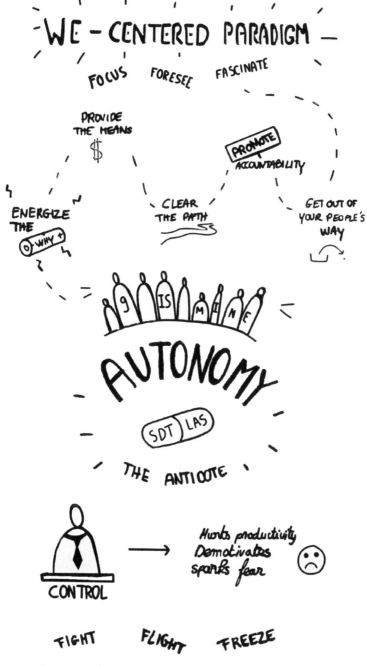

- TRUTH # 9 -

Bring out the gold: A to Z

The Alchemist Within

Every few decades, a book is published that transforms the lives of its readers. At age 18, I read one of the best-selling books in history, *The Alchemist* by Paulo Coelho.[126] This book, which has sold over 65 million copies and has been translated into 80 different languages, changed my perception of life, leadership, and success. The book tells the story of a shepherd, Santiago, who embarks on a journey seeking a grand treasure. Along the journey he learned valuable lessons about hope, friendship, love, failure, faith, perseverance, and happiness. At the end of the journey, Santiago learns the most important lesson of all: The real treasure is in the journey itself. Around the same time I read *The Alchemist*, I recall walking down Al-Bustan Street in Beit-Mery, a beautiful Lebanese village in Mount Lebanon with my friend Raja Touma. That weekly ritual leading us to the top of the village, overlooking Beirut floating under us like a splendid river was a short version of Santiago's journey. On those walks, Raja and I shared our dreams of roaming the world inspiring others, transforming organizations, but most importantly, we learned some of the most vital lessons of our lives: we learned how to be alchemists.

The word alchemist comes from the word alchemy, which has origins in the Greek word "khemeia," meaning the "art of transmuting metals." Alchemy is defined as "a power or process of transforming something common into something special."[127] Historically, one of the goals of alchemy was to find a substance called the "philosopher's stone." This stone, when combined with other metals, would turn into gold. Isn't this what leadership is all about? Transforming the raw talents leaders encounter into gold? Unleashing the precious form of those we serve and lead?

The Truths I have shared so far revolve around this philosophy, and in this Truth, I share additional leadership principles that will enable you to develop the alchemist within—live, learn, leave a mark, and make everything you come across a bit greater. Remember, your habits define you. Therefore, I share a habit under each principle to assist you in bringing those principles to life, make the leap, find your inner gold, and bring out the gold in others.

How to Be an Alchemist: From A to Z

A is for Activate your anchors: Great leaders are true to themselves and aligned with their internal belief system; their leadership ideology. They are principle-centered leaders whose actions are aligned with their purpose, values, and well-defined rules of engagement. The bottom line is, hold firm to your anchors. Without it, you will drift with the wind like a ship lost at sea, sailing towards a vague horizon. Your anchors will enable you to be agile and resilient without compromising what's fundamental to who you are.

Habit A: Set aside 30 minutes a day to assess your actions and decisions against your values and purpose. Think of what you could have done differently to activate your anchors. Align rigorously when needed.

B is for Be unreasonable: Great leaders embark on unreasonable terrains and believe that fear is nothing but "False Evidence Appearing Real." The Irish playwright George Bernard Shaw put it best when he wrote, "Reasonable people adapt themselves to the world. Unreasonable people attempt to adapt the world to themselves. All progress, therefore, depends on unreasonable people."[128] Do not accept the world as it is. Ignore the impossible and add your positive mark on your people, your workplace, the organization, and our world. If they zig, you zag! Scratch the conventional wisdom, go smartly and courageously against the norm, and bring freshness at every turn.

Habit B: At the end of each week, list the norms that prevented you from being unreasonable. Scratch it out and think of one way to bring newness to your life and business.

C is for Choose your own weather: Great leaders create their own circumstances and take full responsibility for their results. Remember, between every stimulus and reaction is a space. A space for you to determine your choices. You can fill that space with hopeless and doubtful voices or hopeful and confident ones. Great leaders reframe negative events and embrace what the psychologist Dr. Martin Seligman referred to as "optimistic explanatory style;" believing that problems are temporary, isolated, and resolvable, and situations will work out for the best in the end if you instill the right belief.[129] When you encounter adversity (e.g., event), how you explain it to yourself (belief) will directly determine the outcomes (consequences). You have the power to choose your own weather by following the ABC (Adversity, Belief, Consequences) approach originally created by psychologist Dr. Albert Ellis. Sometimes though, the event triggers a negative belief leading to negative consequences. Dr. Seligman added the DE to the model to make it more explicit.[129]

Adversity: Facing an event; a stressful or difficult situation (e.g., I didn't get a promotion).

Belief: The event triggers a belief (e.g., I am not good at what I do).

Consequences: The belief generates negative consequences (e.g., I will remain quiet).

Disputation: Dispute the belief and reframe or reshape the adversity in a positive way (e.g., ask for feedback and craft a personal development plan).

Effect (new effect): The results of the healthier beliefs (e.g., commit to learning and the plan).

Remember, the storms and sunny days of your life are the outcomes of your own beliefs and choices. Reframe adversity, create your own self-paradigm, and voice your choices.

Habit C: Practice the ABCDE technique to choose your own weather.

D is for Drive the car of your life: Imagine your life as a car. Where are you sitting right now? In the copilot seat, backseat, or trunk, allowing others to direct your life? Get in the driver seat of your own life, dare to live your own dream, and take ownership of your own road. The world is a true testimony of those who dared to dream and made a way when there was no way. Success stories like Amazon, The Walt Disney Company, Apple, TOMS, Under Armour, Instagram, Groupon, Spanx, Ben & Jerry's, and many others were born from a humble dream. Believe in yourself, put your foot on that gas pedal, and chase your dream.

Habit D: Think of what you would want the world to make for you and then design your own story. Set aside one hour every day to get yourself closer to your dream.

E is for Elevate your measurement of success: Great leaders don't settle for others' measurements. Let go some of the clichés, old perceptions, and traditional concepts. Great leaders constantly challenge themselves and others, pushing the boundaries, raising the bar, and chasing the best version of themselves. We have all created metrics that control the way we live, lead, learn, and love. Maybe the best unit of measurement is your own unmeasurable potentials. Matthew McConaughey said it best in his 2014 Oscar acceptance speech: "So you see every day, every week, every month and every year of my life, my hero's always 10 years away. I'm never gonna be my hero. I'm not gonna attain that. I know I'm not, and that's just fine with me because that keeps me with somebody to keep on chasing."[130]

Habit E: Describe and draw the best version of yourself. Come up with five actions to chase the best of you. Review these actions weekly to ensure momentum.

F is for Focus on the intangibles: Great leaders focus on the intangibles that make them, their people, and organization stand out from the crowd. Whatever you offer is and or will be offered by others. What the competition (another leader or organization) can't offer are your intangibles—reputation, influence, momentum, character, integrity etc. In his celebrated book *The Intangibles of Leadership*, Richard A. Davis wrote about his intensive research and interviews with CEOs to share 10 intangible qualities that define extraordinary leaders—wisdom, will, executive maturity, integrity, social judgment, presence, self-insight, self-efficacy, fortitude, and fallibility.[131] Focus on the intangibles; hire and select for intangibles. Deliver the intangibles. You might not be able to put those intangibles on a scorecard or a spreadsheet, but you can see beyond what's quantifiable because this is there where your power resides.

Habit F: Make a list of your signature intangibles and devise a plan to develop each. Review this plan weekly to ensure momentum.

G is for Get things done: Great leaders execute and deliver. Regulate your conduct and develop the discipline to focus on your goals. At the President Summit, Jack Welch, one of the most respected CEOs in history, stated, "Execution and getting it done is what it is all about."[132] Great leaders understand the reality of their business, connect with others, dig into the why, what and how, question, analyze, formulate a strategy, and ensure a cadence of accountability to get things done, on time, all the time. In their book *Execution: The Discipline of Getting Things Done*, acclaimed CEO Larry Bossidy teams up with the legendary advisor Ram Charan to share seven behaviors that are fundamental for execution. "Know your people and your business; insist on realism; set clear goals and priorities; follow through; reward the doers; expand people's capabilities; and know yourself."[133] The message is clear. Great leaders are disciplined, they think like entrepreneurs, crave smart actions, and are fanatic about making things done.

Habit G: Think of which area in your life and work you would like to be more disciplined. Identify the behavior(s) you need to develop. Craft one weekly action to build this discipline.

H is for Honor your people: Great leaders believe in the "namaste" philosophy. A form of Hindu greeting, namaste is translated as "namah," to bow, and "te," to you. How grand that message is. Every time you greet your people or connect with someone, think of namaste. Ram Dass, the well-known Western Buddhist, defined namaste in his own way: "I honor the place in you in which the entire universe dwells. I honor the place in you which is of love, of truth, of light, and of peace. I honor the place in you where, if you are in that place in you, and I am in that place in me, there is only one of us."[134] So let the divine in you bow to the divine in those you lead. Hold them in the highest regard. Give them your *time* (honor, connect, and engage), your *energy* (cherish, inspire, and elevate), and your *power* (empower, autonomize, and enable).

Habit H: Practice "Namaste" each time you connect with someone. Give them your time, energy, and power. Let the Divine in you bow to the Divine in them. Make every interaction count.

I is for Integrate your life: Great leaders balance all vital areas of their lives to be truly successful. In the introduction section of Principle 2, I shared Dr. Jenson's Seven F's: Family, Firm (career), Fitness, Faith, Friendships, Finances, and Fun.[78] The Seven F's represent the seven buckets of your life, and great leaders commit to live an integrated life and inspire others to live filled and fulfilled lives. In his book, *Discover Your True North*, Bill George states, "If we seek organizations that nourish our souls, permit us to grow into fully functioning human beings, and enable us to integrate our lives, we can find fulfillment."[135] Today's talent seek fulfillment by embracing their humanity in all its dimensions. They look for leaders who bring stability and strike the right balance in the midst of a chaotic, demanding world.

Habit I: Develop one goal for each of your Seven F's. Make these goals part of your weekly calendar. Inspire your people to follow your steps.

J is for Jazz up your language: Like instruments are the tools of musicians and brushes are the tools of painters, language is the tool of leaders. The tool for connecting with others, making decisions, resolving conflict, inspiring creativity, and celebrating results. Much the same as jazz musicians who create harmonious and congruous possibilities from their notes, great leaders inspire a world of possibilities from their words. Our words matter. Because words can either energize or demoralize, empower or suppress, and heal or hurt. Harness the energy of your words to project authenticity, influence others, inspire hope, and promote a winning culture. It was the power of Julia Ward Howe's words in the 1861 hymn, "Battle Hymn of the Republic Glory, Glory, Hallelujah" that inspired solidarity, courage, and faith. It was the power of Martin Luther King's words in his 1963 "I Have a Dream" speech that inspired justice, equality, and freedom. It was the power of Winston Churchill's words in his 1940 speech, "We shall fight on the beaches" that inspired victory. John F. Kennedy once said of Churchill, "He mobilized the English language and sent it into battle. The incandescent quality of his words illuminated the courage of his countrymen."[136] I rest my case with the first verse in the opening chapter of the Gospel of John, "In the beginning was the Word, and the Word was with God, and the Word was God."[137]

Habit J: For the next 30 days, practice the 25/75 Rule (the speaking to listening ratio) and reflect on how you speak to yourself and others. Make a list of powerful words and statements to speak the leadership vocabulary.

K is for Knock off your fears: Great leaders move beyond their fears and build the courage to leap. They know that fear is just an illusion; a matter of perspective, and "is only as deep as the mind allows."[138] If leveraged though, this illusion will serve as an incredible learning experience, prompting us into action and opening unlimited doors. Two decades ago, I read a thought-provoking parable *Who Moved My Cheese?* by Dr. Spencer Johnson, about two mice (Sniff and Scurry) and two little individuals (Hem and Haw) who live in a maze. One morning, they realize that their cheese supply is finished. The two mice accepted the loss and went on to look for new cheese while Hem and Haw, trapped by their fear, kept "hemming and hawing," simmering in a state of inaction. Haw finally moved beyond his fears to wander the maze and share one of the author Spencer Johnson's inspiration lessons, "When you move beyond your fear, you feel free."[139] Fear can be a dreadful emotion if you allow it to control you and paralyze you. But fear is a stellar emotion if you harness it to spur the creation of something new; something special and unique.

Habit K: List the fears that are hindering your success. Think of what you would do if you weren't afraid. Make the transition from fear to excitement. Take the first step.

L is for Lust for passion: In Truth #1, I shared that passion is the hidden force powering your purpose. It is that undeniable and exuberant power pushing us to better ourselves and constantly search for our personal zest. Now, what you will read next might confuse you, but it is true. Passion is an outlet for emotions, and therefore it can possibly change. Different stages of your life serve different things, so don't stop what you do to look for passion, as passion might emerge from what you do. At times, you will find passion, and at other times, passion will find you. And while some believe that their passion should be heroic, something huge and big, others find it in the simplest of things. Commit yourself to what you are passionate about to liberate the flavor you bring to our world.

Habit L: Think of what you love and what separates you from everyone else. Express it by crafting your purpose (refer to Truth #1) and make daily baby steps to serve it.

M is for Make the most of the present: We spend our energy and time dwelling in the past or feeling anxious about the future. Great leaders learn from the past, dream about the future, but embrace the present and seize today's possibilities. Unfortunately, we live in a world where success is defined by control, wealth, titles, and status. None of those make your richer. Life taught me that richness lies in everything I can't buy; those intangible moments. One of the most inspiring biographies I ever came across was that of the former Chairman and CEO of KPMG. In his book *Chasing Daylight*, Eugene O'Kelley writes his memoir in three and a half months, between the time he was diagnosed with brain cancer until he passed away at age 53. Eugene shares how he learned to live in the present, simplifying his life and enjoying the little things that he called "perfect moments." "Just as a successful executive is driven to be as strategic and prepared as possible to "win" at everything, so was I then driven to be as methodical as possible during my last 100 days."[140] He adds, "I marveled at how many Perfect Moments I was having now. I was getting better at it. It was beautiful. And as much as I had loved the hustle and bustle of my previous life, I couldn't help but think back on how rare such moments had been, and how plentiful they were now."[141] Don't wait to come face to face with mortality to find perfect moments in your life. Make the most of your present before your chase for daylight ends.

Habit M: Create one perfect moment, every day.

N is for Nurture your people: Great leaders are constantly looking for possibilities to nurture others. They are gardeners, looking for signs of life in everything they see. They create an environment for growth (developing a learning culture); provide nourishment (coaching, mentoring, etc.); remove impediments (obstacles, barriers, breakdowns, inefficiencies, etc.); and reap the fruits (celebrating growth). Great leaders are givers. They lift their people up and serve them. I started my career as a server and rose through the ranks to learn that to lead is simply to serve. In their book *12 Elements of Great Managing*, Rodd Wagner and James Harter prove that the statement "someone at work cares about me as a person" is critical to employee motivation, retention, productivity, and profit.[142] After almost a decade working for The Ritz-Carlton Hotel Company, their motto, coined by Horst Schulze when he was 16 years old, "We are Ladies and Gentlemen, Serving Ladies and Gentlemen," became the cornerstone of my leadership. They inspired their leaders to take a personal interest in their people, ask about their families, greet them by name, make them feel heard and understood, and most importantly, treat them like internal guests. The saying goes that people don't leave or quit a job, they leave or quit their leader. So, show them in every action you take that you truly care about them and their success.

Habit N: Make it a habit to integrate some of the following questions in your discussions: How can I assist you? What is the one thing I can do differently to become a better leader for you? What can I do to make your job more fulfilling? What can I do to support you?

O is for Own your game: If you study the leaders who positively changed the course of history and those who are inspiring our world today, they share the same core traits. The fact is, Abraham Lincoln, Mother Teresa, Nikola Tesla, and Ingvar Kamprad were ordinary people like us, but they saw the world differently and shaped and played in their own arenas with absolute dedication to their cause. They owned their game and set their own standards, inspired commitment, gained utter loyalty, pursued mastery, and became the change they sought in the world. That same truth applies to organizations like Airbnb, Amazon, Apple, Beyond Meat, FedEx, Lego, Microsoft, Netflix, Tesla, Uber, and Visa, who owned the game and accordingly disrupted our world and permanently changed our society. Whether leaders or organizations, these game changers are purposeful, bold, enablers who recalibrate the measures of progress. Game changers are the "leaders in the arena," who fight for victory despite all obstacles, critics, failures, and roadblocks. The notable passage "The man in the arena," from Theodore Roosevelt's "Citizenship in a Republic" speech encapsulates the essence of owning your game. He said, "It's not the critic who counts, not the man who points out how the strong man stumbles or where the doer of deeds could have done them better. The credit belongs to the person who is actually in the arena, whose face is marred by dust and sweat and blood…who at best knows in the end the triumph of high achievement, and at worst, if he fails, at least fails while daring greatly, so his place shall never be with those cold, timid souls who neither know victory nor defeat."[143]

Habit O: Embrace the 30/60/90+1 Rule. At the beginning of your day, assign 30 minutes to reflect on your purpose; 60 minutes to boost your stamina, e.g., hydrate, exercise, and meditate, and 90 minutes (throughout the day) to connect with your source of inspiration, e.g., books, articles, podcasts, etc. Finally, at the end of each day, reflect on the one thing you have done to own your game (+1).

P is for Pursue learning: At age 87, the famous Italian Renaissance artist Michelangelo was credited for saying, "ancora imparo," which means, "Still, I am learning." Great leaders are lifelong learners. They make the time to power their knowing system (knowledge), doing system (skills), and operating system (inner compass). What do leaders like Warren Buffett, Meg Whitman, Indra Nooyi, Elon Musk, Sheryl Sandberg, Marillyn Hewson, and Tim Cook have in common? A sense of curiosity, a thirst for knowledge, a hunger for learning, and an obsession for renewal. These leaders have learning rituals to ensure the constant flow of freshness in a variety of areas. Giving her advice to the IIM-Calcutta grads, PepsiCo's ex-CEO Indra Nooyi said, "To make an impact in a complex and fast-changing world, you must learn, earn, and return, simultaneously, at every stage of your career…I got to be a CEO, and more importantly, I've stayed a CEO, because I am a lifelong student."[144] Great leaders know that the day you stop learning and growing is the day you start to become stagnant and fade away. We are blessed to have accessibility to the finest minds, and we should deliberately focus on expanding our own. So, hang out with Eleanor Roosevelt, enjoy your coffee with Napoleon Hill, your daily walk with Dale Carnegie, your evening drink with Oprah Winfrey, and at the beginning of each day, sing out loud the words of Michelangelo, "ancora imparo."

Habit P: Build a 90-minute daily learning ritual (refer to the 30/60/__90__+1 Rule). Go for the 30/30/30 rule of thumb. Every day assign 30 minutes to power your knowing system (knowledge), 30 minutes to update your doing system (skills), and 30 minutes to replenish your operating system (inner compass and belief system).

Q is for Question the dots: In his famous 2005 Stanford commencement address, Steve Jobs reflected on connecting the dots when 10 years after taking a calligraphy class, he designed it all into the Mac and married beauty with technology. He said, "You can't connect the dots looking forward; you can only connect them looking backwards. So, you have to trust that the dots will somehow connect in your future.... This approach has never let me down, and it has made all the difference in my life."[145] Great leaders see things from different angles, insights, and perspectives and mold it all into amazing outcomes. Richard Branson's mantra, known as A+B+C+D **Always Be Connecting the Dots,** runs through his companies and empowers lateral thinking, exploration, and discovery. Connecting the dots is also about the understanding that today's seeds are tomorrow's opportunities. In Amazon's 2006 letter to shareholders, Jeff Bezos opened with, "At Amazon's current scale, planting seeds that will grow into meaningful new businesses takes some discipline, a bit of patience, and a nurturing culture."[146] How to connect the dots? First and foremost, see things differently and beyond the current perception. Connect ideas together to create new concepts, connect people together to combine perspectives, connect ideas with people, people with ideas, ideas with products, products with markets, etc. Life is made up of dots. Everything around us was once a dot, and there is a universe of unexplored, missed, ignored, or forgotten dots. Be the one to piece things together.

Habit Q: Question the dots weekly ritual. Plan this ritual to analyze the information you acquired from Habits O (90) and P (20/20/20). Question the dots and think of possible connections.

R is for Replenish your energy: The boxing legend Muhammad Ali once described his ability and strategy by saying, "float like a butterfly."[147] Did you know that at the beginning of every day, butterflies spread their wings to collect energy through their scales' solar cells? This energy is crucial for the butterfly to fly. Likewise, great leaders need their daily dose of energy to continuously energize themselves and others. They manage energy like they manage their time and investments. What follows is the R.E.G. approach to replenish your energy.

R: Replenish your emotional, physical, mental, and spiritual energy: Boost your stamina at the beginning of each day (e.g., 60-minutes rule: hydrate, exercise, and meditate), take a daily virtual vacation (listening to music, reading, indulging in a hot bath, etc.), and keep a gratitude list and add to it weekly.

E: Eliminate energy leaks: Turn off the critics. Eliminate emotionally draining news, negative thoughts and toxic conflicts, discussions and relationships. Minimize distractions.

G: Give back to others: Perform one act of kindness every day. Make the most of the present and create one "perfect moment" with others every day. Compliment someone, thank someone, and praise someone every day.

Habit R: Practice R.E.G. (Replenish, Eliminate, Give back) to replenish your energy.

S is for Stay the course: Great leaders never quit. They possess the courage, passion, and determination to get where the action is, keep pace with change, and finish whatever they begin. When asked by the American talk show host Tavis Smiley if there is something special and unique about him, Will Smith said, "You might have more talent than me, you might be smarter than me, you might be sexier than me, you might be all of those things—you got it on me in nine categories. But if we get on a treadmill together, there's two things: you're getting off first, or I'm going to die."[148] Great leaders persevere, learn from adversity, remove obstacles, and if failure is inevitable, they fail forward. In her book *Grit,* Angela Duckworth studied extra ordinary women and men to find out that the combination of passion and perseverance are the characteristics of highly successful people[148]. How to stay the course? Remember PACE.

P: Push yourself: Act within five seconds from the time you feel the need to take action.[149]

A: Anticipate: Be proactive and anticipate the challenges and obstacles that you might face. Frame challenges, realign, and make the necessary adjustments inside and out.

C: Connect: Power your passion by connecting your actions with your purpose.

E: End strong: March onward and finish strong.

Habit S: Practice P.A.C.E. to stay the course and finish strong.

T is for Tease the monotony: Discomfort = Growth. Full marks! Like any relationship between couples, the relationship between you and those you lead might fall apart because of the irrepressible weight of boredom. Work becomes static, ordinary, and dull. Engagement drops, productivity suffers, and creativity diminishes. Great leaders shake things up to stir newness and promote a playful workplace. They routinely repackage the work environment, throw in some beats, push people beyond their comfort zone, inspire a learning mindset, and plan unwinding activities. While at The Ritz-Carlton corporate office, I really enjoyed the natural, ad hoc twists of energy. The executives would roam our corridors distributing First Class cards (uplifting notes to recognize those who went above and beyond), teams planned yoga sessions, colleagues played music in their offices and revamped their workspaces, and teams executed internal WOW stories (internal surprising acts of kindness to make someone's day). Great leaders inspire a state of mind that brings energy, sparks creativity, and promotes a spirit of oneness.

Habit T: Plan one weekly ad hoc twist of energy to break up the monotony at work (and another to break the monotony in your personal life).

U is for Undo and fix as you go: Confucius once said, "To know what is right and not to do it is the worst cowardice."[150] Great leaders believe that expectations, priorities, measures, and strategies, just like relationships, need to be calibrated to ensure a seamless ride. At times, great leaders apologize, make restitutions, rectify mistakes, address variations, eliminates defects, fix deviations, and repair breakdowns. MR. BIV is a simple, easy-to-implement acronym that The Ritz-Carlton Hotel Company referred to in order to encourage the Ladies and Gentlemen to undo and fix as they work:

Mistakes
Rework
Breakdown
Inefficiencies
Variations.

Whether MR BIV makes an appearance as a damaged product or a worn-down service, the Ladies and Gentlemen are empowered and recognized to spot him, find the remedy, and accordingly check him out of the hotel. Great leaders don't sweep MR BIV under the rug, point fingers, or pass the buck. Instead, they strive to build a culture that encourages, celebrates, and honors those who right wrongs.

Habit U: Be a "MR BIV Chaser" and fix as you go. Empower your people to right wrongs.

V is for Vitalize your emotions: Your emotions can serve you, your people, and the entire organization. You can either ignore them, dismiss them, minimize them, and suppress them, or choose to decode them, navigate them, and harness their energy so you can effectively maximize your leadership impact, promote your people's productivity, and therefore your organizational success. You can learn from your frustration, anger, distress, sadness, and fear to move into action. It is because of anger that I lost 110 pounds; because of frustration that I opened my own firm; because of fear that I secured my financial investments; and because of guilt that I integrated my life. Great leaders are emotionally intelligent. They understand their emotional patterns and navigate emotions to transform and deliver. They vitalize the emotions of love, joy, excitement, kindness, and happiness, because like the Swiss psychiatrist and psychoanalyst Carl Jung, they know that "there can be no transforming of darkness into light and of apathy into movement without emotions."[151] To vitalize your emotions, practice *the A.I.M. technique:*

A: **Acknowledge** the emotion that comes with the situation or the circumstances you are facing. Ask yourself, what is this emotion is trying to tell me?

I: **Investigate** your options and the choices you have. Ask yourself, what will make me feel better?

M: **Make things happen**, decide on the next action step that is most aligned with your purpose.

Habit V: Practice A.I.M to vitalize your emotions.

W is for WOW our world: In her eulogy, Steve Jobs' sister Mona Simpson recalled his last words: "Steve's final words, hours earlier, were monosyllables, repeated three times. Steve's final words were 'OH WOW. OH WOW. OH WOW.'"[152] Nobody will ever know the precise meaning of these last words, but I love to interpret it this way: Great leaders thrive on WOW; they create the life they have always wanted to live, and in the process, they make their mark and WOW our world. Mark Zuckerberg, Facebook's cofounder, posted a public manifesto "Building a global community" to 1.9 billion people to address one vital question, "Are we building the world we all want?"[153] It is accurate to state that our job is about generating profits and growing the business, but in the process, great leaders make our world a better place. You are born to make your mark. Dare to dream, find your calling, and awaken your potential. *Oh, the Places You'll Go!* I have read this book by Dr. Seuss hundreds of times for my kids but also to remind myself that,

"Kid, you'll move mountains! So…be your name Buxbaum or Bixby or Bray…Or Mordecai Ali Van Allen O'Shea, You're off to great places! Today is your day! Your mountain is waiting. So…get on your way!"[154]

Habit W: Draft your leadership manifesto and get on your way.

X is for X-out the pessimism: Pessimism is the shredder of dreams. You might possess all the qualities I shared so far in this list, but if you are pessimistic, you are like a Porsche with flat tires; you will go nowhere unless you change them! I fully understand that human beings are wired for pessimism because it helped us survive the dark ages. We moved beyond those days, but we still carry this "shredder." It steels our inner peace, rips out our energy, and robs us of our dreams and aspirations. The realistic way out of it? Manage your pessimism to optimism ratio. Your optimism ration should be 5:1—five portions of optimism against one portion of pessimism. If you manage that ratio, you will broaden your horizon, open up your perspective, maximize your personal presence, earn more money,[155] build great relationships,[156] and yes, live longer.[157] The grand news? You can control this ratio. When you fall short of optimism, inject your day with doses of positive emotions by counting some blessings; retriggering happy moments from your past; and hanging out with optimistic people, positive books, and affirmative thoughts.

Habit X: Keep track of your emotional ratio throughout the day and work towards a 5:1 ratio. Promote optimism in your workplace by injecting doses of positive emotions.

Y is for Yes! for small victories: Great leaders find a reason to celebrate. Celebrate the good in others, your purpose and values, your new employees, a new product, a new service, a new sale, the close of a deal…. Celebrate small victories on your way to the finish line. These victories bring momentum, fuel confidence, and inspire progress. Every milestone in our lives was tackled by celebrating small victories that made big wins possible. It is with this approach that we inspired our kids to walk, talk, draw, learn, and thrive. Why stop there? Bring this spirit to your organization. In their book *The Progress Principle*, Teresa Amabile and Steven Kramer dissect almost 12,000 journal sections from 238 individuals implementing the most significant advancement ventures in their organizations to find that what spurs individuals on an everyday basis is the feeling of gaining ground; progress. The authors report, "On days when they made progress, our participants reported more positive emotions. They not only were in a more upbeat mood in general but also expressed more joy, warmth, and pride...and were more intrinsically motivated." The authors add, "Even small wins can boost inner work life tremendously."[158] Notice the small victories, reflect on them, communicate them, and make them the stepping-stones towards progress.

Habit Y: Find small victories every day and create a ritual to communicate and celebrate gaining ground.

Z is for Zero in on caring for people: I left this last section to serve as a conclusion to this list and to remind us that all the habits above are there to serve one purpose: to unleash the best version of those you serve and lead. Yes, serve! I meant to use this word. Leadership can only thrive if it's built on service. If you can't serve, you can't lead. I join Stephen Covey's call on leaders to be trim tabbers. A trim tab is a small rudder attached to a big rudder on an airplane or a boat. When you move the trim tab, it creates enough pressure to move the big rudder, which then changes the direction of an A380 or a huge ocean liner. The simplicity of this idea can be compared to the small choices we make in our daily lives that bring about big changes. It also relates to people in our society who chose to be trim tabbers and bring significance to our world. I have met several trim tabbers in many of the organizations I worked with; individuals who spread their influence and enabled transformation regardless of their social status or job title. Former General Electric CEO Jack Welch once visited Stanford Graduate School of Business to talk about leadership where he said, "The day you become a leader, it becomes about them. Your job is to walk around with a can of water in one hand and a can of fertilizer in the other hand. Think of your team as seeds and try to build a garden. It's about building these people."[159] If you ask me about the wildly important lesson I learned throughout my journey roaming the world enabling greatness in individuals and organizations, it would be this: When you strive to enable greatness in others, everything you encounter becomes great too.

Habit Z: Be a trim tab. Identify a need in your team or organization, and then do something about it.

Bring Out the Gold Worksheet

Remember, your habits define you! I invite you to use this Truth's worksheet and choose three habits to develop. Then another three. Then another three. Commit to these habits and practice them systematically for 66 repetitions (days) to reach automaticity. I also challenge you to work with your people and pick three habits to develop as a team. It's time to bring out the gold!

Final Note: Leadership, a Balancing Act!

Let's go back to Paulo Coelho's book *The Alchemist*. In the book, the king of Salem shared a story with Santiago about a boy on a mission to learn the secret of happiness from the wisest man in the world. He traveled 40 days to meet the mysterious wise man, who gave the boy the challenge of balancing oil in a spoon while enjoying the marvels of his castle. The wise man concludes by stating, "Well, there is only one piece of advice I can give you. The secret of happiness is to see all the marvels of the world, and never to forget the drops of oil on the spoon."[160] You can interpret this in many ways, but I like to think of the drops of oil as your own self, personal projects and tasks, etc. (yourself), and the marvels as those you serve and lead (others). When we are only focused on ourselves, we tend to miss others and vice versa. Remember, leadership is a balancing act between focusing inward (self-awareness, self-control, and cultivating your personal operating system) and focusing outward (zero in on uplifting and leading others). Only when you approach leadership with the "alchemist" mindset will you be able to unleash greatness at every level.

Tool # 10: Bring Out the Gold Worksheet

Instructions: Your habits define you. Start the journey by circling the three habits that you commit to embrace in order to find your inner gold and bring out the gold in others. Write the selected three habits below and practice it systematically for 66 repetitions (days) to reach automaticity.

A	J	S
B	K	T
C	L	U
D	M	V
E	N	W
F	O	X
G	P	Y
H	Q	Z
I	R	

Habit ___

Habit ___

Habit ___

THE 'ALCHEMIST' MINDSET

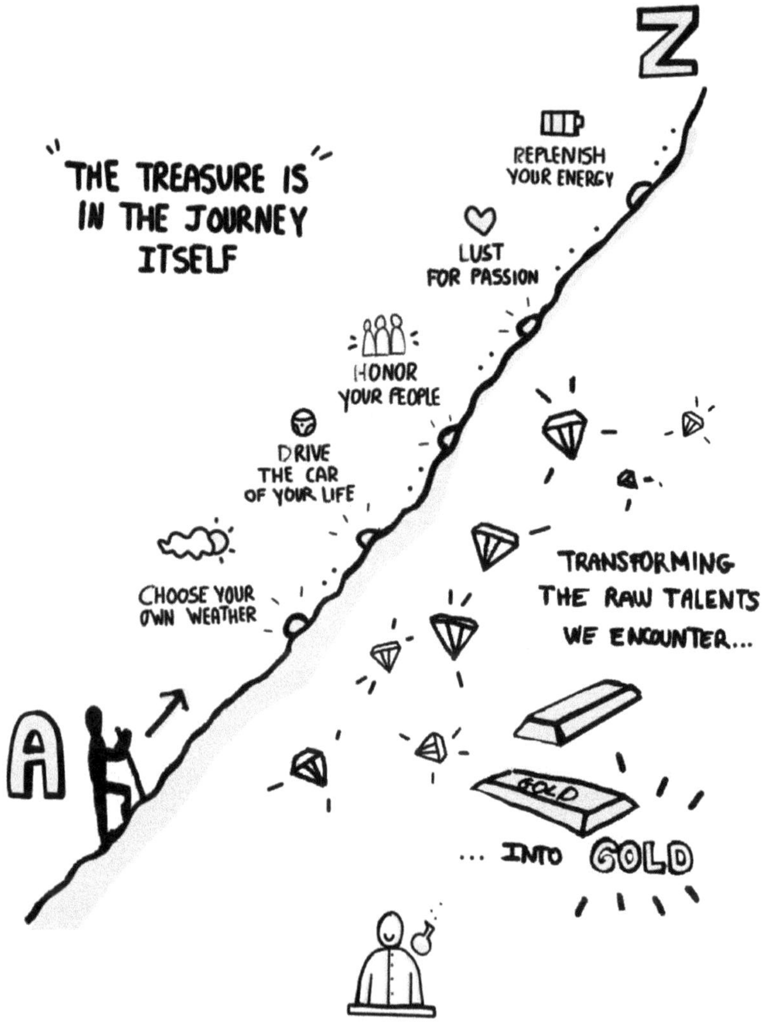

How to be an

ALCHEMIST?

Melkart Rouhana

- TRUTH # 10 -

Energy:
The supreme power

Organizational Energy

An impalpable power lies at the core of your organization. This invisible force makes your culture, and everything for that matter, work. Have you ever wondered why some people display full energy while others suffer from idleness? Why some cultures are vigorous while others project listlessness? Why some organizations buzz with life while others experience inertia?

The answer is: Organizational energy.
The one concealed force that changes everything.

Organizational energy is the "fuel that makes great organizations run."[161] It "can lead to either a wellspring of corporate vitality or the destruction of its very core."[162] Organizational energy drives the intensity, pace, and endurance of the organization's performance.[163] We live in a dynamic and volatile world where organizations are struggling to keep up with the unprecedented pace of change. It is crucial to acknowledge that energy is pliable, and sometimes, even the greatest leaders and the most celebrated companies experience low energy. As a result, today's organizations are hungry for leaders who know how to orchestrate organizational energy and deploy people's passion, creativity, and potential to shift from strength to strength. The founder of modern management Peter Drucker once said, "Your foremost job as leader is to take charge of your own energy, and then orchestrate the energy of others."[164] Like the energy for all life originates from the sun, organizational energy originates from the **culture**, the **connection** between people and the organization, and finally, the **context** or how the organization operates—all of which depends on choices made by leaders.

Organizational energy is shaped by the culture (leading with love),
the connection between employees and the organization (leading with fun),
and the context or how the organization operates (leading with focus).

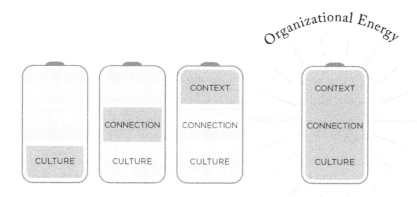

Figure 4. Organizational Energy

A: Organizational Energy Dimension #1
Culture (Lead with Love)

If you want to ensure long-lasting energy, lead with love. I understand that the word love might create some confusion or suggest a soft leadership style. But in the context of energy, love reflects the notion that great leaders touch the hearts of those they serve and lead before they drive action.[165] This notion is inspired by one of the Greek words for love, "agape"—the unconditional commitment and emotional engagement to a person, team and/or the organization. It means being aware of your people's emotions, needs, and adversities. As *New York Times* bestselling author John C. Maxwell writes, "You can't move people to action unless you first move them with emotion. The heart comes before the head."[166] Leading with love is one of the success secrets of self-made billionaire, cofounder, and former executive chairman of the Alibaba Group, Jack Ma. In one of his talks, Jack revealed his secret weapon. He said that to be respected, survive, and continue to be successful, leaders need LQ (Quotient of Love).[167] In his book *Lead With Love*, the internationally acclaimed management guru Gerald M. Czarnecki argues that, "Everything a leader does begins with a capacity and commitment to love."[168] The Quotient of Love is the leader's ability to care, lead, nurture, and express love, encourage loving relationships, show compassion, and fight for their people in a world governed by artificial intelligence.

181

The influence of LQ is enormous. In Truth #4 "With Oxytocin We Charge," I discussed the impact of this "love molecule" on increasing trust, boosting performance, productivity, retention, and joy. As leaders, we are not in the business of leading machines; we are in the business of leading souls, and souls are governed by love.

Hugspedition

During one of our team bonding events and after sharing the power of "leading with love" at Phoenicia Intercontinental Hotel, Beirut, the former general manager, Dagmar Symes, and her team introduced actions of love throughout the hotel. They launched love campaigns such as the "hugspedition," which entailed each member of the executive team providing genuine, six-second hugs to six colleagues in various departments every week. "This hugspedition inspired a positive energy, increased our social connections, and brought a sense of belonging. It was a love investment unlike any other," Dagmar said.[169] Executing a "hugspedition" might not be the answer or even be appropriate in your part of the world. What worked with Dagmar and her team might not be your cup of tea. In his book *Love Leadership*, John Hope Bryant, the founder, chairman, and CEO of HOPE writes, "Love follows one of the primary laws of money: Currency without circulation has no value. Likewise, love without circulation has no value."[170] So the question remains, how are you instilling love in your team and organization?

Leading with L.O.V.E

L: Loyalty: Loyalty is the ability to put people at the core of your business, honor them, and genuinely care for them. By doing so, you elicit greater loyalty from your people and accordingly customers, increase retention, boost energy, and maximize emotional engagement.

Actions: Demonstrate respect; show kindness; give your people credit; be passionate about their development and growth; speak positively about others; be a servant leader; extend smart trust; inspire protection, support, and fidelity; share expectations; and ensure accountability.

Absence of loyalty: Backstabbing, gossiping, and duplicitousness.

O: O(Au)-thenticity: Authenticity is the ability to lead with purpose, have an unshakable set of values, and lead with and from the heart. It empowers people to work as one, cultivates a positive work environment, increases productivity, and inspires trust at every level of the organization.

Actions: Know yourself; find your purpose; craft your values and develop a moral compass; don't take shortcuts; play to your strengths; create transparency; act with integrity; be genuine and humble; give generously; develop a growth mindset; be consistent; and lead with your heart.

Absence of authenticity: Hidden agendas, faking, and manipulation.

V: Vulnerability: Vulnerability is the ability to be "smartly" open, express yourself, and be who you truly are even at risk of losing control. Described by research professor Brené Brown as uncertainty, risk, and emotional exposure, and "the birthplace of love, belonging, joy, courage, empathy, and creativity; it is the source of hope, empathy, accountability, and authenticity."[171] Vulnerability increases your effective power,[172] enables you to approach tough conversations, discourages defensive behavior,[173] and enables relationships to be forged.[171]

Actions: Know your strengths and weaknesses; encourage feedback; be transparent and admit mistakes; embrace an attitude of openness and receptivity; find the "why" behind the flaws; engage in healthy conflicts; understand and accept failure; create a space to discuss emotions; encourage risk taking; request for help; and inspire people to ask for help when needed.

Absence of vulnerability: Divisiveness, entrenched silos, and cynicism.

E: Empathy: Empathy is the art of acceptance,[174] the ability to listen, recognize, and respond to people's feelings, thoughts, and emotions. It is key to build genuine connections, promote collaboration, and develop long-lasting relationships.

Actions: Recognize and relate to the challenges your people face; listen with a virtuous heart; focus on your people's well-being; step outside yourself, step into their shoes and take an interest in their feelings and emotions; be present when they need you; have heart-to-heart talks with them; connect and learn about their stories; lead with a "giving" mindset; and think "them," not "me."

Absence of empathy: Antagonism, resentment, and malevolence.

When Greatness Flourishes

When you lead with love, you will foster positive and enduring energy. The Lead With Love Worksheet at the end of this Truth will guide you to identify some vital actions required to lead with love. Remember, leadership is a human journey; it is about enabling oneself and others by inspiring the mind. But most importantly, it's about touching the hearts of those you serve and lead. As one of the world's top authorities on inspirational leadership, Dr. Lance Secretan once wrote, leadership "is a human activity that comes from the heart and considers the hearts of others."[175]

B: Organizational Energy Dimension #2
Culture (Lead with love)
Connection (Lead with play)

Organizations are made up of teams and teams of human beings with a powerful desire to emotionally connect with one another and the purpose of the organization. Take that element out and you are left with a bunch of disengaged employees working for a paycheck and ready to leave at the first opportunity. Emotional connection is triggered when people a) express themselves; b) love what they do; and c) clearly see their contribution to the purpose and success of the team and the organization. It is pure energy—you do what you love, love what you do, and feel like you're part of something. In Principle 1, I shared tools to connect what your people do with the purpose of the organization, and in Principle 2, I have shared practices to promote powerful associations. In this section, I will share three additional fundamentals to spark emotional connection and lead with play, a) give back to the community; b) restore the FUN in FUNctional; and c) promote a learning culture.

1. Giving back to your community: Great organizations care. They invest their time, resources, and energy to create a lasting mark on their communities and positively impact the lives of others. Giving back paves the way for deeper employee connection, sustainable growth, and meaningful contribution. In their book *Firms of Endearment,* Raj Sisodia and his coauthors share that more companies are now building their corporate cultures around service to society. They call these companies Firm of Endearment ("FoEs"); companies such as Amazon, BMW, Caterpillar, eBay, IKEA, Johnson and Johnson, Starbucks, Timberland, Toyota, Whole Foods, and others that exemplify a high standard of humanistic performance.[176] If you are planning to give back, and you should, below are 10 ideas to consider:

1. Footprints champion: Have a champion within your organization to advocate for community involvement, drive momentum, and integrate "giving back" in the culture.

2. People involvement: Support your community through individual and team volunteering activities.

3. Product donations: Donate products and services to your community partners.

4. Signature fundraising: Plan events to raise funds for charitable and community causes.

5. Pro bono services: Offer services at no charge, promoting and supporting local businesses.

6. Environmental conservation: Implement a range of environmental solutions to conserve and protect our natural resources.

7. Disadvantaged people: Provide a nurturing environment and support people with disabilities.

8. Space donation: Donate your space for meetings, events and fundraisers.

9. Sponsoring events: Partake in a variety of sponsorship opportunities.

10. Mentoring programs: Provide free training programs to local community members.

2. Restoring the FUN in FUNctional: Boredom is the enemy of energy. Great organizations incorporate "fun and play" in the workplace to move from a "have to do" to a "want to do" mindset. Work becomes enjoyable, and organizations generate superior satisfaction, enthusiasm, loyalty, higher productivity, increased innovation, superior positive energy, and organizational citizenship. Today's leaders should "gamify" work; introduce meaningful play at work, and design fun rituals promoting a gratifying and meaningful work environment.

Similar connections are made by many authors, scholars, and practitioners. One of my two favorite statements comes from James Kouzes and Barry Posner in the fifth edition of their book *The Leadership Challenge*: "Every personal-best leadership experience was a combination of hard work *and* fun. In fact, most people agreed that without the enjoyment and the pleasure they experienced with others on the team, they wouldn't have been able to sustain the level of intensity and hard work required to do their personal best."[177] My second favorite statement comes from *On the Brink* by authors Donald T. Phillips and Norman E. Brinker, who write, "If you have fun at what you do, you'll never work a day in your life. Make work like play—and play like hell."[178]

To create a joyful and fun environment, make people part of the decision-making process, let them take initiatives and control the work that affects them. Empower them and put them in charge. I highlighted the importance of autonomy in Truth #8 to free the passion of your people, engage their raw potential, capacities, and talents, and elevate them to design and own their job. The outcome is significant on employee satisfaction, morale, creativity, involvement, performance, and motivation, among others.

Dennis W. Bakke, author of the *New York Times* bestseller *Joy at Work*, states, "Joy at work starts with individual initiative and individual control." He adds, "A joy-filled workplace gives people the freedom to use their talents and skills for the benefit of society, without being crushed or controlled by autocratic supervisors."[179] Remember, a team that plays together, stays together. Not only that, they generate the greatest performance. But for fun and play to work, it should have a purpose. Don't get me wrong, I am totally for introducing fun activities such as decorating the workplace, celebrating holiday and happiness-boosting traditions, observing personal milestones, organizing theme days, planning outside events, designating art and fun labs, and encouraging sports, social, and special interest groups. But to truly harness the power of play and fun, activities should stem from the work itself, with the intention to serve the individual, team, and the organization.

Consider the following 10 ideas:

1. Experimentation time to dig up new ideas.
2. Testing time to experience products and services.
3. Organizational values contests to boost the culture.
4. Cross-generational team bonding to build connections.
5. Healthy competitions to spark innovation.

6. Celebrating wins with rituals to build momentum.
7. Playful morning briefings to raise morale.
8. Experiencing the competition to improve performance.
9. Role-playing; play a customer for a day to refine your customer experience.
10. Wild ideas brainstorming sessions to revamp your business.

3. Promoting a learning culture: When people are learning and sharing, they fuel their commitment and energy.[180] In today's environment, leaders are required to embrace and promote dynamism through continuous evolution and learning. Promoting a learning culture is your ability to integrate learning in every relationship, in every interaction, and in every moment—a culture in which people not only want to learn and apply what they have learned to help their organization, but also feel compelled to share their knowledge with others.

Now, learning can come from many different routes, either external or internal, and can be available 24/7. Learning that occurs in a traditional, formal setting is crucial, especially for some industries that are managed by rules, regulations, and laws, but in general, traditional or formal learning constitutes only 10 percent of learning. Effective learning is the fruits of relationships (through others) and experiences (on-the-job). The 70/20/10 model[181] serves as a guide to help you identify, design, build, and measure your learning activities to create a leaning environment that generates significant business impact.

> • **Formal learning (10%):** Formal education; workshops, seminars; courses; conferences; masterclasses; professional qualifications; eLearning.

> • **Relationship learning (20%):** Formal and informal feedback; performance reviews/feedback assessments; collaboration; peer-to-peer learning; networking; cooperating with experienced colleagues; coaching; mentoring.

• **Experiential learning (70%):** On-the-job experience; problem solving; projects; tasks; stretched goals; expanded job scope and responsibilities; decision making; cross-functional projects; reading/research/applying practices; cross-departmental exposure; substitute for leader in meetings and projects; special assignments.

Whatever learning model you adopt, it is vital to ensure that learning is applied and to align all your learning activities to your culture, business goals, and desired outcomes. Make learning a strategic initiative; it is never about quantity, but quality. Creating a learning organization is about promoting an environment where people work and interact with one another (70% + 20%), maximize their potential, and grow your business. Below are a few tips to promote a learning organization:

Make learning an integral part of the culture

• Connect learning to your purpose and values and make it part of your key performance indicators (KPIs).
• Integrate learning in the selection (hiring) process by selecting people with an appetite to learn.
• Inspire a growth mindset and reward learning by creating links between learning and performance.

Empower the subject matter experts (SMEs) to inspire learning

• Make executives active participants in the learning itself.
• Promote the SME as coaches and mentors.
• Implement "learning sharing programs" to harness the SMEs skills and knowledge.

Make it social and fun

• Plan formal and informal learning rituals.
• Create opportunities for people to associate and cooperate.
• Make learning from feedback a way of work.

Let your people design their learning journeys

• Give people access to learning opportunities and allow them to take charge of their own learning paths.
• Enable people to identify, learn, and overcome the obstacles that prevent them from unleashing their full potential.
• Encourage people to plan what they learn, apply it, and then share it with others.

Make learning a 24/7 activity

• Grant people access to knowledge, talents, and resources, and create autonomous learning opportunities.
• Allow people the freedom to learn at their own pace, take initiatives, and make mistakes.
• Encourage an open-door policy for engagement, openness, seeking assistance, and tough questioning.

From a "team of all stars" to an "all-star team"

• Develop-cross functional teams and encourage peer-to-peer coaching.
• Give teams stretch assignments.
• Un-box people from their roles or departments to learn from one another.

Promoting a learning culture is a perpetual, deliberate journey, and you will only witness its fruits when you pledge to put learning at the heart of what you do, front and center. The Lead with Play Worksheet will guide you to identify some vital actions required to create a joyful environment and live the words of Walt Disney who once said, "You don't work for a dollar—you work to create and have fun."[182]

C: Organizational Energy Dimension #3
Culture (Lead with love)
Connection (Lead with play)
Context (Lead with focus)

Your focus determines your reality and impacts your energy. You are what you focus on. If you only focus on what's wrong in your work and life, you will face mediocre results. If you focus on greatness, you will harness the power of possibilities. This may seem simple, but it is absolutely true. I would like you to take a moment and mentally take note of how many objects around you are red. Try to detect as many red objects as you can. Stop reading until you are done with this task. Now, without looking around anymore, take a pencil and write down on a piece of paper, how many brown objects did you see? It's tricky, isn't it? You might be able to recall one or two. Now gaze around and look at the brown objects you have missed (chairs, desk, carpet, frames, curtain, mud, pencils, etc.) By asking you to focus on red, I created a visual paradigm that filtered and marginalized the other colors for you to achieve the priority at hand. That's the power of focusing your energy on what matters most. The question is, do you harness the power of focus in your organization?

What your people see and how they act is heavily influenced by the paradigms you and the culture create. Now remember, your people are focused on something whether consciously or unconsciously. My message though invites you as a leader to "consciously" direct your people's energy around the organization's top priorities so they can consciously and unconsciously invest their energy to achieve those priorities.

Scientist and innovator Alexander Graham Bell, who is credited with patenting the first practical telephone, once said, "Concentrate all your thoughts upon the work at hand. The sun's rays do not burn until brought to a focus."[183] This quote reminds me of my Boy Scouts days, where I learned how to use glasses to make a fire. Exposed to the sun, the glass produces a more focused beam of light, creating more heat to start a fire.

How do you lead with focus?
How do you mobilize and direct the energy of your people
to achieve the organization's vital priorities?

Quantifiable Mission

Imagine watching a basketball game, or any sport for that matter, without a clearly defined mission, a buzzer, and a simple and understandable scoreboard. Imagine the impact that would have on the focus, momentum, and energy of the game. It would be boring and dreary.... People play and behave differently when they are moving towards a clearly articulated and measurable mission with a well-defined finish line. It is engaging, energizing, and motivating.... Most of the mission statements I have seen are generic and impossible to remember. Your people most probably believe that the mission statement of your organization is nothing but a C-suite executive initiative that requires a squad to explain it.

Today's organizations crave quantifiable missions
that engage and pump people up.

In their book *Built to Last,* Jim Collins and Jerry Porras write that visionary companies like IBM, Ford, Sony, and Disney developed bold missions. They refer to these as Big Hairy Audacious Goals (BHAG). They write, "a BHAG engages people—it reaches out and grabs them in the gut. It is tangible, energizing, highly focused. People 'get it' right away; it takes little or no explanation."[184] What I am proposing in this third dimension is to quantify your mission statement to represent your top three or four priorities—bold but clearly defined priorities that everyone within the organization can relate and contribute to. Once you have defined those bold priorities, select the key activities or leading indicators, craft a scoreboard to create a cadence of accountability, and adjust to the game as it is being played. Picture the energy of your people, the raving fans in the arena, when progress is made.

Project 90

When Ayman Gharib was appointed the general manager of the iconic Raffles Hotel Dubai in 2014, he crafted a quantifiable mission to consciously direct his team's focus towards three priorities: guests, associates, and quality. He launched his quantifiable mission as *Project 90* (90 percent guest satisfaction; 90 percent employee satisfaction; and 90 percent quality assurance). It goes without saying that Ayman's *Project 90* generated the desired energy, buy-in, commitment, and excitement. His team crafted a dashboard and a reward system to promote a cadence of accountability, stimulate progress, and drive sustainable performance. Ayman and his executive team leveraged every opportunity to speak about *Project 90.* They started every call, every town hall meeting, every conversation, and every interaction by reinforcing this mission. "Every department created the disciplines to enliven *Project 90.* From line staff to executives, we made necessary corrections when needed to break through and press forward. The entire workforce narrowed its focus down to *Project 90.* Individuals and teams joined forces and aligned their actions, decisions, and behaviors accordingly. This was the turning point for Raffles Dubai,"[185] Ayman said. Ayman clearly understood that *Project 90* must be the focus of the team, or nothing else they would achieve would really make a difference. He continued to say, "*Project 90* became a way of life at Raffles Dubai, and part of our culture and lingo. Without it, success would have been a matter of chance." Since its inception, *Project 90* has yielded unparalleled results at all levels. Raffles Dubai ranked #1 among Raffles International for guest satisfaction and #1 in the Middle East Region across all Fairmont Hotels for employee satisfaction. The hotel improved its Tripadvisor ranking from #24 to #1 and achieved above 90 percent in quality assurance with a score of 93.4 percent in 2016, ranking the hotel #1 out of 560 hotels in Dubai, UAE. "When we focus, we play differently, and my people played for real.... *Project 90* enabled us to unleash the energy and contribution of our people and generated an emotional commitment around our goals. It directed our energy, talents, and capabilities towards one explicit, bold, and compelling mission." In a nutshell, Ayman channeled the focus of his team and created a system that works independently from him that is focused on the top priorities, the organization's strategy, people's involvement, and sustainable performance. In fact, as I am writing this Truth, Raffles Dubai has been ranked in the top 10 of Tripadvisor's World's Best Hotels 2020 traveler's choice award.[186] More proof that it is a system that truly works. Let's make it work for you!

How to Quantify Your Mission Statement

The Lead With Focus Worksheet will guide you on this ride. The journey starts by defining the three to maximum four bold goals or priorities that if achieved, nothing else really matters. Make sure these goals are easy to remember, tangible, daring, and have a clear finish line. For example, I worked with Mandarin Oriental Jumeira, Dubai, a hotel with a mission to be the heartbeat of Dubai, creating engaging experiences, and building a community of raving fans. Together, we identified their four vital, bold priorities:

1. Colleague Engagement (CE)
2. Guest Voice/Customer Satisfaction (GV)
3. Top Line (TL)
4. Giving Back to the community (GB)

The team then crafted their focused, concrete, daring, and measurable mission that was totally aligned with the Mandarin Oriental culture and ideology:

$$85 \text{ (CE)} \quad 95 \text{ (GV)} \quad 105 \text{ (TL)} \quad + 1 \text{(GB)}^4$$

"This quantifiable mission was celebrated, owned, and energized by all. Simple, easy to remember (85, 95, 105, +1), but daring. Divisions and departments worked together developing and aligning their goals to support the quantifiable mission. Colleagues crafted their

---

4 85 percent Colleague Engagement, 95 percent Guest Voice / Customer Satisfaction, 105 percent Top Line, and executing one event per month to give back to the community.

own individual goals answering the ultimate question, "What is the one thing I can do today to bring us closer to our mission?" The quantifiable mission provoked forward movement unlike anything we have experienced in the past,"[187] the general manager Werner Anzinger told me. Once the mission was defined, the team crafted the four key activities or lead indicators required to achieve the priorities' results. They crafted an exciting scoreboard, visible to everyone within the organization, and updated it monthly to drive momentum. Finally, they created a cadence of accountability and resolved to adjust to the game as it was being played.

Final Note: Can't Start a Fire?

Back in my Boy Scouts days, I have to admit that sometimes I failed to start a fire when I was tasked with doing so. I realized that for some scientific reasons (converging lenses and diverging lenses), certain lenses made out of glass are not powerful enough to start a fire. How do you deal with that? A drop of water on the inside of the lens will make all the difference. This drop of water will bend the light, turning the glasses biconvex, generating enough focus to start a fire.

Reveal your drop of water. And once you find that drop—*your organizational energy*—you will possess the power to move from strength to strength, and most importantly, go out with a bang.

Tool # 11: Lead With Love Worksheet

Instructions: Rate yourself (from 1 low to 10 high) on each component of the acronym L.O.V.E. Reflect on the gaps and identify the vital actions required to lead with love.

Loyalty: The ability to put people at the core of your business, honor them, and genuinely care for them.
1   2   3   4   5   6   7   8   9   10

Consider the following: Demonstrate respect; show kindness; give your people credit; be passionate about their development and growth; speak positively about others; be a servant leader; extend smart trust; inspire protection, support, and fidelity; share expectations; and ensure accountability.

Actions:

O(au)-thenticity: The ability to lead with purpose, have an unshakable set of values, and lead with and from the heart.
1   2   3   4   5   6   7   8   9   10

Consider the following: Know yourself; find your purpose; craft your values and develop a moral compass; don't take shortcuts; play to your strengths; create transparency; act with integrity; be genuine and humble; give generously; develop a growth mindset; be consistent; and lead with your heart.

Actions:

Vulnerability: The ability to be "smartly" open, express yourself, and be who you truly are, even at risk of losing control.

1   2   3   4   5   6   7   8   9   10

Consider the following: Know your strengths and weaknesses; encourage feedback; be transparent and admit mistakes; embrace an attitude of openness and receptivity; find the "why" behind the flaws; engage in healthy conflicts; understand and accept failure; create a space to discuss emotions; encourage risk taking; request for help; and inspire people to ask for help when needed.

Actions:

Empathy: The ability to listen, recognize, and respond to people's feelings, thoughts, and emotions.

1   2   3   4   5   6   7   8   9   10

Consider the following: Recognize and relate to the challenges your people face; listen with a virtuous heart; focus on your people's well-being; step outside yourself, step into their shoes and take an interest in their feelings and emotions; be present when they need you; have heart-to-heart talks with them; connect and learn about their stories; lead with a "giving" mindset; and think "them," not "me."

Actions:

Tool # 12: Lead With Play Worksheet

Instructions: Reflect on the fundamentals needed to spark emotional connection, and identify the vital actions required to lead with play.

Giving back to the community
Consider the following: Footprints champion; people involvement; product donations; signature fundraising; pro bono services; environmental conservation; disadvantaged people; space donation; sponsoring events; and mentoring programs. Actions:
Restoring the FUN in FUNctional
Consider the following: Experimentation time to dig up new ideas; testing time to experience products and services; organizational values contests to boost the culture; cross-generational team bonding to build connections; healthy competitions to spark innovation; Celebrating wins with rituals to build momentum; playful morning briefings to raise morale; experiencing the competition to improve performance; role-playing, play a customer for a day to refine your customer experience; and wild ideas brainstorming sessions to revamp your business. Actions:

Promoting a learning culture

Consider the following: Connect learning to your purpose and values, and make it part of your KPIs; select people with an appetite to learn; reward learning by creating links between learning and performance; make the executives active participants in the learning itself; promote the SME as coaches and mentors; implement "learning sharing programs" to harness the SME's skills and knowledge; plan formal and informal learning rituals; create opportunities for people to connect and collaborate; make learning from feedback "a way of work;" give people access to learning opportunities and allow them to take charge of their own learning paths; encourage people to plan what they learn, apply it, and then share it with others; grant people access to knowledge, talents, and resources, and create autonomous learning opportunities; allow people the freedom to learn at their own pace, take initiatives and make mistakes; encourage an "open door policy" for engagement, openness, seeking assistance, and tough questioning; develop cross-functional teams, and encourage peer-to-peer coaching; give teams stretch assignments.

Actions:

Tool # 13: Lead With Focus Worksheet

Instructions: Work with you team to complete this worksheet and craft your quantifiable mission.

---

1. Top priorities: Define and craft your three to maximum four bold priorities that if achieved, nothing else really matters.

Format:
(Verb) (Variable) from (A) to (B) by (Deadline)
OR (Verb) (Variable) to (X) by (Deadline)

Top Priorities:
1.

2.

3.

4.

2. Priorities analyzer. Are your priorities well crafted?
Use the checklist below to analyze your priorities.
Review the priorities until you nail it.

	Pr. 1	Pr. 2	Pr. 3	Pr. 4
Does it fulfill the purpose?				
Does it fit your ideology?				
Does it stimulate progress?				
Does it generate thrust?				
Is it easy to grasp by everyone?				
Is it specific and highly focused?				
Is it compelling and daring?				
Is it measurable?				
Does it have a clear finish line?				
Can everyone contribute to it?				

3. Get the juices flowing: Reformat your priorities to make it visually memorable, engaging, and concise.

Format: e.g., 85 (CE) – 95 (GV) – 105% (TL) + 1
(variable 1; goal) – (variable 2; goal) – (variable 3; goal), etc.

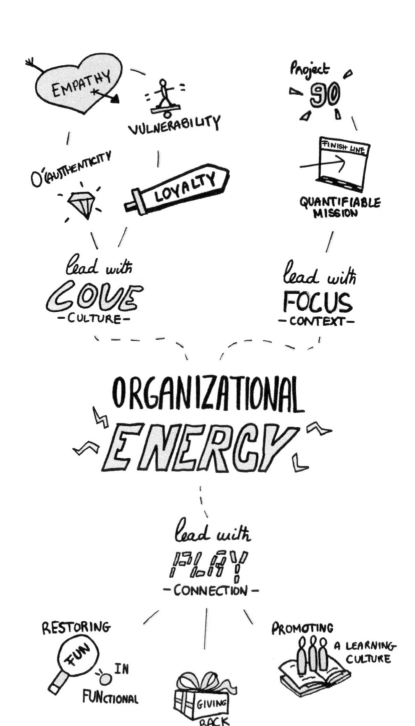

SUMMARY
PRINCIPLE 2

We live in a new world of business where the nature of human resources is going through a major shift. The only way forward is to reimagine the way we treat and lead our people. The problem is, HR people are always viewed as the organization's "admins" and "mechanics" who hire, fire, safeguard regulations, and sometimes monitor productivity. With this mindset, we will go nowhere. That is an epic failure of the imagination. Time to redefine. Sit at the executive table. Recommend talent solutions.

From *in*human resources to talent maximizers. Case Closed.

Truth #6: Talent alone is not enough

Greatness is NOwhere Mindset: Talent alone is everything.
Greatness is NOWhere Mindset: Talent + Deliberate Practice + Inner Drive = Growth
Toolset: Talent Maximizer Worksheet TMW (p.115)

Truth #7: Rethink leadership: All bets are off!

Greatness is NOwhere Mindset: Leadership is a one-size-fits-all approach.
Greatness is NOWhere Mindset: Leadership is a one-size-fits-one choice that ultimately unleashes greatness.
Toolset: It's All About You Worksheet IAAY (p. 133)

Truth #8: Autonomy is the ruling currency

Greatness is NOwhere Mindset: ME-centered paradigm: It's about control.
Greatness is NOWhere Mindset: WE-centered paradigm: It's about autonomy.
Nine is Mine Autonomy Kit (p. 150)

Truth #9: Bring out the gold: A to Z

Greatness is NOwhere Mindset: Leadership is an inward journey, focusing on self-awareness, self-control, and cultivating your personal operating system.
Greatness is NOWhere Mindset: Leadership is a balancing act between focusing inward and focusing outward (bring out the gold in yourself and others).
Toolset: Bring Out The Gold Worksheet (p. 175)

Truth #10: Energy: The supreme power

Greatness is NOwhere Mindset: Organizational energy is shaped by extrinsic factors.
Greatness is NOWhere Mindset: Organizational energy is shaped by the culture (Lead with love), connection (Lead with play) and context (Lead with focus).
Toolset: Lead with Love Worksheet (p. 196) Lead with Play Worksheet (p. 198) Lead with Focus Worksheet (p. 200)

Golden Nuggets

You can't be what your people are not. To win, surround yourself with talented, passionate, and engaged colleagues who go above and beyond, bring your organizational values to life, and serve its purpose.

You and I exist to make a difference, regardless of our position, status, or job title. We are all influential in our own way, and we all have our own pace and place.

If your talents are the cards you were dealt, how you play your hand is what translates talent to performance. Talent will only yield ideal perfect execution if partnered with its vital allies—deliberate practice and inner drive.

The evidence is overwhelming! Maximizing performance requires a deliberate effort to improve. Injecting your talent with deliberate practice leads to change and mastery.

Disruptive times require one-size-fits-one leadership choices that ultimately unleash greatness.

Enable greatness everywhere. Start building. Build a relationship, a team, an organization, or a tower. It doesn't matter. The key to greatness is to start building.

When people have freedom, they transform the automatic, built-in 3F mechanism Fight, Flight, or Freeze into Focus, Foresee, and Fascinate.

Empowerment is not enough. Autonomy is the ruling currency. Give your people the choice on what to do; when to do it; how to do it; whom to do it with; and what's next.

Leaders are alchemists: Transforming the raw talents they encounter into gold—unleashing the precious form of those they serve and lead.

Organizational energy—the concealed force that changes everything, is shaped by your organizational culture, the connection between your people and the organization, and the context or how the organization operates.

PRINCIPLE 3

You can't be
what your investment is not

Repackage best practices, create your own,
and zig when others zag. Maybe your most important task
as a leader is to be a paradigm shifter.

*Once you craft and inspire a powerful winning culture
and select the right people, it is time to bring your investment
to your customers in the form of an experience.*

Investment = Customer experience

Your biggest investment is undeniably your customer experience! You might have the best and most magnetized products and services, but if you don't ensure an exceptional experience, it means nothing. Let us explore that magical word: experience.

The Etymology of "Experience"

Experience—the word: Noun: experience; plural noun: experiences.
Entry 1. "An experience is something that you do or that happens to you, especially something important that affects you."
Entry 2. "Is used to refer to the past events, knowledge, and feelings that make up someone's life or character."
Entry 3. "The act of living through an event or events. Anything observed or lived through."
Entry 4. "Activity that includes personal participation."
Entry 5. "To be emotionally or aesthetically moved by." [188]

First known use of the word: 14th century.

Experience—the mindset: When we think of the word "experience," we tend to imagine a trip to a theme park, a journey with a cruise liner, or a vacation at a hotel. We must accept that the word experience is not limited to organizations like The Ritz-Carlton Hotel Company, Disney, Singapore Airlines, or Seabourn Cruise Liners. This word belongs to YOU and every organization in the business of selling a product or service.

Experience-related words: Act. Adventure. Encounter. Endeavor. Engagement. Event. Happening. Manifestation. Occurrence. Performance. Phenomenon. Quest. State. Turning point. Venture. Voyage. Way of life. MOMENT.

The Metamorphosis of Experience

We currently live in a world where customers' expectations, needs, and demands are shifting. Like butterflies, the perception of value have been through a metamorphosis—from product/production of goods (stage 1) to service/provision of services (stage 2), to finally experience/ crafting of moments (stage 3).

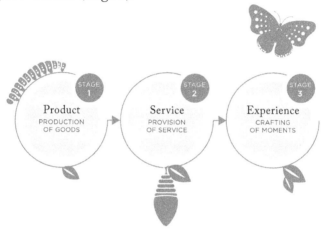

Figure 5. The Metamorphosis of Experience

Your customers are driven by experience, not function. In their classic book, *The Experience Economy*, authors Joseph Pine and James Gilmore make a strong case that "experiences are as distinct from services as services are from goods."[189] Today's customers crave experiences—a call for organizations to rethink and reimagine the packaging of their products and services. To embrace that shift from "product and service" to "experience," organizations must therefore move beyond the convenient delivery of goods and the seamless provision of services to deliver experimental experiences. They have to make the customer experience their mission and accordingly design unique, engaging, memorable, personal, and emotional moments.

In his book *The Experience-Centric Organization*, professor of interaction design Simon Clatworthy discusses the fact that the experience economy resides at the core of people's lives, and those experiences guide our purchase decisions.[190] Like a visit to The Ritz-Carlton or Disney, when customers connect with you, the experience is what they are really seeking. This shift was also predicted 20 years ago by Rolf Jensen, director of The Copenhagen Institute for Future Studies, one of the world's largest future-oriented think tanks, when he predicted that the information society (governed by data) will be replaced by the dream society—a society governed by emotions and stories.[191] The notion of a customer-centric organization is not totally new, but making the shift to this experience economy is still vague and murky.

The first table below summarizes this shift from "product and service centricity" to "experience centricity" and highlights the differences between these economies. This shift inspires a totally different dynamic; a new way of thinking. And this new way of thinking determines the way you embrace your business as a whole. The Ritz-Carlton, Harley-Davidson, Starbucks, Disney, Porsche, Nordstrom, and Club Med, to name a few, embraced this experience economy, and their successes are stories to tell. The second table below shares how some organizations navigated this ambiguity and wrapped their experiences around the experience economy to find their edge.

The shift from "product and service" to "experience"
economy requires organizations
to deliver emotional experiences.

Product/Service Economy versus Experience Economy

Centricity	Product/Service	Experience
Features	Transaction (physical/tangible)	Transformation (abstract/intangible)
Priority	Meeting expectations	Surpassing expectations
Delivery	Budget	Opportunity
Competition	On the basis of price	On the basis of experience
Value	A piece of the puzzle (feature/benefit)	Oh Yes! Moments (memory)
Intensity	Satisfaction/Loyalty	Advocacy
Intent	I am done	I want more

Leveraging the Experience Economy

Company	Product/Service	Experience Economy
The Ritz-Carlton	Rooms	Lasting memories
Harley-Davidson	Motorcycle	Rebel lifestyle
Starbucks	Cup of coffee	The third place, filling souls
Disney	Rides	Sprinkling pixie dust
Nordstrom	Retail	Expressing oneself
Porsche	Sports car	Daring and dreaming
Club Med	Vacations	Unwinding and reconnecting
North Face	Outdoor products	Exploring the world
Apple	Computers	Breaking the status quo
Lego	Toys	Nurturing the child
IKEA	Furniture	The wonderful everyday

At the Heart of the Experience Economy: Emotions!

Think of your finest customer experience; how would you describe it? Typically, people realize that the reasons they cite are related to emotions. Some can't even remember the products or services they paid for (i.e., physical or tangible experience) but they will always remember how they felt—being respected, valued, delighted, surprised, etc. (i.e., emotional experience). This is the reason I define the customer experience as:

The emotional outcome of one or a series of moments
of contact in the customer journey.

Since the inception of my company and due to my heavy travel schedule, I made a commitment to be with my family every weekend. At the end of a consulting week in London and Paris in 2014, I received a call from a very loyal client in Riyadh, Saudi Arabia, requesting my urgent support to facilitate a strategy session that same weekend. I apologized, shared my commitment and explained that I hadn't seen my family for the whole week. The client made an emotional appeal that the team would miss the deadline if I didn't make it, so I deviated from my commitment and flew from Paris directly to Riyadh. After checking into my room, I noticed a stuffed teddy bear on my bed. Don't get me wrong, I love plushies and stuffies, but with age, your preferences tend to change, so I was very intrigued why they did it. Upon further exploration, I noticed a sign on the teddy bear's paw that read, "Press here." Being the curious man I am, I pressed the sign, and to my surprise, I heard my four-year-old son Raphael singing his favorite lullaby, "Twinkle, Twinkle, Little Star." His lifting chant was followed by a moving message, "Pap, I know that you can't come to us, so I am coming to sleep next to you. I miss you and love you." Now imagine this scene: a 38-year-old guy crying like a four-year-old baby in front of a stuffed teddy bear! That is the true essence of an experience; an emotional outcome of that one moment. Truth be told, I don't recall the amenities they offered that day, neither do I remember the color of the curtains or how relaxing the bed was. But I vividly remember the people who evoked those emotions, and most importantly, I will never forget the brand, The Ritz-Carlton, Riyadh.

It is so true what Arnold Bennett, one of the most remarkable English literary figures of his time, once said, "There can be no knowledge without emotion. We may be aware of a truth, yet until we have felt its force, it is not ours. To the cognition of the brain must be added the experience of the soul."[192] If I learned something from my years of experience in the hospitality industry, it would be this: Make emotions a key part of your offerings and deliberately design it into your customer experience. That's the way to the soul. It is crucial to create moments that energize, provoke excitement, and bring a sense of delight to your customers.

Make emotions a key part of your offerings and deliberately design it into your customer experience.

I Feel, Therefore I Buy

Some believe that we know more about the planet Mars than we know about our human brains. I tend to agree. Our brain is pretty complicated, and I will not dare to embark on figuring out how billions of neurons, woven together by trillions of connections operate, but here are a few simple facts. As human beings, we don't think our way to rational solutions, we feel our way to them.[193] Data flows from the emotional side of the brain (the core) to the logic-driven rational side of it (the cortex). The emotional part of the brain is automated, fast, and forms the largest part of the brain, where major decisions are made by the joint effort of the hippocampus (attention, formation, and indexing of new memories), amygdala (emotional responses and reactions), and thalamus (relays motor and sensory signals to the cortex). This is what most business marketers focus on. That part of the brain operates in the background where memories, feelings, preferences, likes, dislikes, and decisions, among other things, originate and most functions exist. On the other hand, the rational, "conscious" part of the brain tries to make sense of it all through analysis, interpretation, and planning.

This is why professor of psychology, philosophy, and neurology Antonio Damasio states, "Emotion is integral to the process of reasoning and decision-making."[194] When you buy products or services, it may seem that your purchasing decisions are rational. They aren't! If our decisions were rational, smokers would stop smoking just from reading the "Smoking Kills" warnings boldly highlighted on cigarette packs. In his 2008 bestselling book *Buyology: Truth and Lies About Why We Buy*, Danish author and *Time* Magazine Influential 100 Honoree Martin Lindstrom shares that people make decisions and choices based on "somatic markers," i.e., intense clusters of emotions and sensations... and that 80 percent of new U.S. products die within a few months. Those that survive are those that engage people emotionally and link to their subconscious drives.[195]

You don't buy a $1,000 Montblanc pen to just take notes; any $1 pen can serve that purpose.

You don't buy a $15,000 Rolex to just tell you the time; any $10 watch can serve that purpose.

You don't buy a $150,000 Porsche to just go from point A to point B; any $1,500 car can serve that purpose.

You buy these products because of how they make you feel—the feeling of carrying a Montblanc, wearing a Rolex, or driving a Porsche. This same truth applies to our day-to-day purchases too. We buy products and services because of the emotions evoked by their stories, sensory associations, and subconscious impact.

Your customers enter your business with emotional expectations, and therefore it is fair to conclude that connecting with your customers' emotions should drive the design of your products and services. I am not suggesting we emotionalize every touch point, but start by defining the customers' state (how they feel, what they think and do) when coming into the experience, their emotional expectations at certain touch points, the emotions to evoke; then finally craft the respective actions to evoke those emotions in order to build connection, predict behavior, and ultimately drive intense loyalty.

Remember, you can't be what your investment is not. Today's organizations are required to make the shift from "product and service" to the "experience" economy and accordingly make emotions a key part of their offerings and deliberately design it into the customer experience. Again, that's the way to your customer's heart—creating moments that energize, provoke excitement, and create raving fans.

Five Truths to Spice up Your Customer experience

In Principle 3, I present five Truths to spice up your customer experience.

Truth #11: The language of emotions

Brands are built on experiences and experiences on emotions. In fact, more than 50% of the customer experience is emotional. Organizations need to focus on deliberately infusing emotions in the customer's journey. This Truth shares three blocks of emotions and their respective key drivers to amplify the intensity of the customer experience, influence perception, and drive advocacy.

Truth #12: The Holy Grail of customer experience

The customer experience is a collection of moments. It is vital for organizations to consider the customer's point of view, decipher and map the customer journey, and convert the experience into an Oh Yes! Moment that adds enormous emotional value. In this Truth, I share three ways to create those Oh Yes! Moments: Scenography, WOWography, and Ethnography.

Truth #13: Spice up your experience

In today's fiercely competitive climate where everyone wants a piece of the cake, organizations must unceasingly exploit our world of thinking for solutions and ideas that could possibly open new doors of opportunities. In this Truth, I present 20 insights that will propel you to search for answers, raise the bar, and reimagine your investment.

Truth #14: Uncover the cream of the crop

Selecting the right people is an indispensable success factor to any organization. They shape every customer's encounter and have the power to design an experience that delivers on your promises, or one that triggers the Chewing Gum Effect and ruins your brand. In this Truth, I uncover the 10 fundamental attributes that I consider the real deal for colleagues in the service industry; attributes that filter and uncover the cream of the crop.

Truth #15: 19 for COVID-19

Every 10 to 15 years, a crisis or something jaw-dropping happens, and in times of turbulence, great organizations reinvent themselves to stay relevant to those they lead and serve. Imagine a crisis as a line. On one side of that line is the status quo; the world as we know it. On the other side of the line is a great chance to thrive, a whole new world of opportunities. In this Truth, I share 19 tips to inspire you and fuel your quest to transform, make things happen, and finish strong.

Enjoy the ride and work with your team to evoke emotions, craft Oh Yes! Moments, spice up your experience, uncover the cream of the crop, and reinvent your investment. Repackage best practices, create your own, and zig when others zag. And remember that maybe your most important task as a leader is to be a paradigm shifter.

- TRUTH # 11 -

The language of emotions

Customer experience is:

- An event, happening, story, memory…and an emotion.
- A physical, tangible performance…and an emotion.
- Holistic, individualized, ingenious…and emotional.
- A sensual, intangible journey…and an emotion.
- An engaging relationship…and an emotion.
- A competitive battleground, and 50 percent of that experience is emotional.

Brands are built on experiences. Experiences are built on emotions. Your business, therefore, depends on emotions.

You Have a Choice to Ignore or Use Emotions

Ignore them and you will unleash a psychological war against yourself and totally disconnect with those you lead and serve; a war that will consume your energy and business. Your organization will throw your customers into an impulsive, emotional rollercoaster, leaving everything to chance and resulting in disengaged customers and reduced business.

Use them and you will harness the power of the messages they present. They will enable you to emotionally connect with those you lead and serve and build relationships for life. Your business will thrive by deliberately evoking emotions in the customer journey, leaving nothing to chance, and resulting in engaged customers and prosperous business.

EXPERIENCES are built on EMOTIONS.

Emotions: Asset or Liability?

Emotions are data and energy. They reveal our preferences, what we like and don't like, and drive our attention and perception. They give us the ammo to create a work environment charged with potential and possibilities and to take actions. Sandi Mann, a senior lecturer in occupational psychology at University of Central Lancashire, author, and emotions expert states, "Emotions and emotion management are a prominent feature of organizational life."[196] They enable us to connect, forge relationships, and enrich the work environment. For example, researchers in organizational behavior and evidence-based management, Barry Staw, Robert Sutton, and Lisa Pelled, found that "Positive emotions on the job have favorable consequences…leading to work achievement, job enrichment, and a higher quality social context."[197] Not only that, but emotions are also the backbone of your customer experience. In fact, over 50 percent of the customer experience is about emotions.[198] They influence the way we and our customers think, communicate, make decisions, and behave. Emotions guide us and help us to process information, reach conclusions, and influence judgments. They help us to thrive and give us the muscles we need to be resilient, learn, and grow.

In simple terms, emotions have the power
to drive or ruin your business.

An asset or liability?
Well, you do the math!
It's time to master emotions.

Emotions and the Customer Experience

How many emotions are there? Philosophers and psychologists have tried to answer this question. In his book *Emotional Intelligence: Why It Can Matter More Than IQ*, the internationally celebrated psychologist Daniel Goleman writes, "There are hundreds of emotions, along with their blends, variations, mutations, and nuances. Indeed, there are many more subtleties of emotion than we have words for."[199] There is no way to agree on a precise number of emotions, but many scholars agree on the primary emotions from which psychologist Robert Plutchik created the "Wheel of Emotions"[200] in 1980. Founded on eight primary bipolar emotions (joy and sadness; anger and fear; trust and disgust; and surprise and anticipation), Plutchik designed a flower-shaped two-dimensional model with petals describing those primary emotions, the relations among them, their similarities, and intensity variations.

Driving Advocacy

We are in the business of selling experiences, and the shift from "product and service" to the "experience" economy requires today's organizations to focus on engaging certain emotions that influence customer perception and drive advocacy. For example, emotions like anger, sadness, disgust, boredom, and anxiety are associated with customer disengagement and service failure, while emotions like safety, trust, and amazement are associated with customer engagement and service excellence. Evidently, for our investment to yield absolute impact, we should minimize those emotions that evoke disappointment and elicit the right emotions at the right time to delight our customers.

How do you define those emotions,
let alone manage and measure them?

That might be the reason why most of today's service quality models and measurements are of cognitive nature. Working with and studying the most recognized global organizations, their cultures and customer services practices, as well as reviewing research findings from multiple scholars in this field (Richins, 1997;[201] Edwardson, 1998;[202] Barsky, 2002;[203] Laros and Steenkamp, 2005;[204] Shaw, 2007;[205] Desmet et al., 2009;[206] Jang and Namkung, 2009;[207] Jani and Han, 2015[208]), I formulated three blocks of emotions with a total of eight emotions that a) encapsulate a number of other emotions, and b) trigger the highest form of emotional connection. I recommend injecting these emotions into your customer's journey to advance from mere satisfaction to absolute advocacy, creating customers for life—customers who are intensely loyal even in the presence of other choices and passionately promote your organization to others. As you will see in Figure 6 below, there are three blocks of emotions (Expected, Connection, and Unexpected) that drive and optimize the intensity of your customer experience. I propose that you first work on the "Expected" block of emotions to eliminate negative emotions, then push ahead to increase the intensity of the experience. By doing so, you will predict your customers' behavior and depict the growth of your organization. I also advise that you use these three blocks as a stepping stone to further define which additional emotions drive most value in your particular business, analyze your customers emotional motivators, needs, and expectations, and then design experiences with your customers in mind. Finally, it would also be rewarding to involve your customers; engage with them in real time to deeply understand the emotions they seek while going through your experience.

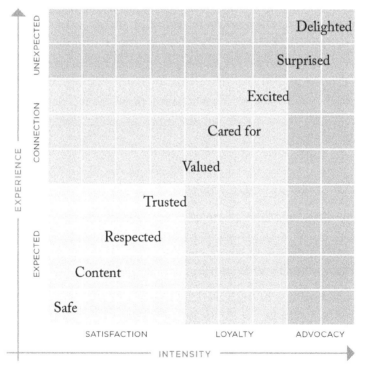

Figure 6. Experience Intensity Model

The degree of intensity is affected by the a) latency and duration of the emotion (how long the emotion lasts), and b) to what extent the emotions will change the customer's belief and/or behavior. I will further discuss this topic in Truth #12, as focusing on specific touch points in the experience cycle yields a higher emotional return. In this next section, I will briefly define each block and its respective emotions[209] and share five key drivers to evoke each of these emotions.

Knowing your customers better than they do is critical to anticipate, envision, and design your experience.

I: The Expected Block of Emotions

Customers seek your services with certain emotional expectations. If those expectations fall below the reality of the experience, it leads to stress, irritation, frustration, helplessness, and disappointment. The expected cluster of emotions is about simplicity, reliability, and usability. It is the price of entry to drive customer satisfaction. The trouble is, satisfaction is not enough. Your customers might feel secure, content, respected, and trusted but remain open to switch service providers when convenient.

Safe:

Definition: An emotional state of being free from harm, loss, or risk; being free from the occurrence or risk of injury or danger.

Key drivers:
1. Operating with high safety standards. Safety first.
2. Projecting signs of safety and speaking the language of safety.
3. Being informed, resourceful, and honest with your customers at all costs.
4. Taking the time to explain the inner workings of your experience to provide reassurance.
5. Prioritizing safety concerns and addressing it with a sense of urgency.

Content

Definition: An emotional state of satisfaction; being at ease in one's situation; being happy with who you are and where you are; being pleased because of a happening or the fact that you got what you wanted.

Key drivers:
1. Simplifying the customer's experience (make it easy and reducing the steps) and speaking their language (not the language of your industry.)
2. Designing and delivering a seamless, stress-free experience.
3. Making the customers feel comfortable and meeting their needs.
4. Providing your customers with accessibility to knowledge and technology.
5. Bringing your personality into the customer experience; avoiding robotic services.

Respected

Definition: An emotional state of appreciation; being considered important to someone; being deferentially regarded.

Key drivers:
1. Living up to your promises and claims.
2. Respecting your customers' views and thoughts and giving them the choice to decide things for themselves.
3. Projecting a friendly, approachable, and helpful character, and living up to your values.
4. Being responsive and attentive toward your customers.
5. Being authentic—saying what you mean and meaning what you say.

Trusted:

Definition: An emotional state of confidence in someone or something; being worthy of trust and confidence; belief in the honesty of others.

Key drivers:

1. Delivering on your commitments and living up to your promises. Understanding your customers and doing what's right for them.

2. Believing that customers are always right. Don't penalize the many for the deceitfulness of the few.

3. Soliciting the customers' reviews and feedback and acting upon it.

4. Doing what's best for your customers, even if you have to bend some rules.

5. Owning the customers' problems and immediately resolving them.

II: The Connection Block of Emotions

This block of emotions builds on satisfaction to engage the hearts of customers and drive loyalty. Nurturing emotional connections will enable you to build deep and strong relationships. When your customers feel valued, cared for, and excited, they tend to support your organization and come back for more. This surely leads to repeat purchases, as these customers rarely seek alternatives. Yet they will not necessarily be your brand advocates. They will share your story, but only when enticed to do so.

Valued:

Definition: An emotional state of importance; being highly regarded; being appreciated and recognized.

Key drivers:

1. Making your customers feel welcome. Addressing them by name and connecting with them as human beings, not a plate number, room number, or invoice number.

2. Treating customers warmheartedly and showing them that you value their business by personalizing the experience.

3. Making customers feel appreciated and special, offering additional value with customized amenities and niceties. Celebrating them as valued customers (birthdays, discounts, memberships, etc.).

4. Showing interest in your customers and adjusting your processes to serve them.

5. Making customers feel that they are truly a part of something to promote a sense of belonging and foster a brand community. Making them your heroes.

Cared for:

Definition: An emotional state of love; being the center of concern for someone or something; being looked after and loved.

Key drivers:
1. Being available and accessible 24/7.
2. Knowing and understanding your customers' preferences, acting on it, and providing meaningful advice.
3. Anticipating customers' needs and taking proactive ownership of those needs. Making your service proactive and agile.
4. Protecting and looking after your customers. Putting them first!
5. Empathizing with your customers; putting yourself in their shoes. Seeing what they see, hearing what they hear, and feeling what they feel.

Excited:

Definition: An emotional state of enthusiasm; being physically and mentally active; being stimulated and interested.

Key drivers:
1. Nurturing your customers to become better, smarter, and more capable.
2. Enlivening the senses of your customers and making the experience educational and entertaining.
3. Injecting a sense of thrill in the customer's experience. Keeping them zeroed in on the experience.

4. Introducing new experiences and involving the customers in designing their own.

5. Injecting fun, energetic, and gratifying events into the customer experience.

III: The Unexpected Block of Emotions

Recent neuroscience studies have shown that our brains yearn for the unexpected.[210] Evoking the emotions of surprise and delight will enable you to intensify the experience and build on loyalty to transition your customers into raving fans. Building on the unexpected emotions of satisfaction and loyalty will yield intense relationships where customers will be living with your brand in a passionate way. They ultimately become your brand advocates and voluntarily offer their time and energy to share your story and recommend you to others.[211] This block of emotions links to the "Net Promote Score" introduced by Fred Reichheld in his 2004 article, "The One Number You Need to Grow"[212] and then in his book, *The Ultimate Question*.[213] Reichheld writes, "When customers act as references…they put their own reputations on the line. And they will risk their reputations only if they feel intense loyalty." He adds, "The only path to profitable growth may lie in a company's ability to get its loyal customers to become, in effect, its marketing department."[212]

Surprised:

Definition: An emotional state of wonder; being stunned; being astonished by something totally unexpected.

Key drivers:
1. Triggering the Expected and Connection blocks of emotions consistently and ensuring consistency in quality and delivery.
2. Building ad-hoc memories and leaving customers with stories to tell.
3. Delivering unusual offerings that take the customers by surprise.

4. Adding extra touches to the customer's experience. Indulging them with something exclusive; a form of luxury.
5. Making promises is good. Keeping them is great. Beating them is the name of the game.

Delighted:

Definition: An emotional state of enchantment (= surprise + (joy, thrill and exhilaration)); being positively overwhelmed; being greatly pleased and filled with amazement.

Key drivers:
   1. Staging the customer experience and including deliberate WOW moments.
   2. Crafting deliberate scenes in the customer experience and transforming needs, desires, and preferences into thrilling, spontaneous acts of kindness.
   3. Driving customers' active participation and enhancing specific touch points in their experience.
   4. Designing experiences that push the customer's self-esteem.
   5. Finishing the experience "strong." Ending the experience with a grand last impression.

Deciphering the Customer Experience

The celebrated painter Vincent van Gogh once wrote, "Small emotions are the great captains of our lives."[214] In this Truth, we learned that emotions are not only the great captains of your life, but also your business. Emotions that your customers seek and buy. If leveraged, this data and energy will mobilize performance, drive behavior, and steer decisions and advocacy.

Remember, the customer experience is the emotional outcome of one or a series of moments of contact in the customer journey. This Truth's worksheet will guide you to deliberately infuse the customer experience with emotions. I also invite you to redefine your measurement tools in order to measure those emotions. There is no one way to measure emotions. You can use the Net Promoter Score (NPS),[212] which is a simple and comparable measure, monitor social media, and redefine your current surveys to measure emotions in order to continuously improve your customer experience.

Final Note: Deliver Your Brand Experience

At every customer encounter, you have a choice to deliver your brand experience or not. Don't hope for things to happen. Instead, center your customer experience around human emotions and put emotions at the heart of your development, sales, marketing, and service strategies. Make a commitment to align your business with this new way of thinking. Embark on understanding your customers, and infuse their journey with emotions, crafting experiences that truly matter to enable advocacy. And always remember what the American poet, memoirist, and civil rights activist Maya Angelou once said: "People will forget what you said, people will forget what you did, but people will never forget how you made them feel."[215]

Tool # 14: Language of Emotions Worksheet

Instructions: Work with you team to map your customer experience and deliberately infuse it with emotions.

Experience: State the experience you want to deliberately design, refine, or redefine.

Customer State and Insights: Who are your customers? How are they entering the experience? What state are they in? What are they feeling, thinking, and doing?

Touch points: State the different experience touch points for each moment of contact.
Duplicate this page as needed to cover all the touch points.

Touch point #1:

Emotional expectations: State your customers' emotional expectations.

Emotions to evoke: Define the emotions to elicit in order to exceed expectations and drive behavior.

Actions: Determine the actions to evoke those emotions.

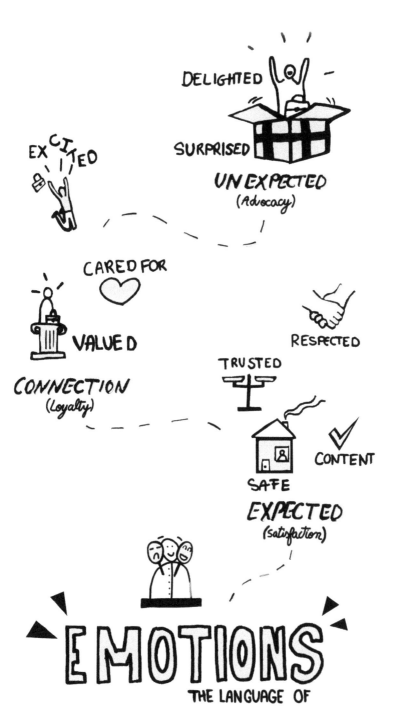

DELIGHTED

EXCITED

SURPRISED

UNEXPECTED
(Advocacy)

CARED FOR

VALUED

RESPECTED

TRUSTED

CONNECTION
(Loyalty)

SAFE

CONTENT

EXPECTED
(satisfaction)

EMOTIONS
THE LANGUAGE OF

– TRUTH # 12 –

The Holy Grail
of customer experience

Driving Advocacy

Many organizations throughout the world still pursue and celebrate customer satisfaction as a point of differentiation. Like I said in the previous Truth, satisfaction is necessary, but it only measures a short-term condition, not the depth of the emotional connection. It is a given these days. Fred Reichheld, a leading authority on loyalty and the author of the bestselling book *The Loyalty Effect,* writes, "If you are mediocre and adequate is your goal, use satisfaction as your target."[216] Today's organizations should go beneath the satisfaction surface, trade up emotionally, and craft vibrant, enriching, and sometimes even dramatic customer experiences. This is the true path to advocacy, the deepest form of emotional connection and customer loyalty.

Consistency drives satisfaction.
Emotional connection drives loyalty.
A state of amazement drives advocacy.

Advocacy might sound like the next buzzword and a complex notion, but in fact, it is simple. In the Experience Intensity Model,[5] I illustrated that when you go above and beyond, surprise and delight your customers, they become your advocates and raving fans. Above all, they will voluntarily offer their time and energy to reward your brand by sharing their stories and recommending your products and services to others. They will grow so loyal that they treat your business as their own, share their feedback, and recommend ways for your business to improve and flourish. They will become your best source of inspiration to further refine, redefine, and achieve sustainable growth. They will take your brand places. And if I were you, I would move heaven and earth to keep them and hide them from this world.

---

[5] Figure 6. Experience Intensity Model. Truth #11.

Three Words: Word of "Mouse"

With the rise of technology and social media, word of mouth happens around the clock, 24 hours day, seven days a week, 365 days a year; and these words are no doubt dramatically affecting your business. People share products, services, experiences, emotions, and brands. But with the presence of technology and social media, word-of-mouth (or shall I call it, *word of mouse*), is faster and louder. Think about this:

- A study conducted by Forrester Research showed that approximately 500 billion word-of-mouth impressions are created every day by social media—and that was in 2010; imagine how many are created today![217]

- A research conducted by McKinsey & Company estimated that two thirds of the U.S. economy is driven by word-of-mouth.[218]

- According to the American information, data, and market measurement firm Nielsen, 83 percent of people trust friends and family recommendations and 66 percent say they trust consumer opinions posted online.[219]

- Bain & Company, working with Earl Sasser of Harvard Business School, published a study showing that a 5 percent increase in customer retention can boost a company's profitability by 25 to 95 percent.[220]

Big, impressive numbers.
Three words: Word of "mouse."
Make these three words the centerpiece of your business strategy.
You can't afford to ignore it.
People talk, people listen; people write, people read.
People follow and brand advocates are born.

The Holy Grail: Oh Yes! Moments

In the previous Truth, I invited you to understand your customers and infuse their journey with emotions, crafting experiences that truly matter to develop customer advocacy. In this Truth, I dig deep into how to evoke "The Unexpected" block of emotions (*Surprised and Delighted*) to convert your customer experience into one that chills and thrills; an OH YES! Moment that adds enormous emotional value.

The customer experience is a journey with multiple touch points—points of interaction between the customer and your organization. Simply put, it is a collection of moments. With this in mind, organizations need to a) walk the customer's journey to see, hear, understand, and feel the experience from the customer's point of view; b) decipher and map the journey to highlight every possible touch point; and c) craft vibrant, enriching, and profoundly memorable and personal moments.

Yes, MOMENTS!
Moments of delight and surprise.
Some big. Some small.
At times you have to stage it by deliberately injecting it at predefined touch points, and at times you spontaneously orchestrate it.
Think in moments!
Enrich the customer's experience with stories to tell.
Don't leave it to chance.

The same way that flowers' colors and fragrances transform insects and birds into pollinators to multiply, organizations' moments and stories turn customers into advocates to grow and thrive.

There are three approaches to creating Oh Yes! Moments: Scenography, WOWography, and Ethnography. In this Truth, I highlight the components of each by sharing a brief definition, purpose, five catalysts for change, the process, return on investment (ROI), terminology, a tool, reflection, and end with a quote. Let's discuss these approaches and how we can create more of them.

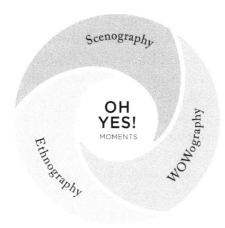

Figure 7. Oh Yes! Moments

A. Scenography

Definition

The essence of scenography is embedded in the subtitle of B. Joseph Pine and James Gilmore's book, *The Experience Economy: Work Is a Theater and Every Business a Stage*. It is the art of staging environments or atmospheres and making spaces "talk."[221] The term scenography is defined as "the art of perspective representation especially as applied to the design and painting of stage scenery."[222] I believe the author and business executive Seth Godin nailed this concept when he shared his experience of gazing at a field of black and white cows right next to the highway.[223] An ordinary scene, you might agree, especially if you drive on that highway every day. But imagine if, in the midst of this field, you suddenly spot a purple cow. What would you do? You would surely be intrigued and might even take a picture of it, right? That is not something that you spot every day, unless you are a "Milka" chocolate lover.[6] So in the customer experience context, scenography is the art of staging key moments in the customer's experience through unique and memorable scenes (think of it as your purple cows).

---

[6] The purple cow (known as Lila) is a strong symbol of Milka, a well-known Swiss brand of chocolate confection.

Today's leaders should recognize the transformational power of scenography as the art of designing experiences in a theatrical way. Companies all over the world are moving in this direction to orchestrate memories. You can see it in hotels, malls, theme parks, airports and restaurants, etc. Take The Ritz-Carlton, for example. When the company launched scenography in 2006, it was an absolute transformation. It enabled the organization to offer distinctive properties and orchestrate remarkable moments that stand out—moments that ignite their guests' (not customers) emotions and bring them closer to local cultures and the uniqueness of the environment properties operate in while unobtrusively preserving and celebrating the true Ritz-Carlton brand.

Purpose
Choreographing the customer experience to:

- Ignite word of mouth and mouse.
- Increase the perceived value of the product and services.
- Leverage the essence of the location.
- Stage one-of-a-kind experiences.
- Engage the customers' senses and make them feel connected.
- Create a sense of place and inspire a sense of belonging.
- Enliven the distinct aspects of the business.
- Create indigenous, authentic, and memorable moments.
- Leave the customers with stories to tell.

Five catalysts for change

1. *Experience analysis:* Implementing rigorous experience analysis through journaling and documentation, role-playing and shadowing to identify potential scenes.
2. *Obsession to delight:* Inspiring an experience culture enabling people to focus on surprising and delighting customers.
3. *Leaders as scenographers:* Leveraging the power of leaders as scenographers who operate their organizations as if they were theaters.

4. *Bottom-up innovation:* Considering employees as a) artists who are empowered to design outstanding productions for the audience (customers), and b) storytellers who bring experiences to life.

5. *Deliberate planning:* Incorporating scenography into your business strategy and budget process. Remember, scenography is a proactive process requiring deliberate planning.

The Process[7]

1. Theme

Start by identifying a descriptive and emotional "theme;" an all-embracing concept to tie the customer's experience together. Themes should be indigenous (stirring a sense of place and inspired by the culture and history of the location), congruent (projecting the brand promise), and anticipatory (considering the customers' needs and your industry's trends). The theme should give your business its unique service identity, make your customers feel connected, and create a true sense of place. Back to The Ritz-Carlton example, hotels developed themes like "Fire and Wine" (The Ritz-Carlton, Half Moon Bay, California), "Experience The Past, Today" (Sharq Village and Spa, The Ritz-Carlton Hotel, Qatar), "The Modern Castle" (The Ritz-Carlton, Wolfsburg, Germany), "An Oasis of Culinary Treasures" (The Ritz-Carlton, Grand Cayman, Caribbean), "East Meets West" (The Ritz-Carlton, Tokyo, Japan), and "The Source of Life" (The Ritz-Carlton, Bali, Indonesia).

2. Theme Audit

Once you identify your theme, it is time to put yourself in the customers' shoes and audit the experience to ensure that all the touch points are aligned with the theme, supporting and enhancing it. Make a list of every touch point and assess if the props (furniture, costumes, decoration, stationary, amenities, ornaments, etc.), tone (service language, uniforms, behaviors, internal and external communication, handwritten or

---

[7] This process is inspired by The Ritz-Carlton Hotel Company and IDEO, a creative firm that was involved in the creation of this scenography approach.

printed messages etc.), and mood (fragrances, aromas, light, music, etc.) reinforce the theme. Remember, the goal is to look through the eyes of the customer to evaluate every aspect of the experience and find ways to intensify the theme and ultimately enrich the experience.

3. Scenes

The next step is to deliberately design scenes that bring the theme to life. These scenes are moments that might occur at any part of your business with the purpose of enlivening the senses and enchanting your customers. The scenes could be rituals, signature services, ceremonies, spiritual moments, sensuous moments, family moments, or special activities—staged moments that will be remembered and cherished. It is important to deliberately design these scenes and also fine-tune it to the needs of your different customers. To keep your experience fresh, it is also imperative to introduce new, fresh scenes every year. Below are a few examples:

Theme: "Discover The District" (The Ritz-Carlton, Washington, D.C., U.S.).

Scene 1: Offering the President's and First Lady's favorite cookies every evening while featuring aspects of Washington, D.C. in the lobby.

Scene 2: Placing conversation cards with fun facts about Washington, D.C. around the hotel and with employees.

Theme: "Bedouin Rituals" (The Ritz-Carlton Ras Al Khaimah, Al Wadi Desert, UAE).

Scene 1: Celebrating the Bedouin lifestyle with a daily sunset falcon show—where guests are actors in the process.

Scene 2: Planning yoga sessions amongst the sand dunes while discovering the local fauna and flora.

Return on investment (ROI)
In addition to the significant word of mouth and mouse, consider this:
Cost of a homemade lemonade: A
Price of a lemonade at a luxury hotel: (Cost price A) x 22
Net Profit: 60%
ROI: 1,220%
PS: Staging is everything!

Terminology
Scenography; scenographers (leaders); guests (customers); memory makers (employees); orchestrating (providing or delivering); stories to tell (experiences); theme; scene; props; mood; tone; touch points.

Tool
Refer to the Scenography Worksheet at the end of this Truth.

Reflection
Do you have a theme for your business? Which part of your experience is not clearly visible or attracting attention? What can you do to create scenes that enchant your customers?

Quote
"The senses don't just make sense of life in bold or subtle acts of clarity, they tear reality apart into vibrant morsels and reassemble them into a meaningful pattern."[224] – *Diane Ackerman, American poet, essayist, and naturalist.*

B. WOWography

Definition
WOWography is the art of celebrating special emotional moments in customers' lives and transforming needs, desires, and preferences into thrilling spontaneous acts of kindness—scenes that will take your customers by surprise. The keyword here is "spontaneous." The experience, like anything in life, is made up of patterns that at times

make things unnoticeable. In psychology, this phenomenon is known as "habituation;" the decrease of a response to a certain stimulus that we became accustomed to.[225] In the experience context, customers become habituated to the experience, and at times, they won't remember any aspect of it. And if you agree with me, we live in a copy/paste customer experience world. Everything looks the same! I stay in luxury hotels 300 days a year, and at times I can only recognize certain brands because of their logo at the entrance of the building. Winning the experience game is about breaking that pattern. Imagine you are driving your car to suddenly witness an accident; what would you do? Stop, most probably! Why? Because it is an unusual event; not part of the ordinary. In the same way, WOWography simply entails taking individualization to a whole new level by injecting spontaneous, personalized scenes into the customer experience to interrupt the experience's routine, grab attention, and make the experience stand out above the rest. It doesn't have to be complex or expensive. It is simply a call to go off-script to break a pattern, but in a meaningful way that enriches the experience. Like scenography, you make the most out of that moment if you make your customers part of it and at times, allow them to even discover the journey themselves.

Purpose

Complement scenography to:
- Motivate word of mouth and mouse marketing.
- Increase the perceived value of products and services.
- Connect with customers' individuality to craft bespoke moments tailored to their specific needs, desires, and preferences.
- Go off-script to break the experience's routine and enrich the customer's experience.
- Show that you truly care about customers' well-being.
- Turn customers' complaints into opportunities to win their hearts again.
- Move the needle from ordinary to awesome.

Five catalysts for change

1. *The art of anticipation:* Selecting and training people who are capable of harnessing all sensory data and learn about the customers' needs, desires, and preferences.

2. *Integrate your systems:* Integrating all your apps, databases, and software solutions to support and cultivate anticipatory service.

3. *The granting of power:* Providing a structure that empowers people to improvise and go above and beyond the call of duty.

4. *Lateral service and collaboration:* Encouraging cross-functional teams to collectively interpret customers' data and design spontaneous scenes.

5. *Seamless communication:* Implementing daily briefings and simulations to constantly share customers' data and celebrate Oh Yes! Moments.

The Process

1. Observe

It's about the art of engagement and artful attentiveness. The first pivotal step is to motivate your people to strike up conversations with your customers and notice and anticipate their underlying expectations, needs, desires, and preferences. As the Ladies and Gentlemen say at The Ritz-Carlton, all employees should have their radar on and antenna up to read customers' signals, preferences, and unspoken needs.

2. Record

Design a system to record the information you collected about your customers. At The Ritz-Carlton, for example, employees carry guest preference pads on which they can record their observations and submit them to be documented in the company's guest relationship management software accessible across all properties. I also encourage you to investigate using portable technology that employees can use to record and have access to the customer information for prompt execution.

3. Empower

Shift from anticipation to fulfillment. After all, collecting and recording information isn't a deal breaker unless you share and make the information useful. Plan and execute customer data briefings and simulations to constantly encourage your people to craft and celebrate Oh Yes! Moments. Empower your people and enable them to go above and beyond to turn the information into memories.

Return on investment (ROI)

Consider this:

You most probably have heard of the customer who walked into a Nordstrom store—a store that doesn't sell tires—to return four snow tires, and he did.

Cost: Today's value for a pair of tires: $250 to $300.

PS: Google "Nordstrom Tires" and you will find 5,920,000 results.[8]

ROI: Significant word of mouth and mouse publicity.

Terminology

WOWography; preferences; Oh Yes! Moments; Oh Yes! celebrations; radar on, antenna up; empowerment; go above and beyond; lateral service; spontaneous acts of kindness; anticipation and fulfillment.

Tool

At the end of this Truth, I share a sample of a preference pad on which employees can record the customer's observations. As mentioned above, investigate using portable technology that employees can use to record and have access to the customer information for prompt execution

Reflection

How do you notice and anticipate the underlying needs, expectations, and preferences of your customers? What processes and systems do you have in place to inject spontaneous scenes in the customer's experience? Are your people empowered to craft spontaneous Oh Yes! Moments?

---

[8] As per a Google search, May 2021.

Quote
"The most memorable moments in life are the ones you never planned."
— *Unknown.*

C. Ethnography

Definition
Ethnography is the study of how people behave in a certain environment. In business, it is the art of directly observing how your customers interact with your products and services. When the Danish businessman Jorgen Vig Knudstorp took the helm of the LEGO group in 2004, the company was struggling, losing hundreds of millions every year. He knew something major needed to happen to turn the ship around. In addition to the traditional key moves such as cutting cost, restructuring, slashing the number of Lego parts, and managing cash flow, he invested in a new project, ethnography. In a nutshell, he involved LEGO's fans (customers) in the reinvention of LEGO by researching and observing how these fans interact with their toys, and most importantly, how they like to play—"A deep ethnographic study of how kids around the world really play."[226] Equipped with these observations, the company redefined the business, and a year later, they reported $81 million net profit.[227]

You might be thinking that you already leverage the power of ethnography within your organization in the form of focus groups, surveys, and research. Throughout the years though, I've learned that people say one thing yet act in a different way. I invite you to "directly observe" how your customers interact with your products and services. Analyze the hundreds of signals that your brand sends to customers to truly learn about their behavior, expectations, and motivations, and then take action accordingly to magnify the impact of your customer experience.

Purpose
Directly observe how your customers interact with your products and services to gain insight into what they are really like to:

• Increase the perceived value of products and services.
• Find solutions to defined service problems.
• Learn about your customers' behavior, expectations, and motivations while going through the experience. Align your design and delivery accordingly.
• Refine current products and services and design new products and services.
• Target and enhance specific touch points in the customer's experience.
• Spot opportunities to shape specific moments and make your customers tick.

Five catalysts for change

1. *Outside-in orientation:* Starting with your customers in mind to enable an experience focused on them, not your own organizational needs.
2. *Fieldwork, a necessity:* Being where the action is; moving from the dance floor to the balcony to observe how customers interact with your product and services.
3. *Leaders as ethnographers:* Leveraging the power of leaders as ethnographers who continuously look for opportunities to improve the customer's experience.
4. *Data! Data! Data!* Collecting customers' data is a foundational success factor. It is about quantity; gather as many behavioral and sensory-related intelligence as possible.
5. *Everything is relevant:* Customer perception is reality. Accept that some of what you think is irrelevant might be vital for your customer's experience.

The process

1. Objective
The first step is to define the ethnography objective. Are you planning

to introduce a new product or service, evaluate an existing product or service, boosting your sales, enhancing and enriching your customer experience at a particular touch point, etc.? This is the starting point that will guide you along this journey. The more specific you are, the greater the outcomes, and this exercise will yield amazing results.

2. Direct observations and data collection

Once you define your objective, you directly observe customers in the real environment where they connect with your products and services. For example, if you want to enhance your welcome experience, observe your customers in the welcome center, at the front desk, in the lobby, etc. How are they behaving when they come into the experience? What are they looking at? What are they hearing? Think of who they are, what they are doing, and why they are doing what they are doing. Take notes of the conscious and unconscious signals you send to your customers, and be mindful of their feelings, facial expressions, body language, and lingo. You can also conduct direct interviews with your customers to gain further insights. I recommend that you collect at least 15 hours of data from direct observations for simple touch points, but bear in mind, at times this exercise might take days or weeks.

3. Analysis

Now it is time to dive into the data, identify patterns, and formulate impactful actions. Are there any negative signals or emotional withdrawals (pain points) that detract from the customer's experience? What about potential positive signals or emotional deposits that add to the experience? Are there any opportunities to inject new deposits and or turn withdrawals into deposits? Any opportunities to further align the products and services to the needs of your customers? Any opportunities to make the touch point unique and fresh?

4. Action

Equipped with these findings, leaders then introduce actions to make meaningful changes, improve the customer's experience, and ultimately boost profitability.

Return on investment (ROI)
Consider this:
LEGO post-ethnography: LEGO surpassed Mattel to become the largest toy maker in the world.[228]
ROI: The rebirth and rise of an organization.
PS: A matter of life and death.

Terminology
Ethnography, ethnographers (leaders); emotional withdrawals (negative signals); emotional deposits (positive signals); direct observation; touch points; fieldwork.

Tool
Refer to the Ethnography Worksheet at the end of this Truth.

Reflection
Are you an inside-out organization (starting with your needs in mind) or an outside-in organization (starting with your customers in mind to enable an experience focused on them)? How can you apply ethnography to turn your ship around?

Quote
"There's the famous quote that if you want to understand how animals live, you don't go to the zoo, you go to the jungle." – *Jorgen Vig Knudstorp, Former LEGO CEO*[226]

Final Note: Experience Is Everything

In this Truth, we learned that you should deliberately evoke emotions in your customers and convert the experience into moments that chills and thrills. At times you have to stage it (Scenography), and at times you spontaneously orchestrate it (WOWography). I also discussed the importance of observing how your customers interact with your brand to magnify the impact of your customer experience (Ethnography). Experience is everything! It is central to our lives.

It is not a program; it is an Oh Yes! Moment; a memory for life.
Think in moments!
Enrich the customer experience with stories to tell.
Don't leave it to chance.
Get it right. Do it big.
It's time for a different measuring stick.

Tool # 15: Scenography Worksheet

Instructions: Follow steps one to three highlighted in the process under the scenography section and hereunder (identify a theme, conduct a theme audit, and deliberately design scenes to bring the theme to life.)

1. THEME: An all-embracing concept to tie the customer experience together. Criteria: indigenous, congruent, and anticipatory.

2. AUDIT: Step into your customer's shoes and align the touch points with the theme. Any elements to enhance, add, or remove? Consider the language, uniform, handwritten and prinn, fragrances, light, music, decoration, stationaries, amenities, etc.

Touch points	Notes

3. SCENE: Deliberately design scenes that bring the theme to life (rituals, signature services, ceremonies, spiritual moments, sensuous moments, family moments or special activities, etc.).

Scene 1:

Props (furniture, costumes, decoration, stationaries, amenities, ornaments, etc.)

Tone (service language, uniforms, behaviors, internal and external communication, handwritten or printed messages, etc.)

Mood (fragrances, aromas, light, music, etc.)

COST/FEASIBILITY/IMPACT

Tool # 16: WOWography—Customer Preference Pad

Instructions: This is a sample of a preference pad on which employees can record the customer's observations. Investigate using portable technology for efficient and effective execution.

Customer Name: Date:
Personal information (business card, contact details, etc.)
Routine (frequent behavior, habits, etc.)
Events (anniversary, birthday, special occasion, etc.)
Favorites (music, beverage, snack, magazines, time, etc.)
Interests (activity, industry, specific sport, show, etc.)
Needs (expectations, likes, dislikes, etc.)
Employee name: Department: *Ideas for Oh Yes! Moments:*

Tool # 17: Ethnography Worksheet

Instructions: Follow steps one to four highlighted in the process under the ethnography section and hereunder (objective, direct observations and data collection, analysis, and action).

---

1. Objective: define the ethnography objective:

---

2. Direct observations and data collection—Touch point/location (15 hrs. of data):
How are customers behaving when they come into the experience? What are they hearing? What are they looking at? Think of who they are, what they are doing, and why they are doing what they are doing. Take notes of the conscious and unconscious signals, customers' feelings, facial expressions, body language, and lingo.

3. Analysis: Any negative signals or emotional withdrawals (pain points)? Any opportunities to inject new deposits and or turn withdrawals into deposits? Any opportunities to further align the products and services with the needs of your customers? Any opportunities to make the touch point unique and fresh?

4. Action: List the actions to make meaningful changes.

DIRECT OBSERVATIONS
AND DATA COLLECTION

OBJECTIVE

ACTION

ANALYSIS

Emotional
deposits

Offering insights into
what customers are really like

ETHNOGRAPHY

OH YES!
MOMENTS

SCENOGRAPHY

Choreographing the
customer experience

THEME

leaders as
scenographers

THEME
AUDIT

design scenes

SCENES

WOWOGRAPHY

Designing spontaneous
acts of WOW

OBSERVE

RECCORD

EMPOWER

- TRUTH # 13 -

Spice up your experience

Raise the Bar and Reimagine Your Investment

We live in the age of abundance and in a fiercely competitive climate where everyone wants a piece of the cake—your cake. This is why you must unceasingly exploit our world of thinking for insights, practices, and techniques to open new doors and relentlessly enrich the customer experience. In his landmark bestseller *Think and Grow Rich*, Napoleon Hill writes, "All achievements, all earned riches, have their beginning in an idea."[229] I'm all for a revolution of ideas, and I call upon you to turn any idea on its head. But I am also an advocate for tuning ideas, re-expressing old concepts, and repackaging notions. That's how the most successful individuals and organizations stimulate progress and transform the world we live in.

- It was a trip to Swift and Company's slaughterhouse in Chicago that gave Ford engineer William Pa Klann the idea to design an assembly line for cars that revolutionized the industry and ultimately made cars affordable for everyone.

- It was an encounter with a biker that inspired the veterinarian John Boyd Dunlop to invent the first practical pneumatic (inflatable) rubber tire that fueled the personal transportation revolution.

- It was the need to share resources that inspired the engineer Lawrence Roberts to invent the first workable prototype of the internet, which ignited the internet revolution and transformed every aspect of our lives.

- It was the concept of connecting consumers with manufacturers that inspired Jeff Bezos to start Amazon from his garage and lead it to become the "Everything store," an organization that changed and shaped the retail industry.

• It was the idea of test-driving from the automotive industry that inspired Jim Stewart and Jeffery Sears to lead the reinvention of the appliance showroom and position Pirch as a place where you can test-drive everything, even ovens and showers.

The above examples boil down to this fact:
One simple idea can open a world of opportunities.

What follows is a series of 20 insights that I trust will inspire you to look for answers, raise the bar, and reimagine your investment. I believe that these ideas will bring up some AHA! moments, empower you to see connections that maybe were not previously obvious, and enable you to go beyond the normal, shape your customers' perception, and spice up your customer experience. As Kjell Nordstrom and Jonas Ridderstrale state in their book *Funky Business*, "To succeed, we must stop being so goddamn normal…. At its best, normal output will produce normal results. In a winner-takes-all world, normal = nothing."[230]

Genius resides everywhere.
Explore ideas and force connections.
Nothing is given. Search for differentiation.
Stay in motion. Stay ahead of the curve.
Welcome to the revolution.

1. Think "Guests," Not Customers

Think for a moment about the power of the words we use in our businesses. For example, what comes to mind when you think of the word customer? What about the word guest? Think of how you treat a customer versus how you treat a guest. What if you start referring to your customers as guests? Makes a big difference, right? Now being called a guest might sound a bit over-the-top for some. If that's the case, call them whatever you like, but at least make them "guests" in the eyes of your own people. Treat them like human, not numbers. It is a big deal.

2. Focus on Systems and Smiles

Invest in smiles, but by all means, don't ignore the systems. Your systems are crucial to collect and analyze customers' intelligence, improve communication, promote consistency, and enable you to design experiences and deliver smiles. It is true what the legendary car dealer Carl Sewell points out in his book *Customers for Life*, that smiles are the icing on the cake, and the cake is the systems that allow you to make things happen.[231] It is vital for organizations to streamline and synchronize their processes and systems to design immaculate experiences. Yes, systems are invisible but necessary.

3. Observe the Peak Rule

According to behavioral psychologists, not every part of an experience is equally memorable.[232] In fact, what we truly remember is the intensely high (positive or negative) emotional event of an experience. In the experience context, customers remember the details of intensely emotional events. This is why it is critical to take this rule into account in order to rethink the design of the customer's experience, inject the right emotions at peak moments, and manage customers' memories. In other words, deliberately create a positive peak.

4. Uphold the End Rule

Behavioral psychologists have also proved that we remember the end of a cycle best.[232] In the experience context, customers also favor the most recent event or last moment of an experience (the end point). Screenwriter Robert Towne, who wrote some of the greatest screenplays, such as *The Last Detail* (1973), *Chinatown* (1974), and the first two *Mission Impossible* films (1996, 2000), states: "If you don't have a strong finish to a film, you are in serious trouble. It can be explosive. It can be a bang or a whimper, but it better be memorable, or else people will remember very little about the movie."[233] In simple terms, if an experience has a compelling end, customers will overlook its earlier shortfalls, just like viewers. But if it has a disappointing finale, they will overlook nearly everything that they enjoyed about it. So, go out on a high note.

5. Honor the Primacy Rule

Another concept in psychology is the serial-position effect, also known as the primacy and recency effect.[234] This term was conceived by the German psychologist Hermann Ebbinghaus, who discovered that human beings recall not only the last items (recency effect; see point four above) but also the first items (primacy effect) more frequently than the middle. The lesson here is that first impressions count, and we should focus on injecting the first encounter with positive emotions to form a memorable mental image and create a strong foundation for the way in which customers perceive the organization.

6. Mind the Pre- and Post-Experience

When we think of the customer experience, we mostly think of the "time" in which the customer is interacting with our brand—the actual experience that we have control of. But what about stretching this experience to understand their needs and learn about their intent, concerns, and questions before and after the actual experience? Think of ways to influence and enrich the customer moments before the actual experience (the pre-experience) and after the actual experience (the post-experience). It's a call to own the entirety of the customer journey and also influence what you can't control.

7. Design from the Outside-In

One of the problems that organizations face today is that they are so focused on their own organizational needs, products, and sales—an inside-out perspective. The solution is to design your experience through the eyes of your customers and walk in their shoes. Understand your customers' environment and gain real insights into their needs, expectations, and feelings. Sit where they sit, drink what they drink, eat what they eat, see what they see, hear what they hear, and feel what they feel—an outside-in perspective. Powered by these observations, you can totally move your customer's experience to the next level. It's about your customers' needs and perceptions (them), not your own traditional product and service functions (you).

8. Empower the Zero-WOW

In Truth #12, I discussed the importance of going above and beyond to transform needs, desires, and preferences into thrilling Oh Yes! Moments—scenes that will take your customers by surprise. The truth is, going above and beyond could also be achieved with a zero budget. What about getting your response time down? Over-delivering? Following up when your customers least expect it? Personalizing your responses? Anticipating and fulfilling their needs? Bending rules and processes to surpass their expectations? Being spontaneous and prompt? Personalizing your experience? With your team, think of ways you can surprise and delight your customers without paying a penny. Invest in small acts of kindness.

9. Discern the Expectation Inflation

Inflation is usually associated with prices of goods and services, but it also plays a crucial role in designing your customer experience. Like prices of goods and services, customers are more demanding, and their expectations are always changing. Today's unique experience is surely interesting, but only for a moment in time as it becomes the norm for tomorrow; the new reference point. Organizations have to continuously research and understand their new customers' expectations to design an experience that truly differentiates and exceeds their expectations. Exploiting this shift in expectations is a significant value driver.

10. Deal with the Great, Bad, and Ugly

Did you know that around 90 percent of consumers rely on reviews to make a shopping decision and 94 percent avoid a particular business because of negative reviews?[235] Reviews are a fact of life. It influences your customers' behavior at every turn. We all seek and celebrate great reviews but should also be ready for the bad and the ugly. Welcome those reviews, respond efficiently and effectively, and address the emotions and facts—because customers will learn about the character of your business from how you react to these reviews. Not only that, these reviews are the driving force behind improving and revamping your business. The message is clear: Stay on top of customer reviews.

11. Combine and Manage the Pain Early

Every experience includes traces of undesirable elements like waiting for a service, reviewing and signing boring documents, waiting for approval, completing paperwork, receiving bad news, etc. If you split those undesirable events, the negative impact will appear to be longer and harmfully affect the overall experience. Behavioral science shows that people prefer to go through the undesirable events first so they can enjoy and positively remember the rest of the experience.[236] So, combine and get rid of the pain early in the experience. Enough said!

12. Split the Pleasure

In the same spirit, you also need to split the desirable elements of your experience so that the overall positive experience seems longer. Years ago, I celebrated a friend's 23rd birthday by giving her 23 gifts, all at once. The impact: Great! On her 30th birthday, I did the same trick but shared the gifts throughout the entire day at different touch points. The impact: OH MY...GRAND. In brief, make the fun longer by splitting the pleasure. The message is clear: apply the principles of behavioral psychology to improve the intensity and impact of your customers' interactions and experience.

13. Give Them Control

Since the beginning of our existence, we have had a strong need to be in control—to be powerful and free. That is also true in the world of customer experience. When customers have a certain level of control over the experience, their satisfaction intensifies and you positively impact their perception of the experience.[237] Delegate some of the decisions, allow customers to track the progression of the experience, give them options, introduce self-service, and involve them in the design of their experience. To sum it up, enabling your customers to control certain aspects of the experience will ultimately benefit your brand and the bottom line.

14. Simplify Decision-Making

Have you ever been so overwhelmed by the number of choices that you finally decided to exit a sale or maybe made a necessary sale but questioned the decision? Think about it! How do you feel when opening a menu to find five-dozen offerings? Not a pleasurable experience I bet. In his book *The Paradox of Choice*, Barry Schwartz argues that the presence of too many choices causes self-blame and harms our psychological and emotional well-being.[238] I firmly advise organizations to offer less because the chances are that customers would be happier and more fulfilled. Yes, less is more!

15. Educate Your Customers

Giving your customers control will only yield great benefits if they are knowledgeable and able to make educated choices. Think of the complexity of some experiences that are very difficult to grasp at times. Put yourself in the shoes of your customers, spend time listening to them, understand them, and learn about their preferences and needs. Companies like Apple, Nike, IKEA, Pirch, and Whole Foods provide a hands-on experience, community blogs, social media, tutorials, mobile applications, case studies and more to educate their customers and optimize their experience. Make customers' education a major part of your experience strategy. Remember, investment in this education equals an investment in customers' loyalty.

16. Manage the Passage of Time

How many times have you endured the torturous act of waiting? You surely know what I am referring to. The boring tune filling the silence while placed on hold, the dreadful wait in a long queue, the aimless gaze at the ceiling in a waiting room.... And time seems to drag on forever. How can you transform that experience and make the waiting time efficient? By transforming the "waiting time" to "occupied time." How? You can give your customers control over the waiting time (e.g., offering the option to call them back; unchaining them by using technology notifications; offering self-service etc.), or injecting the waiting time with relevant, value-added activities (e.g., Porsche offers their customers the opportunity to participate in the service examination of their cars at the Porsche Dialogue Bay; Haidilao, the Chinese hot pot restaurant chain, offers board games, free nail polishing services, and more for waiting customers; Singapore Changi Airport offers amazing facilities such as the butterfly garden, a movie theater, and more to kill the passage of time, etc.). Make managing your customers' time a priority!

17. Consider Adaptation

Think of the last nice watch you bought. Do you still recall the excitement you felt every time you looked at it? If you are like most human beings, you will have noticed that this excitement faded away with time. Psychologists refer to this concept as adaptation. In the service experience context, customers adapt to certain experiences as they get used to it, and at times, they even take it for granted. This is why it is crucial to camp on the doorstep of novelty by finding new ways to serve customers and continuously evolve the customer experience. In his 2012 letter to shareholders, Jeff Bezos encapsulated this evolution by stating, "When we're at our best, we don't wait for external pressures. We are internally driven to improve our services, adding benefits and features before we have to…. We invent before we have to. These investments are motivated by customer focus rather than by reaction to competition. We think this approach earns more trust with customers and drives rapid improvements in customer experience—importantly—even in those areas where we are already the leader."[239] Never give up on your organizational quest for newness!

18. Shrink the Survey

How do you feel when you receive a call or an email requesting your feedback about an experience? Customers hate being bombarded with these lengthy phone calls or completing long-winded series of redundant questions. In fact, 80 percent of customers abort this hectic task.[240] Maybe the one question to ask is "What is it like to take a survey?" I am being dramatic here, but the point is, organizations need to realize that soliciting feedback is part of the experience itself and accordingly work to eliminate survey fatigue, as it damages the brand. How? Start by shrinking feedback surveys by focusing on the vital few relevant questions; questions that customers can answer in three to five minutes. And remember to follow through and do something about it to close the loop.

19. Empower a CExO

The position of Chief Customer Officer has been on the C-suite for some time now. I say let's rethink this "figurehead" position and bring a Chief Experience Officer (CExO) on board, empowered with his team to define the experience strategy, break down silos, drive customer experience, and inspire an experience-centric organization. Think of the CExO as your organization's experience activist; a partner at the table who spearheads the mission of bringing customer experience to the heart of the organization's culture, processes, and structure. It's time to truly put customer experience on the executive table!

20. Design Your Employee Experience

Everything being said and done, one fact stands true: Your customer experience is only half of the equation. What is the second driving force of your business? Your employee experience. A study conducted by MIT Sloan Center for Information Systems Research showed that organizations in the top quartile of employee experience (i.e., low work complexity and strong behavioral norms for collaboration, creativity, and empowerment) achieved industry-adjusted Net Promoter Scores twice as high as those in the bottom quartile.[241] It is undeniable that the quality of your employee experience predicts your customer experience. It is not about the tyranny of the OR (focusing on customer experience OR employee experience) but the power of the AND (focusing on customer experience AND employee experience).

Final Note: Experience Role Model

Remember, regardless of your title, you are the experience role model, and whether you like it to not, everyone within your organization is watching you. Choose to lead and serve with purpose because everything you do has a direct or indirect impact on your customer experience. At the end of this Truth, I would like to issue a personal challenge to you to make the 20 insights actionable. Use the chart on the following worksheet to mark where you think your organization stands on the continuum with regards to each of the 20 insights (1–low to 5–high). I further challenge you and your team to think of at least one actionable step for each of the 20 insights to spice up your customer experience.

Go down to where the action is.
Promote a common experience language.
Crash silos and build new bridges.
Experience your customer experience.
Do what you ask your people to do.
Interact with your customers.
Along this ride you will find untapped opportunities at every turn. That I promise!

Tool # 18: Spice up Your Experience Worksheet

Instructions: Mark where you think your organization stands on the continuum with regards to each of the 20 insights (1–low to 5–high). With your team, think of at least one actionable step for each of the 20 insights to spice up your customer experience (CX).

CX Insights	1	2	3	4	5	Actions
1. Think "guests," not customers						
2. Focus on systems and smiles						
3. Observe the peak rule						
4. Uphold the end rule						
5. Honor the primacy rule						
6. Mind the pre- and post-experience						
7. Design from the outside-in						
8. Empower the zero-WOW						
9. Discern expectation inflation						

CX Insights	1	2	3	4	5	Actions
10. Deal with the great, bad, and ugly						
11. Combine and manage the pain early						
12. Split up the pleasure						
13. Give them control						
14. Simplify decision-making						
15. Educate your customers						
16. Manage the passage of time						
17. Consider adaptation						
18. Shrink your survey						
19. Empower a CExO						
20. Design your employee experience						

- TRUTH # 14 -

Uncover the cream of the crop

Fit Is Your Gateway to the Experience Economy

We all know that selecting the right people is an indispensable success factor to any organization. They shape every customer's encounter and play a pivotal role in designing and delivering a compelling customer experience. Actually, having the right people onboard is far more important than having a great product or service, as they hold the key that unlocks the power of your organization and enliven your brand. The Ritz-Carlton Employee Promise states this fact clearly, "Our Ladies and Gentlemen are the most important resource in our service commitment to our guests."[242] And if I can take the liberty to add a twist to this statement, I would add "right" just before Ladies and Gentlemen.

In his book *Good to Great,* Jim Collins and his research team analyzed the performance of 1,435 organizations over 40 years to identify what systemically distinguishes the good from the great. They identified 112 elite companies that made the transition from good to great and sustained their performance for at least 15 years. Collins found that one of the reasons companies become great is their focus on who, then what. He states that "the executives who ignited the transformations from good to great did not first figure out where to drive the bus and then get people to take it there. No, they *first* got the right people on the bus (and the wrong people off the bus) and *then* figured out where to drive it."[243]

Let's examine one of the best companies to work for, Google. The multibillion-dollar technology company's selection process is the cornerstone of their culture and the reason for their success. The company receives over two million job applications every year from which around 0.3 percent are selected. Backed up with years of practice and experimentation, their disruptive selection process is key in attracting and selecting ideal Googlers who fit in with the Google culture and are passionate to drive its long-term business objectives.

The Ritz-Carlton Hotel Company, which has most probably received all the awards and accolades in the hospitality industry, is also celebrated for meticulously selecting the right people who have the spirit to serve. During my tenure with The Ritz-Carlton, I roamed the world in search of potential Ladies and Gentlemen who were the right match for The Ritz-Carlton culture. The Ritz-Carlton partnered with Talent Plus[9] in Lincoln, Nebraska to select the right people. They believe that if employees have the right attributes, skills can be taught. During those days, I interviewed more than 30 applicants to fill one open entry-level position. The Ritz-Carlton referred to the new joiners as the top 1 percent of all service professionals in the world!

*If we examine the best customer-centric organizations in our world,
it is impossible but to find that having the right people
is one of their guiding principles.*

In the introduction of Principle 3, I introduced the experience economy and shared insights about evoking emotions, creating Oh Yes! Moments, and spicing up your experience. The plain fact is that all of these Truths are at the mercy of your people who can make or break your business. No wonder that 68 percent of customers leave a brand because of the indifferent attitude of a company employee.[244] Every employee has the power to design and craft an experience that delivers on your promises, or one that triggers the Chewing Gum Effect and ruins your brand!

The Chewing Gum Effect

Have you been at a restaurant or bar where the experience seemed so great until suddenly your fingers touched an unmistakable lump of gum stuck under your table? How did you feel? Disgusted, right? What happened next? Your brain most probably forced you to focus, find and dwell on other negative signs, and the spiraling of negative thoughts and observations took over the experience. That's what I call

---

[9] Talent Plus, our partner in greatness, helps organizations select individuals that have the talent to enliven the brand of the organization and maximize growth potential at every level.

The Chewing Gum Effect. It is not a secret that human beings have a bias toward the negative, and it is this bias that leads us as customers to focus on and exaggerate the bad things.[245] In the experience context, all it takes is an employee's indifferent attitude to trigger the Chewing Gum Effect, stirring up a chain reaction of negative and toxic customers' emotions, and the rest is history.

Years ago, I was invited to speak at a conference in Africa. I boarded what I considered to be a gorgeous new airplane to finally reach my spacious, lavish first-class seat. The enchanting music in the background, refreshing fragrance, welcoming smiles, and luxurious signs prepped me for a royal flight and a whole new level of customer experience. While settling down, I noticed some breadcrumbs on my seat and coffee stains on the side table. These irregularities could definitely happen with anyone, but my perception was that if they couldn't deal with the small details, they would most likely miss the important ones. So, I called the attention of the flight attendant.

"I believe something is wrong with my seat," I said.

"Nothing is wrong, Sir," she answered.

"Have you ever heard that the guest is always right?" I calmly declared.

"Yes, I agree, Sir," the flight attendant replied.

"Well, if the guest is always right, then how come you told me that I am wrong?" I exclaimed.

"Sir, when you bought the ticket, you were a guest. Today on the plane, you are just a passenger!" the flight attendant proudly proclaimed, with emphasis on the word "just."

Well, to her credit, she said it with a smile. But the truth is, if this flight attendant wanted to send a strong signal that I was worthless, she had found it.

Like the Chewing Gum Effect, the flight attendant triggered a chain reaction of negative emotions, and minute after minute, this employee's attitude impacted my ability to enjoy the experience and all the wonders designed for this flight.

The Real Deal

Your "right" people are your most important asset. Before you take your first selection (hiring) step, it is vital to decide what attributes you are looking for in those who are designated to design and deliver your experience. A lot goes into selecting the right people, and I highly recommend selecting people whose values are aligned with the values of the organization. But when it comes to frontline colleagues, it is also crucial to select those who have the passion to serve.

I have studied the most celebrated leaders and researched the most renowned organizations and talent developers around the globe to find out that some attributes kept popping up time and again. I believe that the 10 attributes listed below are the real deal for colleagues in the service industry; attributes that filter the cream of the crop and uncover the right people. I found that the impact of these 10 attributes are significant on inspiring a winning work environment, fashioning customer excitement, producing sustainable performance, and leaving a distinct footprint.

I will define each, share some counterproductive behaviors related to each, and provide some coaching recommendations. I also invite you to refer to The Cream of the Crop Worksheet at the end of this Truth to assess yourself and each of your team members against these attributes and define the coaching strategies to uncover the cream of the crop.

1. Humility

Individuals associated with this attribute are humble and voluntary modest. They listen to and acknowledge customers, show respect, welcome different viewpoints, and own irregularities and mistakes. They have a healthy ego and a deep sense of self-worth that enable them to act beyond themselves in order to get things done and serve others. In the work environment, humility drives openness, transparency, respect, accountability, continuous learning, and constant improvement.

Counterproductive behaviors: Being arrogant, nosy, self-flattering, having an overinflated opinion of oneself, and seeing others as threat.

Coaching recommendations:
- Be honest and straightforward with your customers.
- Be open for advice and feedback from customers and colleagues.
- Admit mistakes, learn from them, and take ownership of them.
- Ask for help and assistance when needed.
- Put your ego and needs aside to serve others.

2. Empathy

Individuals associated with this attribute put themselves in customers' shoes, understand their needs, see their uniqueness, feel what they feel, and seek to build fulfilling connections. They see the experience through the eyes of their customers and accordingly provide anticipatory service to enrich that experience. In the work environment, empathy promotes diversity, unity, inclusion, positive interactions, and trusting relationships.

Counterproductive behaviors: Feigning empathy, stereotyping others, and being insensitive to colleagues and customers.

Coaching recommendations:
- Cultivate interest about your customers' feelings, priorities, needs, and perspectives.
- Go where the action is and live your customers' experience (walk a mile in their shoes).
- Take actions to build rapport, anticipate customers' needs, and create a bond of trust.
- Listen with a virtuous heart, validate customers' points of view, and make them feel respected.
- Recognize customers' challenges and make them feel safe and understood.

3. Optimism

Individuals associated with this attribute are resourceful, take a proactive perspective of possibilities, embrace a solution-oriented approach, and have a cheerful disposition. They innovate, persevere, connect with customers, and look for what's possible versus what's wrong. These individuals are great problem solvers who constantly look for opportunities to learn, improve, and make things better. In the work environment, optimism boosts decision-making, motivation, positive energy, creativity, innovation, and well-being.

Counterproductive behaviors: Overemphasizing the downside, being negative, blaming others, using victim thinking, and feeling powerless.

Coaching recommendations:
- Master the power of emotions to manage yourself and others.
- See an opportunity in every customer encounter.
- Embrace every customer complaint, negative feedback, and frustration as an opportunity.
- Use positive language, tone, and attitude to promote a positive customer perception.
- Adopt a "can do" attitude and take more risks.

4. Care

Individuals associated with this attribute have a natural desire to take care of others and a passion to serve. Not only that, they go above and beyond to build strong relationships and create customers for life. They are dedicated to their customers and care to the extent that they make their colleagues heroes. In the work environment, caring fuels ownership and commitment. It also fosters a work environment of pride, joy, and meaningful relationships.

Counterproductive behaviors: Displaying a "just a job" attitude, working and serving half-heartedly, being apathetic, and showing signs of negligence and irresponsibility.

Coaching recommendations:
- Show interest in others and display acts of kindness.
- Be in the moment and personalize customer encounters.
- Be approachable and accessible around the clock and provide immediate support.
- Go the extra mile and make everything you come across a little bit better.
- Appreciate your customers and take ownership of their experience.

5. Curiosity

Individuals associated with this attribute are hungry to learn about customers, unlock their insights, and deliver one-size-fits-one experiences. No matter what situation they are in, these creative thinkers and natural learners seek to explore, think out of the box, solve problems effectively, connect the dots, and discover new ways of serving others. In the work environment, this attribute powers imagination, newness, innovation, smarter decision-making, and effective problem-solving.

Counterproductive behaviors: Showing no interest or concern in others and displaying an absence of inquisitiveness.

Coaching recommendations:
- Be inquisitive. Master your products and services and learn more about your customers' expectations and objectives.
- Question and explore things. Start your questions with what, what if, where, when, why, and how. Look for clues in your customers, patterns in your job, and trends in your industry.
- Engage in conversations and practice smart listening; use these three magical words during conversations, "Tell me more…."
- Be gracious and discreet; not in the way, but always there when needed.
- Commit to mastery and acquire different functions outside of your role.

6. Authenticity

Individuals associated with this attribute are honest, transparent, and congruent with their outward persona. They are reliable, trustworthy, and genuine with words and actions. Authentic individuals wholeheartedly relate to others, foster personal interactions, and make every relationship count. In the work environment, authenticity cultivates trust, acceptance, respect, confidence, loyalty, and happiness.

Counterproductive behaviors: Being fake, political, and superficial; bluffing and showing excessive formality.

Coaching recommendations:
- Go "off script" and use language you and your customers are comfortable with.
- Relate to your customers. Be welcoming, friendly, and courteous. Convey an authentic enthusiasm to serve them.
- Be yourself, unveil your individuality, and also appreciate the authenticity of others.
- Deliver on your promises and give credit where it is due.
- Find and live the purpose of your job.

7. Personal Presence / Charisma

Individuals associated with this attribute communicate with credibility and significance. They project self-confidence, look professional and charismatic, speak with clarity, radiate uplifting energy, and positively influence the customer experience. These individuals make a grand first impression, act with intention, and create lasting impact. In the work environment, personal presence elevates commitment and motivation, fuels effective communication and influence, and strengthens your brand image and mystique.

Counterproductive behaviors: Having a flippant and laid-back attitude, being too intense, looking nervous, and being too stiff, unmannered, and unprofessional.

Coaching recommendations:
- Be visible, mind your appearance, and look professional at all times.
- Exhibit a positive body language and choice of words to build rapport with your customers. Be assertive, confident, but warm.
- Cut through the clutter, speak clearly, and summarize conversations.
- Practice storytelling and have a sense of humor.
- Create amazing first and last impressions.

8. Agility

Individuals associated with this attribute welcome change and adapt expediently in order to efficiently and effectively respond to fluctuating customers' expectations and changing business conditions. They have a flexible mindset and the ability to find creative ways around ambiguous situations and challenges as well as ways to exploit and capitalize on new opportunities. In the work environment, agility spurs empowerment, autonomy, and decentralized decision-making. It also promotes ingenuity and powers flexibility and adaptability.

Counterproductive behaviors: Resisting change; being rigid, directionless, and indecisive.

Coaching recommendations:
- Embrace and navigate change. Be resilience in the face of setbacks, make mid-course corrections, and remove barriers.
- Solicit customers' feedback, recalibrate priorities, and continuously improve the experience.
- Anticipate and recognize customers' demands, expectations, problems, and challenges and respond to them quickly.
- Allocate and deploy resources to meet and exceed expectations.
- Leverage collaboration and technology to accelerate execution.

9. Focus

Individuals associated with this attribute prioritize actions, have a passion for details, and deliver on their promises to customers. They are disciplined, organized, and most importantly, purposeful. They pay attention to themselves and also have a great eye for what is important to customers and the organization. In the work environment, focus builds alignment and persistence, facilitates mastery, and enables execution.

Counterproductive behaviors: Being easily distracted, sloppy, and engaged in time-wasting activities. Underachiever; keeping things unfinished and missing deadlines.

Coaching recommendations:
- Engage in focused preparation. Prioritize, attach timelines, and execute.
- Strive for closure. Follow up and follow through.
- Allocate and deploy resources to meet and exceed deadlines.
- Cut the clutter, eliminate distractions, and refocus your attention.
- Practice mindfulness. Focus on the moment but also on the larger context of your customer experience.

10. Team Spirit

Individuals associated with this attribute have the ability to cooperate and collaborate with others, form strong bonds with their colleagues and customers, and step in to assist when needed. As bridge builders, they are catalysts for trusting relationships and actively participate, contribute, and commit to the team and the customer experience. In the work environment, team spirit builds a sense of community, trust, and harmony, amplifies collaboration, and stimulates a culture of camaraderie.

Counterproductive behaviors: Being unhelpful and uncooperative, hijacking credit for others' work, and showing a "not my job" attitude.

Coaching recommendations:
- Assist others to be successful and fulfilled.
- Celebrate others' uniqueness and find ways to work with them.
- Extend smart trust and form strong relationship with your colleagues and customers.
- Offer lateral service when needed to ensure a seamless customer experience.
- Be an active participant and show commitment to the team.

Final Note: Assemble Your A-Team

Your selection process can't be a trial-and-error guessing process. Assembling your A-team for your customer experience requires having the right people on board. All the right people onboard.

In his book *Excellence Wins*, Horst Schulze writes, "Customer service isn't just for those who face the public. It also extends to people inside an organization who deal with each other. Really, it's all connected."[246] The attributes I shared in this Truth are just the tip of the iceberg, and they do not exist in isolation. When you investigate the many interactions amongst them and your organization's values, you have the winning formula to attract, select, develop and retain the right people; those who are engaged from the start and have the spirit to serve.

The "war for fit" has never been more intense.
Each selection decision makes your organization stronger or weaker.
Select the best people you can get your hands on and unload those who don't fit.
Uncover the cream of the crop.
It is your gateway to the experience economy.
Over and out!

Tool # 19: The Cream of the Crop Worksheet

Instructions: Integrate the 10 attributes in your selection process. I also recommend you assess yourself and each of your team members against these attributes[10], then define coaching strategies to uncover the cream of the crop.

Part I: Assessment

Employee: Date:

Counterproductive behaviors	-3	-2	-1	0	1	2	3	Attributes
Arrogant Self-centered								Humility
Inconsiderate Self-centered								Empathy
Pessimistic Blamer								Optimism
Apathetic Irresponsible								Care
Uninquisitive Indifferent								Curiosity
Fake/bluffing Disingenuous								Authenticity
Unprofessional Unmannered								Charisma/ Personal Presence
Hard-headed Stiff and Rigid								Agility
Underachiever Sloppy								Focus
Uncooperative Nonparticipant								Team Spirit

---

[10] To simplify this worksheet, I summarized the counterproductive behaviors. Please refer to the entire list presented in this Truth for an accurate assessment.

Part II: Coaching Strategies

Attributes	Coaching Strategies[11]
Humility	
Empathy	
Optimism	
Care	
Curiosity	
Authenticity	
Charisma/ Personal Presence	
Agility	
Focus	
Team Spirit	

[11] Refer to the coaching strategies shared in this Truth for each attribute.

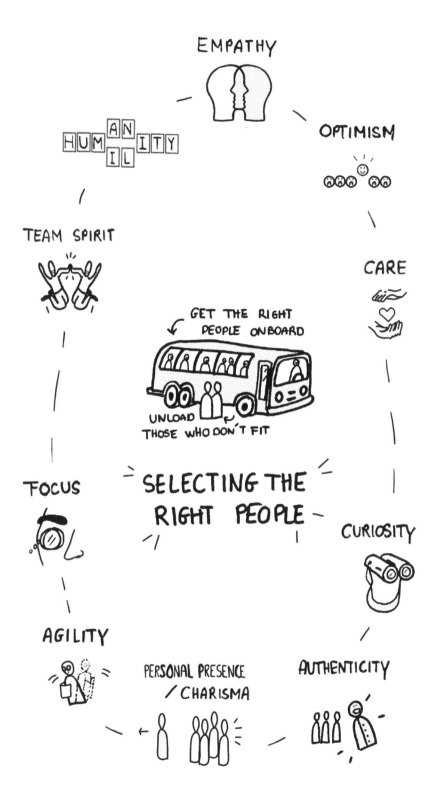

-TRUTH # 15-

19 for COVID-19

Cross the Line

You might be reading this Truth after the COVID-19 crisis has passed. Well, this Truth is not only about managing your investment in turbulent times, but also about reinventing your organization to stay relevant to those you lead and serve. I purposely left this Truth until the end of the journey, as it impacts all three principles and beautifully reinforces some of the messages I shared so far.

Every 10 to 15 years, a crisis or something jaw-dropping happens. And if you think that this COVID-19 turmoil is the last, you are way off. A few years ago, I read a book with a great message, *Cross the Line*[247] by Sam Parker. Sam encourages us to commit, work hard, focus, and bounce back when things get tough in order to cross the line where there is a greater chance to make great things happen. Imagine a crisis as a line. On one side of that line is the status quo; the world as we know it and the old ways of doing things. On the other side of the line is a great chance to thrive; a whole new world of opportunities. What would you do? You have three options:

1. Wait for things to happen.
2. Wonder what in the world just happened.
3. Make things happen.

The right choice is obvious to me. It would be insane not to cross that line and explore the unknown.

Embrace the challenges ahead and rethink boundaries.
Redefine the new normal and navigate the new reality.
Uncertainty is a good thing, and it is time to cross the line.

The Power of Questions

Human evolution is the byproduct of asking questions. It is our innate ability to ask questions that makes us different, enables us to expand our horizon of thinking, and triggers the chain of evolution and transformation. In one of my favorite books, *A More Beautiful Question* by Warren Berger, the author analyzes leading companies such as Netflix, Nike, Airbnb, Apple, and Zappos, and finds that asking questions is the starting point of innovation and breakthroughs. Warren shares a three-part questioning framework. It starts by asking "Why or why not?" to seek understanding of the situation, then "What if?" to imagine the possibilities, and finally "How?" to make things happen.[248]

Asking stimulates ideation.
Asking sparks innovation.
Asking boosts engagement.
Asking fuels progress.

Don't miss the opportunity to ask questions, even if the answers might scare you or put you off track temporarily. Accept the challenges ahead and explore the hidden by asking questions. It has been said that great leaders might not have answers, but they do one thing exceptionally well; ask great questions.

This Truth, 19 for COVID-19, shares 19 tips designed to inspire you and fuel your quest for innovation and change. At the end of each tip, I present some great questions to support you on this expedition. Some questions might work better for you than others. Most importantly, don't stop there—continue this questioning voyage to move from ideation to progress. This Truth also shares 19 calls to action that you could further fine-tune in order to take the first step. Using the Reimagine Worksheet highlighted at the end of this Truth, work with your team to reflect on the 19 tips and think of four measurable, pragmatic actions to take you across the line!

Section I: Culture

1. A Declaration of Ideology

Staying true to your core ideology and culture in a time of turbulence is the true test of your foundation and character. In moments of crisis, people need that anchor to steady the organization, instill a sense of stability and oneness, be connected, engaged, and resilient. Here's the twist though. Along this ride, you should inject agility into the heart of your culture. How? **Embrace a four-eyed paradigm** (maintain a stable internal environment while yearning to identify patterns, act on them, grow, and reproduce); **be like water** (change with the change and take the shape of your new environment); **play with a full deck** (leverage diversity and amplify innovation, speed, and impact); and **put people over processes** (investigate your processes and simplify them to promote engagement, autonomy, and experimentations.)

Questions: How can we stay true to our culture? How can we uphold our core ideology and at the same time inspire agility?

Call to action: Celebrate your culture (e.g., culture appreciation day, reorientation, values in action competitions, and workshops). Make decisions aligned with your values. Plan cross-functional think tanks to explore how to further express your values to promote agility.

2. MESS = MESSage

Visionary organizations love a mess. Enjoy the mess and always remember that failure supported by imagination always leads to freshness and better outcomes. The secret to "fast success" is "fast failure." Denying the message is insanity! Approach the mess with a leverage mindset.

Questions: How can we approach this crisis with a leverage mindset? How can we get more with less? What is the message behind the mess? What are the new norms and how will it affect our culture and the way we do business?

Call to action: Your people need a sense of hope. Find a message of hope and spread it all over the organization, energize it daily in your briefings, meetings, and forums, and find ways to translate this hope into action.

3. Reinvent Yourself

Weathering a storm is never enough. Life is a race, and you constantly need to evolve with time and push your limits with your passion, imagination, and persistence. Think about it; how many of us have changed our lifestyle due to an unforeseen crisis? We sometimes adjust our diet, habits, hobbies, and even clothing to accommodate a change. The same is true for the survival of your organization in the midst of these disruptions. Reinvent your business before it is too late. Don't wait for the dust to settle, as the consequences of waiting are dire.

Questions: What will the business look like 10 years from now, and how can we reinvent ourselves to remain competitive? Where is the opportunity and how can we fill the gap? How can we promote a smarter and more effective culture?

Call to action: With you team, craft your post-crisis rules of engagement by clarifying the new leadership expectations. Empower your entire team to bring purposeful freshness to the organization (think of one or two new business opportunities for growth).

4. Control-Alt-Delete

For those of you using a Windows Operating System, you'll know that you press Control-Alt-Delete at the same time to terminate an application or reboot the system. At times, you have to destroy to rebuild, release to win, stop to start again. Remember, every great leader knows when to let go. You might need to terminate, change, or alter a certain service, task, product, or application, and at times you might need to reboot the entire operating system. I encourage you to adopt new tools, build new collaborations, inspire new partnerships, investigate new products and services, etc. Be comfortable breaking things as long as you move forward toward your purpose.

Questions: Are there any collaborations, partnerships, tools, products, and services that we can stop, continue, and start? How can we do more with less?

Call to action: Think of the projects, products, or services that you can say no to without jeopardizing your culture. Think of the new yesses to address the new norms, opportunities and expectations.

5. Keep It Simple

The most fruitful way to deal with a crisis is to strip it down and make it simple. Simplify the way you lead, communicate, collaborate, and do business. Cut to the chase. Simplify your processes, your hierarchy, your technology, and everything about running your business. People look at you to bring clarity in the midst of chaos. Simplify the chaos, the facts, and the data to create a culture of success.

Questions: How can we clearly articulate our purpose? How can we cut through the clutter, simplify the way we deliver our values, and focus on what really matters?

Call to action: Pick one process, ritual, or procedure and challenge your team to simplify it to ensure a purpose-driven business.

6. Think Possibilities

The best way to get things done: Think possibilities. Six words that change everything: "You are what you think about!" Don't entertain negativity! You are a dealer of hope, and I beg you to awaken the child within you and your organization. It is there. It is that child within that enabled your very existence. So, create an adventurous culture where people seek possibilities at every turn. Remember, in every negative situation there is a degree of positivity, so reframe the negatives as positives to unlock potentials.

Questions: How can we harness the diversity, strengths, and capabilities of our team to create a culture that whirrs with possibilities? How can we turn worries and concerns into opportunities?

Call to action: Introduce a ritual where people can openly share their worries and concerns and work together to transform them into possibilities (e.g., opportunity board, possibilities greenhouse, ideation forums).

Section II: People

7. Tend Your Garden

Whether you are a sports team, an orchestra, a hospitality team, or any other team for that matter, it is the shift from a team of all stars to an all-star team that matters. During challenging times, tend your garden, be a talent maximizer, and fertilize your work environment. Put your people truly first and inject a daily dose of oxytocin. Show that you truly care and turn empathy from a noun to a verb. Lead from the front and take out the weeds (negativity and pessimism), be visible, encourage and affirm your people, inject learning opportunities and create a coaching and feedback mechanism, plan team bonding activities, and celebrate achievements and growth.

Questions: What can we do to put people at the heart of our business equation? What are the tools, means, resources and tech we can give to our people to embrace and lead the change? How to foster continuous learning and improvement?

Call to action: Be visible, encourage and affirm your people. Inject informal learning opportunities from within and introduce well-being forums to address your people's mental and psychological considerations (e.g., round table meetings, bonding activities, support groups).

8. The "One-Minute Rule"

Years ago, I was introduced to WeChat, China's equivalent of WhatsApp. In WeChat, though, you can send a voice note of up to one minute. "ONE MINUTE! Are you kidding me?" I thought. I admit that I struggled at first, but this application made me understand the power of a minute and how to get more out of it. Think about this! How long does it take to show you truly care? To uplift someone? Genuinely hug, give a high-five, listen, smile, and praise someone? Yes, one minute. I invite you to bring these simple acts of caring and appreciating of others to your work environment, and you will witness its marvelous impact on engagement at every level.

Questions: What one-minute action(s) we can bring to our culture to engage our people? What are the acts of kindness we can exhibit to uplift one another?

Call to action: Invest 15 "one-minute actions" a day with the aim of connecting with your people, uplifting them, and being a cheerleader.

9. Hire a "What If" on Your Board

I am not a fan of the word "aggressive," but I truly have to say it: aggressively pursue "What if!" These two words are and will always be your greatest companions. In fact, put them on your board. They are your status quo, static thinking, and complacency fighters. Start by asking "What if?" Encourage proactive thinking and make your organization a mind gym. I have never heard of someone dying from a "What if?" overdose. Inspire your people to be bold thinkers. "What if?" is your gateway to the future, and remember that ideas come from the most unexpected places.

Questions: What if...? (state your rhetorical question, *i.e., activate our talents, attract new talents, introduce a new product, gain a new market, maximize productivity, minimize cost, increase profitability, etc.)*

Call to action: Launch a "What if lab" or introduce a "What if cross-functional team" within your organization and encourage your people to question the norms, voice their concerns, and share their thoughts and ideas.

10. Celebrate Witty Mistakes

Like most kids, we have been taught that it is not okay to fail. I will never forget the days where the principal of my school visited our class at the end of each month to distribute our scorecards. He always started by praising the best in class and moved slowly and tormentingly down the line to reach those who failed. That is by far the most humiliating journey to experience as a kid. Kids survived those days, but I wish we all learned the words of David Kelley, the founder of IDEO, who once said, "Fail faster, succeed sooner."[249] It is time for organizations to accept that failure is a stepping-stone towards success. Go and inspire your people to explore, wonder, investigate, create; and let them know that screwups are welcome.

Questions: How do we inspire our people to experiment, explore, wonder, and investigate? How do we clearly communicate that honest mistakes are welcome here?

Call to action: Design a program that would encourage people to experiment with new products and services. Think of Google's 20 percent rule or Merck's "permitted" bootlegging practice (refer to *Nine is Mine* Autonomy Kit, Truth #8).

11. Cross-Functional Teams: The Way Forward

How many times have you witnessed the same project in flight at the same time but by two different teams, reporting to two different board members (who might be waiting for one another to fail)? Make the change to cross-functional teams. This is a "everyone is a partner" mindset. Everyone contributes. Forget about the support functions.

Think collectively, work collectively, and celebrate collectively. Your team's ability to communicate and collaborate is a game changer at times of crisis. Everyone and every function matters.

Questions: What ways have we developed to successfully work across functional lines? Do we leverage the power of all our people to improve the organization? If yes, did we establish clearly defined goals, governance, and accountability?

Call to action: Say goodbye to siloed teams and make cross-functional teams as routine as breathing. Grant team members action to information, find a system to instantly notify your teams about urgent updates, and create forums to engage the whole organization in important conversations.

12. Celebrate Small Wins

Celebrating small wins is a precondition for keeping yourself and others fired up and geared towards making things happen. Celebrate the small steps—a number, task, prototype, call, idea, practice, etc. Like in basketball, every ball is a cause for celebration. I personally believe that during uncertain and challenging times you have to exaggerate the small wins. It boosts morale and confidence, injects energy, and brings meaning to the work environment. And it is the accumulation of those small wins that create what we call victory. The message is clear; by celebrating incremental meaningful progress, you can generate momentum and fun to get up, go, and keep going. Remember, wins are like diamonds, they come in small packages.

Questions: How do we acknowledge our people's progress? How do we celebrate incremental, meaningful small wins?

Call to action: Design a daily ritual to celebrate your people and share and applaud small wins and success stories.

Section III: Investment

13. Relish Technology

Technology touches every aspect of our business, including our customers' habits. It is a vital part of our present and will continue to transform our future. It is not about technology versus people. It is about making technology work for people. It empowers flexibility, productivity, transformation, and growth, and enables artificial intelligence, speed, and effective decision-making. Embrace the digital revolution and find ways to integrate it into your organization and the customer experience. It is the new market reality, so force yourself to fall in love with it. That's not an option!

Questions: How do we take advantage of the new technological opportunities to improve our products and services? How do we embrace technology to design a seamless and unique customer experience? How do we leverage technology to educate our customers, engage with them, and maximize sales?

Call to action: Invest in your online presence. Use the wide range of available channels to connect with your customers. Invest in a Customer Relationship Management System. Embrace social selling.

14. A Pinch of Weirdness Is a Must

We are all weird, and are subsequently attracted by weirdness. A pinch of weirdness unleashes creativity and empowers unconventional experiences. Think of weirdness as your differences, and it is this weirdness that brings a twist of freshness to your investment. No one put it as plainly as Robert Fulghum, the author of *All I Really Need to Know I Learned in Kindergarten*, when he wrote, "We are all a little weird and life's a little weird, and when we find someone whose weirdness is compatible with ours, we join up with them and fall in mutual weirdness and call it love."[250] Maybe we should all be Chief

Weirdness Officers and bring a sense of uniqueness to everything we touch. Remember, weirdness breeds success.

Questions: How do we tap into our people's inner weirdos and unleash their creative potential? How do we capitalize on our people's differences to uplift our investment?

Call to action: Find, connect, and select (hire) interesting people, engage in weird projects, review unconventional ideas, introduce original experiences, and investigate remarkable thoughts to transform your business.

15. The Power of Play

Partner with those who dare to play. They push you forward and design a customer experience that is playful and fun. We owe our social, emotional, intellectual, and physical development to the power of play. True leaders love to play. They religiously seek out those who want to play and ride the fun wave of the customer experience. Honor the spirit of play.

Questions: How do we deliberately design playful and fun experiences? How do we encourage our people to improvise, go off-script, and inject fun into every customer encounter?

Call to action: Find ways to make your customer experience playful (e.g., include them in the design of the experience, inject physical and mental activity into the experience, make use of customers' senses, and turn your people into storytellers).

16. It's the Age of Emotions

It's not about your products and services; it's all about emotions and experiences. Embrace this fact or you will become extinct. Invest in emotions and continuously ask yourself: What are the emotions we need to evoke in those we serve? Remember, people don't buy your products and services, they seek the emotions your products and services evoke in them. It's the age of emotions.

Questions: What emotions do our products and services evoke in those we serve? What emotions do our customers seek?

Call to action: Start your meetings by sharing customers' emotional expectations and the emotions to evoke them, then design everything accordingly.

17. Knock Their Socks Off

Forget about loyalty or customer engagement. We live in the world of advocacy and creating raving fans. Push the experience boundaries and design an experience that keeps your customers coming back for more. Does your experience provide so much value that your customers can't wait to tell others about it? If the answer is no, don't settle for mediocrity. Throw everything in the garbage and start over.

Questions: Are we embracing a raving, fan-centered mindset? How do we exceed customers' expectations and inspire advocacy?

Call to action: Think of the customer experience, map and review every touch point. Think of ways to add massive value to the customer experience through the power of scenography, ethnography, and WOWography.

18. The Days of Ready, Aim, Fire Are Over

Don't overanalyze. Don't overthink. Don't wait until everything is perfect. If you wait to be ready to take the shot, you will be surprised that it is too late. In turbulent times, we live in a world of ready, fire, aim! Prepare and fire away. If you miss, learn, adjust, realign rigorously, then fire again. Get ready, start with the end in mind, plan when you have to and look things around, but by all means, turn your ideas into reality or you might be left behind.

Questions: Are we paralyzed by planning excessively and over-analyzing? How can we make meaningful actions using ready, fire, aim?

Call to action: Determine quick wins to execute in order to move closer towards your goal. Make a list of the decisions your people can't take without going through the bureaucracy of approval and eliminate them. Overcome inertia and take a leap in the right direction.

Summary: Putting It All together: Greatness

19. Aim to Change the World

Great leaders and organizations put our world first and contribute time and energy to leave their positive footprints in many ways, shapes, and forms. Whether hunger and poverty relief, education, development, or environmental conservation, there's never been a more important time to support a cause and leave a humanitarian and environmental imprint to impact the lives of others. Remember, your people and customers love to contribute to something bigger than your bottom line. Greatness will never flourish without giving. Social activist Ethel Percy Andrus's words should echo through the hallways of your organization, "The human contribution is the essential ingredient. It is only in the giving of oneself to others that we truly live."[251]

Questions: How do we nurture our community and the world? Are we contributing to something bigger than ourselves? Are we volunteering our time and energy to make a meaningful difference?

Call to action: Develop an annual footprint plan, support a noble cause, and become an eco-friendly organization.

Final Note

We are witnessing a new world of business. To endure and flourish, it is vital to face and navigate tomorrow's uncharted waters. This Truth is not only about managing your investment in turbulent times, but also about reinventing your organization to stay relevant to those you lead and serve. Remember, beyond the line is a world of endless opportunities. And again, it would be insane not to make the leap and explore the unknown.

The question is: Are you ready for a world of endless opportunities?

Tool # 20: Reimagine Worksheet

Instructions: Work with your team to complete the four sections below. Ready, fire, aim!

Section 1. Culture
Reflecting on tips 1 to 6, think of one measurable, pragmatic action to jazz up your culture.

Section 2. People
Reflecting on tips 7 to 12, think of one measurable, pragmatic action to pep up your people.

Section 3. Investment
Reflecting on tips 13 to 18, think of one measurable, pragmatic action to spice up your customer experience.

Section 4. Greatness
Reflecting on tip 19, think of one measurable, pragmatic action to leave your footprint in our world.

SUMMARY
PRINCIPLE 3

We currently live in a world where customers' expectations, needs, and demands are shifting. Like a butterfly, the perception of value goes through a metamorphosis—from product/production of goods (Stage 1) to service/provision of services (Stage 2), to finally experience/crafting of moments (Stage 3). Today's organizations are required to make the shift to the "experience" economy and accordingly make emotions key to their offerings, deliberately designing Oh Yes! Moments into the customer experience.

That's the way to your customers' hearts.
Create memories that energize and provoke excitement.
Drive customer advocacy.
Make your investment a story to tell.
Period!

Truth #11: The language of emotions

Greatness is NOwhere Mindset: Products and services are the only backbone of customer experience.
Greatness is NOWhere Mindset: Emotions are at the heart of understanding, measuring, and designing the customer experience.
Toolset: Language of Emotions Worksheet (p.235)

Truth #12: The Holy Grail of customer experience

Greatness is NOwhere Mindset: Celebrate customer satisfaction as a point of differentiation.
Greatness is NOWhere Mindset: Design and deliver Oh Yes! Moments to drive advocacy.
Toolset: Scenography Worksheet (p.256) WOWography Customer Preference Pad (p. 258) Ethnography Worksheet (p. 259)

Truth #13: Spice up your experience

*Greatness is **NO**where Mindset:*   If the experience works, don't touch it!
*Greatness is **NOW**here Mindset:*   Relentlessly ride the value-added wave   of the customer experience.
Toolset: Spice Up Your Experience Worksheet (p.274)

Truth #14: Uncover the cream of the crop

*Greatness is **NO**where Mindset:*   People are the most important resource in the service   commitment to customers.
*Greatness is **NOW**here Mindset:*   The "right" people are the most important resource   in the service commitment to customers.
Toolset: The Cream of the Crop Worksheet (p.291)

Truth #15: 19 for COVID-19

*Greatness is **NO**where Mindset:*   Wait for things to happen.
*Greatness is **NOW**here Mindset:*   Reimagine your business and make things happen.
Toolset: Reimagine Worksheet (p.310)

Golden Nuggets

You might have the best and most magnetized products and services, but if you don't ensure an exceptional experience, it means nothing.

Brands are built on experiences. Experiences are built on emotions. Therefore, emotions have the power to drive or ruin your business.

Knowing your customers better than they know themselves is critical to anticipate, envision, and design your customer experience.

Consistency drives satisfaction. Emotional connection drives loyalty. A state of amazement drives customer advocacy.

The same way flowers' colors and fragrances transform insects and birds into pollinators to multiply, organizations' moments and stories turn customers into advocates to grow and thrive.

Oh Yes! Moments = Scenography + WOWography + Ethnography.

People. NO! The "RIGHT" people are your most important resource in your commitment to your customers.

The Chewing Gum Effect: One employee's indifferent attitude stirring up a chain reaction of negative and toxic customers' emotions…and the rest is history.

10 attributes that filter the cream of the crop: Humility, Empathy, Optimism, Care, Curiosity, Authenticity, Personal Presence/Charisma, Agility, Focus, and Team Spirit.

19 for COVID-19: Embrace the challenges ahead, rethink boundaries, redefine the new normal, and navigate the new reality. Uncertainty is a good thing, and it is time to reimagine and redefine.

Genius resides everywhere! One simple idea can open a world of opportunities and spice up your customer experience.

A Final Message

Inspiration exists, but it has to find you working.[252]

Pablo Picasso

This famous quote by Pablo Picasso reminds me that our world is filled with moments of inspiration. These moments come in different ways, shapes, and forms, bringing new possibilities and paving the way for greatness. Capture your moment, and with your tools in your hands, activate it and create something incredible. Stop limiting yourself with defined averages, explore the unknown, transcend your limitations, break the status quo, and invest in novelty.

Some of us are surrounded by people who steal our voice, force the rules, and push us to follow the existing conditions. Many experiments have confirmed that we tend to follow others at the expense of our own voice. One of those experiments conducted by Brain Games on National Geographic featured a test subject in an optometrist's waiting room surrounded by patients (actors) behaving oddly, like standing up and sitting down at the sound of a beep. After three beeps, the test subject followed the actors' behavior for no apparent reason other than wanting to feel like part of the group. In fact, she continued to exhibit this behavior even after all the actors had left the room. Not only that, but she also passed that norm to new test subjects who joined that same waiting room during the experiment. And the worst part of it was that none of them had any idea why they did what they did.

You think you won't fall for that, but this happens to all of us. Have you ever joined a standing ovation simply because others were doing it? Let's change this together. I invite you to draw your own journey and be ready to go when inspiration strikes. Whatever the function of your job is, you can always repackage what you do and walk the unconventional path that many would think is impossible or at least unreasonable. In this book, I shared three principles, 15 Truths, and 20 tools to enable greatness. It is not the number of tools that matters, but the possibilities of fine-tuning and spicing up those tools to achieve your objectives and ultimately greatness. Let me clarify this point with the following puzzle.

Instructions: This activity is inspired by a mathematical puzzle entitled "Four Fours." Use exactly four 4's and any operation (+, −, ×, /, () (brackets), . (decimal point), √ (square root), etc.) to make the numbers from 1 to 16. For example, (4 + 4) / (4 + 4) = 1.

Note: There is more than one solution for each number.

1 (4 + 4) / (4 + 4)	2	3	4
5	6	7	8
9	10	11	12
13	14	15	16

Answers:

1 ~ (4 + 4) / (4 + 4)	9 ~ (4 + 4) + (4 / 4)
2 ~ (4 / 4) + (4 / 4)	10 ~ (4 + 4 + 4) - √4
3 ~ (4 + 4 + 4) / 4	11 ~ (4 / .4) + (4 / 4)
4 ~ (4 - 4) x 4 + 4	12 ~ 4 × (4 - (4 ÷ 4))
5 ~ (**4 × 4** + 4) / 4	13 ~ (4^2 - 4) + (4 / 4)
6 ~ (**4 + 4** / 4) + 4	14 ~ (4 × 4) - (4 ÷ √4)
7 ~ (4 + 4) - (4 / 4)	15 ~ (4 x 4) - (4 / 4)
8 ~ (4 + 4) - (4 - 4)	16 ~ 4 + 4 + 4 + 4

As you can see, it is not about how many tools you have (the four 4's), but how you use these tools. Just as exploring different operations empowered you to achieve 16 different results with the same four 4's, i.e., four tools, I believe that the way you explore, tweak, repackage, experiment with, and implement this book's 20 tools will empower you to connect the dots, raise your own flag, and write your own song.

Raise Your Own Flag

"Some people will think you are crazy, and others will support your vision."[253] With that statement, my friend David Medawar shared with me his message of unity, yearning for one global state. "You have to constantly ask yourself 'why' until you find your song (purpose) that ultimately fuels your life, and then invest every bit of your energy to raise your flag," David said.

He reminded me of the song "Raise Your Flag" by the Japanese rock band, Man with a Mission:[254]

Raise your flag
With all your voice
With all your voice
Shout it out loud with all your voice
One day… Someday somewhere
Believing that we will reach the goal

Come on and raise your flag
So just raise your flag
No matter how many times we feel defeated or lost
As long as we breathe
As long as we carry on
Dream on as we wander

The real pain today is that we crave diversity. We follow the crowd, and in the process, we lose our uniqueness and sing someone else's song. I invite you to investigate every practice, question, and tool in this book, but I also challenge you to focus forward, explore, experiment, and reimagine. Yes, be unreasonable. If Steve Jobs was reasonable, he wouldn't have changed the way our world communicates and connects. It is because of leaders like Marie Curie, Martin Luther King, Nelson Mandela, Rosa Parks, Henry Ford, and Walt Disney that we enjoy the world we know today. These leaders accepted that reality isn't fixed. They set unreasonable goals, worked on unreasonable projects, partnered with unreasonable people…. Be unreasonable; your success depends on it. And don't be afraid of failure, "At least if you fail, what a spectacular failure," David told me. He added, "When you focus on your purpose, and as long as you are not prepared to give up, many will show up to contribute and support you. Never, ever give up!"

Don't see things the way they are today. Dream and ask, "Why not?" David's purpose of inspiring a "one global state" is a call for change in a world that craves it. "If we are all global citizens, if we have a single government, if we join hands and work together instead of fighting over resources and different agendas, we will reach out to one another and make our world a better place," David believes. David went on to break the world record by visiting every sovereign country on the face of the earth in three years, two months, and 20 days. Along this ride, he raised a "one world flag" and planted a tree on the foundation of the rocks he collected from every nation. "This tree's strength is drawn from every part of our world, and I will continue to nurture it and sing out loud the song of unity," David proudly told me.

I deeply believe in our ability to bring greatness to those we lead and serve. And in the process, we become the hope for those seeking to sing their songs and raise their own flags. I invite you to make your first unconventional step, transform your life, your team, your organization, and leave the world with a story to tell.

I don't claim to know all the facts, and I hope that your reading experience has triggered more questions than it gave you answers. There are many facts to investigate and answers that I don't know. But there is one thing I do know: There are billions of people in our world, but you are the only "you" there is, and that, my friend, is a wonderful thing.

Capture your moment. Raise your flag. Sing your song.

And with this Lebanese poem from my father, the poet Rafik Rouhana, I end my journey with you:[12]

> *T*ebliictaq ! Tescal: cu hiyyi l yazami ?
>
> *W* baydayn ! Xelmaq rax ylaciilaq jawaab…
>
> *H*uwwi cenet cewwi mgallefha xjaab…
>
> *C*eccu b hadaf saami w masiira mnazzami,
>
> *B* sacaafit ec cerqi w ciyam yazm ec cabaab…
>
> *W* saayeta ? Camsaq ma biyyedla gyaab.

c: ش   c: ء   y: ع   x: ح

[English]

Before all else, ask what is greatness.
And listen to your dream as it whispers the answer.
"It is your own power shrouded in a veil," it says.
Arm yourself with a purpose, embrace your values,
and with an unwavering march, shatter that veil....
Then witness as your sun ceases to set on your wonderful journey.

---

[12] This poem is written in the letters of the Lebanese alphabet, reformed by the philosopher Said Akl.

Afterword

Three Universal Principles in a Time of Unprecedented Change

It's been said, "If you don't like change, you're going to like irrelevance even less." Change is upon us and as a modern-day leader, creating a winning ideology and engaging the hearts, souls, and minds of your people is one of the biggest challenges facing most companies today. This has been further amplified during these difficult times of COVID-19, and that pace of change is only accelerating.

With this speed of disruption, employees' and customers' expectations heighten, and organizations are constantly looking for ways not only to survive but also thrive. I genuinely believe and can prove that the solutions are not found in redefining your key performance indicators or shuffling the company balance sheet, they are in fact found in these words: *Culture, Leadership, and the Customer Experience.* And that's what Melkart's book is all about.

Are You Prepared for Greatness?

In my experience, one of the most common throwaway statements that I frequently hear in business circles is, "Our people are the most important resource. Put people first!" This always leads me to the question, "Well, how important are they? And what is it that you do as a leader and organization to recognize and support this statement?" After considerable head-scratching and at best some package benefits, the list is remarkably short! For me, one of the greatest tragedies for any business is to have a team full of talent that is never heard. A common myth is that a good remuneration package should be enough to fuel success and keep talent motivated, but I can tell you that it isn't!

I believe that if you want to demonstrate how important your people are, then create a winning culture that enables your people to have a voice and a choice—allow them to use their talents and shine. Inspire them to be the best that they can be and recognize their achievements. It's as simple as that!

Question Is, What Is the Recipe for That Simplicity?

This book provides all the answers. I have had the honor of knowing Melkart Rouhana not only as an inspirational leader, life coach, speaker, trainer, culture and business transformer, and now author, but also as someone I am proud to call my friend. I first met Melkart in 2014 at a Porsche conference in Istanbul, Turkey where he introduced his formula for creating a winning culture and inspiring leadership and its impact on our teams, customers, and ultimately results. During my 30-plus years in the automotive industry, I attended thousands of speeches and was presented with hundreds of theories but as it would turn out, none as impactful! On the morning I met him, Melkart's light shone brightly. His infectious energy, passion, wit, and humor had everyone captivated as he introduced his three Principles to enable greatness. It was with this in mind that I invited Melkart to the Latin America region to help us on our journey of enabling greatness...and oh my, what a journey it has been!

The fact remains, Melkart's Principles are universal— it resonates anywhere and in any industry! Period.

The Dance of Greatness

During my career, I have seen leaders turn down job applicants as they felt threatened that the candidate would eventually take their job! As a leader, I learned a long time ago that it wasn't important to be the smartest person in the room or have all the answers. What is important is to unleash talents, inspire a sense of togetherness, and create an environment that allows teams to work as a collective force—think of it as the dance of greatness....

What Melkart has successfully achieved with this book is to break down the fundamentals that go into creating great leaders and building teams for greatness. He shares the *steps* and a distinctive *rhythm* supported by examples and practices from industry leaders like Apple, Disney, Virgin, The Ritz-Carlton, Amazon, and Google—inspirational brands that are globally appreciated by their raving fans (customers) not only for providing unique and memorable experiences, but for being great employers that fire up talent.

In this fascinating book, Melkart shares pragmatic tools for every step of that dance guiding us on this incredible journey. At no point are you ever left wondering what your next move might be. Think of this book as the definitive guide on how to continue your journey as a great leader. A journey in which you define your own steps and rhythm to lead an organization that adds value to everyone's lives—team members, customers, and your own.

Rome Wasn't Built in a Day

This book brings together structure, explicitness, and tools essential for any successful modern-day business leader. Just remember that "Rome was not built in a day," and neither is creating a culture for greatness. It takes time and consistent leadership. If you are a seasoned professional or starting on your leadership journey, there is something in this book for you. It is your reference guide to building greatness in your organization!

Change is inevitable! You need to prepare.
Figure out the three things you can embrace from this book.
Use the tools, disrupt the status quo.
Redefine your steps and rhythm.
Move from success to success.
I did it, and trust me: the rewards are great for everyone!

George Wills
President & Managing Director
Porsche Latin America, Inc.

Acknowledgments

Starting this journey was startling. I sketched the map, assembled the tools, and embarked on this ride of greatness. Truth be told, taking the first step was like jumping off a cliff. At first it was frightening; then things settled down as the parachute opened. I admit that I worked the parachute hard, but I owe all thankfulness and appreciation to those who enabled me to control the wind and proudly reach my landing spot.

This book could not have been written without the labor of many authors, scholars, and practitioners whose findings and insights are highlighted throughout this book. And to the following executives who were kind enough to share their stories through interviews, listed here in order of their appearance in the book: Ahmed Tharwat, Max Zanardi, Rainer J. Bürkle, Darrell Schaeffer, Bachir Zeidan, Raja Touma, Werner Anzinger, Dagmar Symes, Ayman Gharib, and David Medawar.

Thank you to our business partners (clients) who believe in our philosophy and their tremendous support to experience and validate every tool shared in this book. And to my friends and the great people that I had the opportunity to lead, be led by, and partnered with, for challenging me and sparking my philosophy about life and business.

I am grateful to Leopoldine Vittori, who magically connected the dots and transformed each Truth into a dazzling illustration. To Jenine Davidson for putting my words into memorable figures. To Joris Roozen, Hoss Vetry, Tarik Temucin, Jeff Smith, and Taha Mohamed for being this book's advocates. To Hanady Assaf for giving my father's poem an English voice. It wouldn't have been the same without their magical touch.

Heartfelt thanks to Andreas Löhmer, Andre Bisasor, Diana Oreck, Hagop Doghramadjian, Horst Schulze, Jacqueline Moyse, Kimberly Rath, Marc Dardenne, and Shelley Perkins who dedicated time and energy to read the early manuscript and share their precious praise. Each of these leaders will forever have my gratitude.

This book would have been incomplete without the guidance, insight, and support of my editors Susan Gaigher and Brian Baker as well as my designer Xavier Comas. Their unique talents made the pages of this book shine.

With deep gratitude, I acknowledge Bob Kharazmi, a gracious friend who inspires me to raise my flag. And to George Wills, who sings along with the song of greatness.

I am forever grateful to my father, Rafik, for shaping my life, to my mother, Siham, for bestowing me with all her values, to my brother, Anis, for believing in my dreams, and to my sister, Elissa, for her endless love and care.

And two truly special mentions. My wife, Nancy, whose love inspires me every day to break every boundary, walk the unconventional path, and sing my own song. And to my two angels, Raphael and Matteo, who fuel my purpose and teach me to find happiness in the smallest things.

Honor to God, my silent partner and the source of all greatness.

Last but not least, to you. You are the reason of this book. This one's for you.

Notes

[1] Buchan, J. (1930). *Montrose and leadership.*
Oxford University Press. p 24.

[2] Wiraeus, D., & Creelman, J. (2018). *Agile strategy management in the digital age: How dynamic balanced scorecards transform decision making, speed, and effectiveness.* Palgrave Macmillan. p. 70.

[3] Gerstner, L. V. Jr. (2003). *Who says elephants can't dance? Leading a great enterprise through dramatic change.*
Harper Business. p. 181.

[4] Kaul, A. (2019). Culture vs strategy: which to precede, which to align? *Journal of Strategy and Management, 12*(1), 116-136. https://doi.org/10.1108/jsma-04-2018-0036.

[5] Coffman, C., & Sorensen, K. (2013). *Culture eats strategy for lunch: The secret of extraordinary results, igniting the passion within.*
Liang Addison Press. p. 19.

[6] Ron, B. (1999). When is corporate culture a competitive asset? *Financial Times.* November 1. pp. 14-15.

[7] Bagher Arayesh, M., Golmohammadi, E., Nekooeezadeh, M., & Mansouri, A. (2017). The effects of organizational culture on the development of strategic thinking at the organizational level. *International Journal of Organizational Leadership, 6*(2), 261-275. https://doi.org/10.33844/ijol.2017.60385.

[8] O'Reilly, C. A., & Chatman, J. A. (1996). *Culture as social control: Corporations, cults, and commitment.* In B. M. Staw & L. L. Cummings (Eds.), *Research in organizational behavior: An annual series of analytical essays and critical reviews, Vol. 18,* pp. 157-200. JAI Press, pp. 157-200.

[9] Lok, P., & Crawford, J. (2004). The effect of organisational culture and leadership style on job satisfaction and organisational commitment. *Journal of Management Development, 23*(4), 321-338. https://doi.org/10.1108/02621710410529785

[10] Mohanty, J., & Rath, B.P. (2012). Influence of organizational culture on organizational citizenship behavior: A three-sector study. *Global Journal of Business Research, 6*(1), 65-76. https://ssrn.com/abstract=1946000

[11] Kowalczyk, S. J., & Pawlish, M. J. (2002). Corporate branding through external perception of organizational culture. *Corporate Reputation Review, 5*(2-3), 159-174. https://doi.org/10.1057/palgrave.crr.1540172

[12] Schein, E. H. (1992). *Organizational culture and leadership.* Jossey-Bass.

[13] Kotter, J. P., & Heskett, J. L. (1992). *Corporate culture and performance.* The Free Press.

[14] Kotter, J. P. (2011, February 10). *Does corporate culture drive financial performance?* Forbes. https://www.forbes.com/sites/johnkotter/2011/02/10/does-corporate-culture-drive-financial-performance/?sh=2654310c7e9e.

[15] Connors, R., & Smith, T. (2011). *Change the culture, change the game: The breakthrough strategy for energizing your organization and creating accountability for results.* Penguin Group. p. 214.

[16] Schein, E. H. (1991). *The role of the founder in the creation of o rganizational culture.* In Frost P. J., Moore, L.F., Louis, M.R., Lundberg, C.C., and Martin, J. (eds.) *Organizational cultures* (pp. 14-25). Sage.

[17] Frieberg, J., & Frieberg, K. (1998). *Nuts! Southwest airlines' crazy recipe for business and personal success.* Broadway Books. pp. 144-145.

[18] Gibran, K. (1988). *The prophet.* Alfred A. Knopf. p. 50.

[19] Sinek S. (2009). *Start with why: How great leaders inspire everyone to take action.* Penguin Books Ltd.

[20] Pink, D. (2009). *Drive: The surprising truth about what motivates us.* Riverhead Books. p. 91.

[21] Freedman, J. (2007). *At the heart of leadership: How to get results with emotional intelligence.* Six Seconds.

[22] EY Beacon Institute. (2016). *The business case for purpose.* Harvard Business Review Analytic Services, Boston.

23 Collins, J. C., & Porras, J. I. (1997). *Built to last: Successful habits of visionary companies.* HarperBusiness.

24 Schulze, H., & Merrill, D. (2019). *Excellence wins: A no-nonsense guide to becoming the best in a world of compromise.* Zondervan. p. 111.

25 Ibid., p. 140.

26 Munger, T. T., (1880). *On the threshold.* Houghton, Mifflin & Co. pp. 25-26. https://www.kobo.com/ww/en/ebook/on-the-threshold-6.

27 Blanchard, K. & O'Connor, M. (1997). *Managing by values: How to put your values into action for extraordinary results.* Berrett-Koehler. p. 3.

28 Buchko, A. A. (2007). The effect of leadership on values-based management. *Leadership & Organization Development Journal, 28*(1), 36-50. https://doi.org/10.1108/01437730710718236.

29 Posner, B.Z., & Schmidt, W.R. (1983). *Managerial values in perspective: An AMA survey report.* AMA Publication Division.

30 de Geus, A. (1997). The living company. *Harvard Business Review.* https://hbr.org/1997/03/the-living-company.

31 Peters, T.J., & Waterman, Jr., R.H. (1982). *In search of excellence.* Harper & Row.

32 Argandoña, A. (2003). Fostering values in organizations. *Journal of Business Ethics* 45, 15–28. https://doi.org/10.1023/A:1024164210743.

33 Hitt, W.D. (1990). *Ethics and leadership: Putting theory into practice.* Battelle Press. pp. 14-16.

34 Nagel, K.F. (1998). *Organizational values and employee health initiatives: Influence on performance and functioning* [Doctoral dissertation, University of Victoria]. https://dspace.library.uvic.ca/handle/1828/8608.

35 Berry, L.L. (1999). *Discovering the soul of service: The nine drivers of sustainable business success.* The Free Press. p. 21.

36 Biblica – The international bible society. (n.d.).
Online Bible | Biblica – The International Bible Society. Biblica.
https://www.biblica.com/bible/niv/luke/6/.

37 *We Deliver Happiness.* (n.d.). Zoom Video. https://zoom.us/about

38 *Intuit®: Company | Our Operating Values.* (n.d.).
Intuit. https://www.intuit.com/company/operating-values/

39 Whatley, S. (2016, September 2). *Spotify's core values.*
https://hrblog.spotify.com/2016/09/02/spotifys-core-values/.

40 *The LEGO Brand.* (n.d.). LEGO. https://www.lego.com/en-us/
aboutus/lego-group/the-lego-brand/.

41*Netflix Jobs.* (n.d.). Netflix. https://jobs.netflix.com/culture.

42 Milton, J. (1909). *The complete poems of John Milton.* P.F. Collier & Son. p.
52. https://mthoyibi.files.wordpress.com/2011/03/
complete-poems-of-john-milton.pdf.

43 Merriam-Webster. (n.d.). Silver lining. In *Merriam-Webster.com.*
Retrieved April 1, 2020, from https://www.merriam-webster.com/
dictionary/silver%20lining.

44 Dalton, C. M. (2006). When organizational values are mere
rhetoric. *Business Horizons, 49*(5), 345–348. https://doi.org/
10.1016/j.bushor.2005.12.005.

45 Ringer R. (1990). *Million dollar habits.* Wynwood Press. pp. 9-10.

46 Durant, W. (1926). *The story of philosophy: The lives and opinions
of the great philosophers of the western world.* Garden City Publishing Co.,
Inc. p. 87.

47 Neal, D. T., Wood, W., & Quinn, J. M. (2006). Habits—A repeat
performance. *Current Directions in Psychological Science, 15*(4), 198-202.
https://doi.org/10.1111/j.1467-8721.2006.00435.x.

48 Duhigg, C. (2012). *The power of habit: Why we do what
we do in life and business.* Random House. p. 100.

[49] Lally, P., van Jaarsveld, C. H. M., Potts, H. W. W., & Wardle, J. (2009). How are habits formed: Modelling habit formation in the real world. *European Journal of Social Psychology, 40*(6), 998-1009. https://doi.org/10.1002/ejsp.674.

[50] Zak, P. J. (2017). The neuroscience of trust. *Harvard Business Review.* https://hbr.org/2017/01/the-neuroscience-of-trust.

[51] Covey, S. M. R., & Merrill, R. R. (2006). *The speed of trust: The one thing that changes everything.* Simon & Schuster Audio.

[52] Ferres, N., Connell, J., & Travaglione, A. (2004). Co□worker trust as a social catalyst for constructive employee attitudes. *Journal of Managerial Psychology, 19*(6), 608-622. https://doi.org/10.1108/02683940410551516.

[53] Rich, G. A. (1997). The sales manager as a role model: Effects on trust, job satisfaction, and performance of salespeople. *Journal of the Academy of Marketing Science, 25*(4), 319–328. https://doi.org/10.1177/0092070397254004.

[54] Driscoll J. A. (1978). Trust and participation in organizational decision-making as predictors of satisfaction. *Academy of Management Journal,* 1978, 21, 44-56. *Group & Organization Studies, 3*(4), 511. https://doi.org/10.1177/105960117800300422.

[55] Pillai, R., Schriesheim, C. A., & Williams, E. S. (1999). Fairness perceptions and trust as mediators for transformational and transactional leadership: A two-sample study. *Journal of Management, 25*(6), 897-933. https://doi.org/10.1177/014920639902500606.

[56] Muchinsky, P. M. (1977). Organizational communication: relationships to organizational climate and job satisfaction. *Academy of Management Journal, 20*(4), 592-607. https://doi.org/10.5465/255359.

[57] Zak, P.J., Kurzban, R., Matzner, W.T. (2005). Oxytocin is associated with human trustworthiness. *Hormones and Behavior, 48*(5), 522-527. https://doi.org/10.1016/j.yhbeh.2005.07.009.

[58] Kosfeld, M., Heinrichs, M., Zak, P. J., Fischbacher, U., & Fehr, E. (2005). Oxytocin increases trust in humans. *Nature, 435*(7042), 673-676. https://doi.org/10.1038/nature03701.

[59] Morhenn, V.B., Park, J.W., Piper, E., Zak, P.J. (2008). Monetary sacrifice among strangers is mediated by endogenous oxytocin release after physical contact. *Evolution and Human Behavior, 29*(6), 375-383. https://doi.org/10.1016/j.evolhumbehav.2008.04.004.

[60] Coelho, P. (2007, August 14). *The impatient disciple*. Paulo Coelho. https://paulocoelhoblog.com/2007/08/14/the-impatient-disciple/.

[61] Tharwat, Ahmed. Interview. Conducted by Melkart Rouhana, 15 April 2016.

[62] Ibid.

[63] Digital transformation is racing ahead and no industry is immune (2017, July 19). *Harvard Business Review*. https://hbr.org/sponsored/2017/07/digital-transformation-is-racing-ahead-and-no-industry-is-immune-2.

[64] Patel, N. (2015, July 16). *90% of startups fail: Here's what you need to know about the 10%.* Forbes. https://www.forbes.com/sites/neilpatel/2015/01/16/90-of-startups-will-fail-heres-what-you-need-to-know-about-the-10/?sh=4a252ab16679.

[65] Project Management Institute. (2017). *Achieving greater agility: The essential influence of the c-suite.* p. 2. https://i.forbesimg.com/forbesinsights/pmi/achieving_greater_agility.pdf.

[66] Economist Intelligence Unit. (2009). *Organisational agility: How business can survive and thrive in turbulent times.* https://qtxasset.com/cfoinnovation/field/field_p_files/white_paper/Organisational%20Agility_EIU.pdf.

[67] Talent International. (2014). *87% of executives want to be CEO, yet only 15% of execs are Learning Agile, find Korn Ferry.* https://www.recruitment-international.co.uk/blog/2014/10/87-percent-of-executives-want-to-be-ceo-yet-only-15-percent-of-execs-are-learning-agile-find-korn-ferry.

[68] Lawrence, B. (2018, June 12). *Organizations are getting agile, but not quickly enough.* HRCI. https://www.hrci.org/community/blogs-and-announcements/hr-leads-business-blog/hr-leads-business/2018/06/12/organizations-are-getting-agile-but-not-quickly-enough.

[69] Institute for the Future IFTF. (2017). *Emerging technologies' impact on society & work in 2030.* https://www.delltechnologies.com/content/dam/delltechnologies/assets/perspectives/2030/pdf/SR1940_IFTFforDellTechnologies_Human-Machine_070517_readerhigh-res.pdf.

[70] Bazigos, M., De Smet, A., & Gagnon, C. (2015). Why agility pays. *McKinsey Quarterly.* Retrieved from https://www.mckinsey.com/business-functions/organization/our-insights/why-agility-pays.

[71] Yusuf, Y. Y., & Adeleye, E. O. (2002). A comparative study of lean and agile manufacturing with a related survey of current practices in the UK. *International Journal of Production Research, 40*(17), 4545-4562. https://doi.org/10.1080/00207540210157141.

[72] Accenture Talent and Organization for FS. (2019, January 11). *Enterprise agility explained with five statistics.* Accenture. https://financialservicesblog.accenture.com/enterprise-agility-explained-with-five-statistics.

[73] Zanardi, Max. Interview. Conducted by Melkart Rouhana, 01 November 2017.

[74] Ibid.

[75] McBride, T.L. (2013, August 15). *Bruce Lee be as water my friend* [Video file]. YouTube. https://www.youtube.com/watch?v=cJMwBwFj5nQ.

[76] Vitullo-Martin, J., & Moskin, J.R. (1994). *The executive's book of quotations.* Oxford University Press. p. 293.

[77] Boone, L. E. (1992). *Quotable business: Over 2,500 funny, irreverent, and insightful quotations about corporate life.* Random House. p.137

[78] Jenson, R. (2006). *Achieving authentic success.* Future Achievement International. p.3.

[79] Maxwell, J.C. (1995). *Developing the leaders around you.* T. Nelson. p. 12.

80 Bartlett, J. (1968). *Familiar quotations (14ᵗʰ ed.).* Little, Brown and Company. p.1032.

81 Merriam-Webster. (n.d.). Talent. In *Merriam-Webster.com.* Retrieved April 10, 2020, from https://www.merriam-webster.com/dictionary/talent.

82 Colvin, G. (2010). *Talent is overrated: What really separates world-class performers from everybody else.* Penguin Group Inc.

83 Ibid., p. 7.

84 Fullan, M. (2011). *Change Leader: Learning to do what matters most.* Jossey-Bass. p. 5.

85 Ericsson, K.A., & Pool, R. (2016). *Peak: Secrets from the new science of expertise.* Houghton Mifflin. p. 207.

86 Simon, H. A., & Chase, W G. (1973). Skill in chess. *American Scientist, 61,* 394-403.

87 Gladwell, M. (2008). *Outliers: The story of success.* Little, Brown and Company.

88 Simmons, M. (2016, July 22). *Bill Gates, Warren Buffett, and Oprah Winfrey all use the 5-hour rule.* Inc.com. https://www.inc.com/empact/bill-gates-warren-buffett-and-oprah-all-use-the-5-hour-rule.html.

89 Herzberg, F. (2003, January). One more time: How do you motivate employees? *Harvard Business Review.* https://hbr.org/2003/01/one-more-time-how-do-you-motivate-employees.

90 Csikszentmihalyi, M. (1990). *Flow: The psychology of optimal experience.* HarperCollins. p. 3.

91 *Top 9 quotes of David Goggins.* (n.d.). Inspiring Quotes. https://www.inspiringquotes.us/author/8197-david-goggins.

92 Rainer J. Bürkle. Interview. Conducted by Melkart Rouhana, 20 September 2016.

⁹³ O'Bryant, F. (n.d.). *Fred O'Bryant's quote collection – volume 5.* Fred O'Bryant's. http://people.virginia.edu/%7Ejfo/quotes/quotes5.html.

⁹⁴ Bass, B. M. (1990). *Bass & Stogdill's handbook of leadership.* (3rd ed.). The Free Press. p. 20.

⁹⁵ Stogdill, R. M. (1974). *Handbook of leadership: A survey of the literature.* Free Press. p. 259.

⁹⁶ Bennis, W. (1989). *On becoming a leader: The leadership classic.* Perseus Books Group. p. 1.

⁹⁷ Blaydes, J. (2003). *The educator's book of quotes.* Corwin Press. p. 2.

⁹⁸ Foster, N. (2007, January). *My green agenda for architecture* [Video]. TED Conferences. https://www.ted.com/talks/norman_foster_my_green_agenda_for_architecture/transcript?language=en.

⁹⁹ Zeidan, Bachir. Interview. Conducted by Melkart Rouhana, 01 December 2016.

¹⁰⁰ Demakis, J. (2012). *The ultimate book of quotations.* CreateSpace. p. 13.

¹⁰¹ Mandela, N. (n.d.). *Speech by President Mandela at the Chief Albert Luthuli centenary celebration, 25 April 1998, KwaDukuza | South African history online.* South African History Online. https://www.sahistory.org.za/archive/speech-president-mandela-chief-albert-luthuli-centenary-celebration-25-april-1998-kwadukuza.

¹⁰² Henry, P. (2011, April). *Speech to the second Virginia convention.* Gleeditions. https://www.gleeditions.com/speechtothesecondvirginiaconvention/students/pages.asp?lid=414&pg=4.

¹⁰³ Chambers, H. E. (2004). My way or the highway: The micromanagement survival guide (1st ed.). Berrett-Koehler Publishers. pp. 22-25.

¹⁰⁴ Shuford, J. A. (2019). Micromanagement: The enemy of staff morale. *Corrections Today, 81*(5), 36-41. https://teamcrs.org/corrections-today-micromanagement-the-enemy-of-staff-morale/.

¹⁰⁵ Blanchard, K. (1982). *The one minute manager.* William Morrow & Co, Inc.

106 Guo, L., Decoster, S., Babalola, M. T., De Schutter, L., Garba, O. A., & Riisla, K. (2018). Authoritarian leadership and employee creativity: The moderating role of psychological capital and the mediating role of fear and defensive silence. *Journal of Business Research*, *92*, 219–230. https://doi.org/10.1016/j.jbusres.2018.07.034.

107 Gonzalez-Mulé, E., & Cockburn, B. (2016). Worked to death: The relationships of job demands and job control with mortality. *Personnel Psychology*, *70*(1), 73-112. https://doi.org/10.1111/peps.12206.

108 Ayres, I. (2010). *Carrots and sticks: Unlock the power of incentives to get things done.* Bantam Books.

109 Doshi, N., & McGregor, L. (2015). *Primed to perform: How to build the highest performing cultures through the science of total motivation.* HarperCollins Publishers.

110 Merriam-Webster. (n.d.). Empowerment. In *Merriam-Webster.com*. Retrieved November 1, 2020, from www.merriam-webster.com/dictionary/empowerment.

111 Quinn, R. E., & Spreitzer, G. M. (1997). The road to empowerment: Seven questions every leader should consider. *Organizational Dynamics*, *26*(2), 37–49. https://doi.org/10.1016/s0090-2616(97)90004-8.

112 Ryan, R. M., & Deci, E. L. (2000). Self-determination theory and the facilitation of intrinsic motivation, social development, and well-being. *American Psychologist*, *55*(1), 68–78. https://doi.org/10.1037/0003-066x.55.1.68

113 Deci, E. L., & Flaste, R. (1995). *Why we do what we do: The dynamics of personal autonomy.* Putnam's Sons.

114 Slemp, G. R., Kern, M. L., Patrick, K. J., & Ryan, R. M. (2018). Leader autonomy support in the workplace: A meta-analytic review. *Motivation and Emotion*, *42*(5), 706-724. https://doi.org/10.1007/s11031-018-9698-y.

115 Covey, S. R. (2004). Th*e 8th habit: From effectiveness to greatness.* Free Press. p. 314.

[116] Marquet, L.D. (2012). *Turn the ship around! How to create leadership at every level.* Greenleaf Book Group Press.

[117] Erickson, T. (2007, March 22). Think task, not time. *Harvard Business Review.* https://hbr.org/2007/03/think-task-not-time.

[118] Huston, L., & Sakkab, N. (2006, March). Connect and develop: Inside procter & famble's new model for innovation. *Harvard Business Review.* https://hbr.org/2006/03/connect-and-develop-inside-procter-gambles-new-model-for-innovation.

[119] Mankins, M., & Garton E. (2017). How Spotify balances employee autonomy and accountability. *Harvard Business Review.* https://hbr.org/2017/02/how-spotify-balances-employee-autonomy-and-accountability.

[120] *International Dance Music Awards (IDMA) presents 2018...* (2018, March 22). We Rave You. https://weraveyou.com/2018/03/international-dance-music-awards-idma-presents-2018-winners/.

[121] *IDMA 2019 Nominees & Winners.* (n.d.). WMC · Winter Music Conference. https://wintermusicconference.com/idma-2019-winners/.

[122] *IDMA 2020 winners announced.* (2020, April 01). We Rave You. https://weraveyou.com/2020/04/idma-2020-winners-announced-aviciis-tim-named-as-the-best-album/.

[123] Robertson, B. J. (2015). *Holacracy: The new management system for a rapidly changing world.* Henry Holt and Company.

[124] Chouinard, Y. (2005). *Let my people go surfing: The education of a reluctant businessman.* Penguin. p. 69.

[125] Hoover, H. (1964, August 10). *Text of Hoover's message for Birthday.* The New York Times. https://www.nytimes.com/1964/08/10/archives/text-of-hoovers-message-for-birthday.html.

[126] Coelho, P. (1998). *The alchemist.* HarperSanFrancisco.

[127] TSL Encyclopedia. (n.d.). Alchemy. In *summitlighthouse.org.* Retrieved December 18, 2020, from https://encyclopedia.summitlighthouse.org/index.php/Alchemy.

128 Shaw, B. (1903). *Man and superman.* The University Press. p. 238.

129 Seligman, M. (1991). *Learned optimism: How to change your mind and your life.* Knopf.

130 Oscars. (2014, March 11). *Matthew McConaughey winning best actor* [Video file]. YouTube. https://www.youtube.com/watch?v=wD2cVhC-63I.

131 Davis, R. A. (2010). *The intangibles of leadership: The 10 qualities of superior executive performance.* John Wiley & Sons.

132 Presidents Summit. (2016, June 1). *Jack Welch: My greatest leadership learnings from a life in business* [Video file]. YouTube. https://www.youtube.com/watch?v=xsEtVQCHYpE.

133 Bossidy, L., & Charan, R. (2002). *Execution: The discipline of getting things done.* Crown Business. p. 57.

134 Dass, R. (1976). *Grist for the mill.* Unity Press. p. xiii.

135 George, B. (2015). *Discover your true north: Becoming an authentic leader.* John Wiley & Sons. p. 166.

136 HelmerReenberg. (2020, April 09). *April 9, 1963 – President John F. Kennedy declares Sir Winston Churchill an honorary citizen of USA.* [Video file]. YouTube. https://www.youtube.com/watch?v=q-Qh4YTXM1s.

137 Biblica – The International bible society. (n.d.). *Online Bible | Biblica – The International Bible Society.* Biblica. https://www.biblica.com/bible/niv/john/1/.

138 Diekhof, E. K., Geier, K., Falkai, P., & Gruber, O. (2011). Fear is only as deep as the mind allows. *NeuroImage, 58*(1), 275-285. https://doi.org/10.1016/j.neuroimage.2011.05.073.

139 Johnson, S. (1998). *Who moved my cheese? An amazing way to deal with change in your work and in your life.* G. P. Putnam's Sons. p. 63.

140 O'Kelly, E., & O'Kelly, C.(2006). *Chasing daylight: How my forthcoming death transformed my life.* McGraw-Hill. p. 4.

141 Ibid., p. 116.

142 Wagner, R. & Harter, J. K. (2006). *12: The elements of great managing.* Gallup Press.

143 Griggs, F. E. (2013). Citizenship, character, and leadership: Guidance from the words of Theodore Roosevelt. *Leadership and Management in Engineering, 13*(4), 230-248. https://doi.org/10.1061/(asce) lm.1943-5630.0000237.

144 Law, A. (2018, January 23). *Don't ever take your parents for granted: Indra Nooyi.* The Hindu Business Line. https://www.thehindubusinessline. com/news/education/dont-ever-take-your-parents-for-granted-indra-nooyi/article7068412.ece.

145 Stanford. (2008, March 07). *Steve Jobs' 2005 Stanford Commencement Address* [Video file]. YouTube. https://www.youtube.com/ watch?v=UF8uR6Z6KLc&feature=emb_logo.

146 Bezos, J. P. (2006). *Amazon 2006 letter to shareholders.* Amazon.com, Inc. https://www.sec.gov/Archives/edgar/data/1018724/000119312507093886/ dex991.htm.

147 Whitaker, M. C. ed. (2008). *African American icons of sport: Triumph, courage and excellence.* Greenwood Press. p. 2.

148 Duckworth, A. (2016). *Grit: The power of passion and perseverance.* Scribner. p. 46.

149 Robbins, M. (2017). *The 5 second rule: Transform your life, work, and confidence with everyday courage.* Savio Republic.

150 Sabock, R. J. (1985). *The coach.* Human Kinetics. p. 87.

151 Barcomb, B. (2016). *The change agent: From 30,000 feet.* Dorrance Publishing. p. 41.

152 Simpson, M. (2011, October 30). *A sister's eulogy for Steve Jobs.* The New York Times. https://www.nytimes.com/2011/10/30/opinion/ mona-simpsons-eulogy-for-steve-jobs.html.

153 Zuckerberg. M. (2017, 16 February). Building global community. Facebook.com. https://www.facebook.com/notes/mark-zuckerberg/building-global-community/10154544292806634.

154 Seuss, Dr. (1990). *Oh, the places you'll go!* Random House.

155 Gielan, M. (2019, March 12). The Financial upside of being an optimist. *Harvard Business Review*. https://hbr.org/2019/03/the-financial-upside-of-being-an-optimist.

156 Assad, K. K., Donnellan, M. B., & Conger, R. D. (2007). Optimism: An enduring resource for romantic relationships. *Journal of Personality and Social Psychology, 93*(2), 285–297. https://doi.org/10.1037/0022-3514.93.2.285.

157 Lee, L. O., James, P., Zevon, E. S., Kim, E. S., Trudel-Fitzgerald, C., Spiro, A., Grodstein, F., & Kubzansky, L. D. (2019). Optimism is associated with exceptional longevity in 2 epidemiologic cohorts of men and women. *Proceedings of the National Academy of Sciences, 116*(37), 18357-18362. https://doi.org/10.1073/pnas.1900712116.

158 Amabile, T. M., & Kramer, S. J. (2011, May). The power of small wins. *Harvard Business Review*. https://hbr.org/2011/05/the-power-of-small-wins.

159 Joss, R. L. (2005). It's not about you. *Stanford Business*. August. https://www.gsb.stanford.edu/sites/gsb/files/2005August.pdf.

160 Coelho, P. (1998). *The alchemist*. HarperSanFrancisco. p. 31.

161 Dutton, J. (2003). *Energize your workplace: How to create and sustain high-quality connections at work*. Jossey-Bass.

162 Bruch, H., & Vogel, B. (2011). *Fully charged: How great leaders boost their organization's energy and ignite high performance*. Harvard Business Press.

163 Etzioni, A. (1975). *The active society: A theory of societal and political processes*. Free Press.

164 Freedman, J. (2007). *At the heart of leadership: How to get results with emotional intelligence*. Six Seconds. p.13.

[165] Maxwell, J. C. (2007). *The 21 irrefutable laws of leadership: Follow them and people will follow you.* HarperCollins Leadership.

[166] Ibid., 115.

[167] MacLellan, L. (2017, September 20). *Alibaba's Jack Ma says successful leaders need EQ, IQ, and "LQ" (BABA).* Quartz. https://qz.com/1082709/alibabas-jack-ma-says-successful-leaders-need-eq-iq-and-lq-baba/

[168] Czarnecki, G. M. (2010). *Lead with love: 10 principles every leader needs to maximize potential and achieve peak performance.* Morgan James Publishing. p. 17.

[169] Symes, Dagmar. Interview. Conducted by Melkart Rouhana, 06 February 2018.

[170] Bryant, J. H. (2009). *Love leadership: The new way to lead in a fear-based world.* Jossey-Bass. pp. 104-105.

[171] Brown, B. (2012). *Daring greatly: How the courage to be vulnerable transforms the way we live, love, parent, and lead.* Gotham Books. p. 34.

[172] Greenleaf, R. (2002). *Servant leadership: A journey into the nature of legitimate power and greatness* (25th anniversary ed.). Paulist Press.

[173] Brown, B. (2018). *Dare to lead. Brave work. Tough conversations. Whole hearts.* Random House.

[174] Autry, J. A. (2001). *The servant leader: How to build a creative team, develop great morale, and improve bottom-line performance.* Three Rivers Press.

[175] Chonko, L. B. (2007). A Philosophy of teaching...and More. *Journal of Marketing Education, 29*(2), 111–121. https://doi.org/10.1177/0273475307302013

[176] Sisodia, R.; Wolfe, D.; & Sheth, J. (2007). *Firms of endearment: How world-class companies profit from passion and purpose.* Wharton School Publishing.

177 Kouzes, J. M., & Posner, B. Z. (2012). *The leadership challenge: How to make extraordinary things happen in organizations (5th ed.).* Jossey-Bass. p. 313.

178 Brinker, N.E., & Phillips, D.T. (1996). *On the brink: The life and leadership of Norman Brinker.* Summit Publishing Group. p. 195.

179 Bakke, D. W. (2005). *Joy at work: A revolutionary approach to fun on the job.* PVG. p. 25.

180 Gill, S. J. (2010). *Developing a learning culture in nonprofit organizations.* SAGE Publications, Inc.

181 Arets, J.; Jennings, C.; & Heijnen, V. (2015). *70:20:10 towards 100% performance.* Sutler Media.

182 Smith, D. (1994). *Walt Disney: Famous quotes (1994).* Disney's Kingdom. p.80.

183 Robert, W. ed. (2002). *The best advice ever for leaders.* Andrews McMeel Publishing. p. 58.

184 Collins, J. C., & Porras, J. I. (1997). *Built to last: Successful habits of visionary companies.* HarperBusiness. p. 94.

185 Gharib, Ayman. Interview. Conducted by Melkart Rouhana, 12 September 2016.

186 *Top 25 Hotels in the world—Tripadvisor travellers' choice awards.* (2020). Trip Advisor. https://www.tripadvisor.co.uk/TravelersChoice-Hotels

187 Anzinger, Werner. Interview. Conducted by Melkart Rouhana, 17 October, 2019.

188 Collins Dictionary. (n.d.) Experience. In *collinsdictionary.com.* Retrieved September 15, 2020, from https://www.collinsdictionary.com/dictionary/english/experience.

189 Pine, J. B., & Gilmore, J. H. (1999). *The experience economy: Work is theater & every business a stage* (1st ed.). Harvard Business School Press. p. 3.

[190] Clatworthy, S. D. (2019). *The experience-centric organization: How to win through customer experience* (1st ed.). O'Reilly Media.

[191] Jensen, R. (2001). *The dream society: How the coming shift from information to imagination will transform your business* (1st ed.). McGraw-Hill Education.

[192] Zeidner, M., Matthews, G., & Roberts, R. D. (2012). *What we know about emotional intelligence: How it affects learning, work, relationships, and our mental health.* MIT Press. p.13.

[193] Praet, D. V. (2014). *Unconscious branding: How neuroscience can empower (and inspire) marketing.* Palgrave Macmillan.

[194] Damasio A. R. (2000). A second chance for emotion. In Lane, R. D. & Nadel, L. (Eds.), *Cognitive neuroscience of emotion* (1st ed., pp. 12-23). Oxford University Press.

[195] Lindstrom, M. (2008). *Buyology: Truth and lies about why we buy.* Doubleday.

[196] Mann, S. (1999). Emotion at work: To what extent are we expressing, suppressing, or faking it? *European journal of work and organizational psychology, 8*(3), 347–369. https://doi.org/10.1080/135943299398221.

[197] Staw, B.M., Sutton, R. S., Pelled, L.H. (1994). Employee positive emotion and favorable outcomes at the workplace. *Organization Science,* 5(1), 51–70. https://doi.org/10.1287/orsc.5.1.51.

[198] Shaw, C., & Ivens, J. (2005). *Building great customer experiences.* Basingstoke: Palgrave Macmillan. pp. 43-44.

[199] Goleman, D. (1997). *Emotional intelligence: Why it can matter more than IQ.* Bantam. p. 289.

[200] Plutchik, R. (2001). The nature of emotions: Human emotions have deep evolutionary roots, a fact that may explain their complexity and provide tools for clinical practice. *American Scientist, 89*(4), 344–350. https://www.jstor.org/stable/27857503.

[201] Richins, M. L. (1997). Measuring emotions in the consumption experience. *Journal of Consumer Research, 24*(2), 127-146. https://doi.org/10.1086/209499.

[202] Edwardson, M. (1998). Measuring consumer emotions in service encounters: an exploratory analysis. *Australasian Journal of Market Research, 6*(2), 34-48.

[203] Barsky, J. (2002). Evoking emotion: Affective keys to hotel loyalty. *The Cornell Hotel and Restaurant Administration Quarterly, 43*(1), 39–46. https://doi.org/10.1016/s0010-8804(02)80007-6.

[204] Laros, F. J., & Steenkamp, J. E. (2005). Emotions in consumer behavior: A hierarchical approach. *Journal of Business Research, 58*(10), 1437-1445. https://doi.org/10.1016/j.jbusres.2003.09.013.

[205] Shaw, C. (2007). *Dna of customer experience: How emotions drive value.* Palgrave Macmillan.

[206] Desmet, PMA., Guiza Caicedo, D., & van Hout, M. (2009). Differentiating emotional hotel experiences. In T. Tokko (Ed.), *Proceedings of the International Hospitality and Tourism Educators EuroCHRIE Conference* (pp. 1-6). Haaga-Helia.

[207] Jang, S. C. S., & Namkung, Y. (2009). Perceived quality, emotions, and behavioral intentions: Application of an extended Mehrabian–Russell model to restaurants. *Journal of Business Research, 62*(4), 451–460. https://doi.org/10.1016/j.jbusres.2008.01.038.

[208] Jani, D., & Han, H. (2015). Influence of environmental stimuli on hotel customer emotional loyalty response: Testing the moderating effect of the big five personality factors. *International Journal of Hospitality Management, 44*, 48-57. https://doi.org/10.1016/j.ijhm.2014.10.006.

[209] Ryan, P. M. (2014). *Dictionary of emotions: Words for feelings, moods, and emotions.* PAMAXAMA.

[210] Berns, G. S., McClure, S. M., Pagnoni, G., & Montague, P. R. (2001). Predictability modulates human brain response to reward. *The Journal of Neuroscience, 21*(8), 2793-2798. https://doi.org/10.1523/jneurosci.21-08-02793.2001.

[211] Schneider, B., & Bowen, D. E. (1999). Understanding customer delight and outrage. *Sloan management review, 41*(1), 35-45.

[212] Reichheld, F. (2004). The one number you need to grow. *Harvard Business Review.* https://hbr.org/2003/12/the-one-number-you-need-to-grow.

[213] Reichheld, F. (2006). *The ultimate question: Driving good profits and true growth* (1st ed.). Harvard Business School Press.

[214] van Gogh, V. (1889). *To Theo van Gogh. Saint-Rémy-de-Provence.* Van Gogh Letters. http://vangoghletters.org/vg/letters/let790/letter.html

[215] Gallo, C. (2014, May 31). *The Maya Angelou quote that will radically improve your business.* Forbes. https://www.forbes.com/sites/carminegallo/2014/05/31/the-maya-angelou-quote-that-will-radically-improve-your-business/.

[216] Boyd, T. (2016, April 06). Loyalty effect author Fred Reichheld says customer satisfaction is not enough. *Financial Review.* https://www.afr.com/work-and-careers/management/uncovering-the-profitable-link-between-customers-and-employee-loyalty-20160303-gn9jb5.

[217] Forrester. (2010, April 20). *Announces Peer Influence Analysis: An Analytical Framework To Inform Social Media Marketing Strategy* ·. https://go.forrester.com/press-newsroom/forrester-announces-peer-influence-analysis-an-analytical-framework-to-inform-social-media-marketing-strategy/

[218] Dye, R. (2000). The buzz on buzz. *Harvard Business Review.* https://hbr.org/2000/11/the-buzz-on-buzz.

[219] *Digital formats are among the most trusted advertising sources despite slow growth.* Nielsen. (2015, September 28). https://www.nielsen.com/us/en/insights/article/2015/digital-formats-are-among-the-most-trusted-advertising-sources-despite-slow-growth/.

[220] Reichheld, F.F., & Schefter, P. (2000, July). E-loyalty: Your secret weapon on the web. *Harvard Business Review.* https://hbr.org/2000/07/e-loyalty-your-secret-weapon-on-the-web.

221 Bruckner, A. (2011). *Scenography / Szenografie: Making spaces talk, projects 2002-2010 Atelier Bruckner* (Bilingual ed.). Avedition Gmbh,Csi.

222 Merriam-Webster. (n.d.). Scenography. In *Merriam-Webster.com*. Retrieved October 22, 2020, from https://www.merriam-webster.com/dictionary/scenography.

223 Godin, S. (2003). *Purple cow: Transform your business by being remarkable.* Portfolio.

224 Ackerman, D. (1991). *A natural history of the senses.* Vintage Books. p. 2.

225 Bouton, M. E. (2018). *Learning and behavior: A contemporary synthesis.* Sinauer Associates.

226 Ringen, J. (2015, August 1). *How Lego became the Apple of toys.* [online] Fast Company. https://www.fastcompany.com/3040223/when-it-clicks-it-clicks.

227 The Associated Press. (2016, February 15). *Lego reports return to profitability in 2005.* NBC News. https://www.nbcnews.com/id/wbna11367083.

228 Solomon, B. (2014, September 4). *Everything is awesome: Lego leaps Barbie for world's largest toy maker.* Forbes. https://www.forbes.com/sites/briansolomon/2014/09/04/everything-is-awesome-lego-leaps-barbie-for-worlds-largest-toy-maker/#5c60e7742991.

229 Hill, N. (2004). *Think and grow rich* (revised and expanded by A.R. Pell). Vermillion. p. 9.

230 Ridderstrale, J., & Nordstrom, K. A. (2002). *Funky business: Talent makes capital dance* (2nd ed.). Financal Times Management. p. 277.

231 Sewell, C., & Brown, P. B. (1990). *Customers for life: How to turn that one-time buyer into a lifetime customer.* Doubleday.

232 Kahneman, D., Fredrickson, B. L., Schreiber, C. A., & Redelmeier, D. A. (1993). When more pain is preferred to less: Adding a better end. *Psychological Science, 4*(6), 401–405. https://doi.org/10.1111/j.1467-9280.1993.tb00589.x

[233] Farber, S. (2001, August 27). *Savviest filmmakers put last things first.* Los Angeles Times. https://www.latimes.com/archives/la-xpm-2001 -aug-27-ca-38811-story.html.

[234] Coleman, A. (2006). *Dictionary of psychology* (2nd. ed.). Oxford University Press.

[235] Otar, C. (2018, October 05). *Council post: How review sites can affect your business (and what you can do about it).* Forbes. https://www.forbes. com/sites/forbesfinancecouncil/2018/10/05/how-review-sites-can-affect-your-business-and-what-you-can-do-about-it/?sh=568582d2266a.

[236] Chase, R. & Dasu, S. (2001, June). Want to perfect your company's service? Use behavioral science. *Harvard Business Review.* https://hbr.org/2001/06/want-to-perfect-your-companys-service-use-behavioral-science.

[237] Dasu, S., & Chase, R. (2013). *The customer service solution: Managing emotions, trust, and control to win your customer's business* (1st ed.). McGraw-Hill Education.

[238] Schwartz, B. (2004). *The paradox of choice.* ECCO.

[239] Bezos, J. P. (2013). *2012 letter to shareholders.* Amazon.com, Inc. https:// s2.q4cdn.com/299287126/files/doc_financials/annual/2012-Shareholder-Letter.pdf.

[240] Dishman, L. (2014, March 7). *Retailers: Your surveys are making customers suffer.* Forbes. https://www.forbes.com/sites/lydiadishman/2014/03/07/retailers-your-surveys-are-making-customers-suffer/?sh=4f7ab06b2b4f.

[241] Dery, K., & Sebastian, I. M. (2017). Building business value with employee experience. *MIT Sloan CISR Research Briefing, 17*(6), 6–9. https://cisr.mit.edu/publication/2017_0601_EmployeeExperience_DerySebastian.

[242] The Ritz-Carlton. (n.d.). *Gold Standards.* https://www.ritzcarlton.com/en/about/gold-standards.

[243] Collins, J. (2001). *Good to great: Why some companies make the leap... and others don't.* Random House. p. 41.

²⁴⁴ Phelps, S. (2015, August 16). *Losing customers over poor service? Lessons from TD Bank & Big Ass Fans on overcoming indifference.* Forbes. https://www.forbes.com/sites/stanphelps/2015/08/16/losing-customers-over-poor-service-lessons-from-td-bank-big-ass-fans-on-overcoming-indifference/?sh=1607ca9a7534.

²⁴⁵ Baumeister, R. F., Bratslavsky, E., Finkenauer, C., & Vohs, K. D. (2001). Bad is stronger than good. *Review of General Psychology, 5*(4), 323–370. https://doi.org/10.1037/1089-2680.5.4.323.

²⁴⁶ Schulze, H., & Merrill, D. (2019). *Excellence wins: A no-nonsense guide to becoming the best in a world of compromise.* Zondervan. p. 49.

²⁴⁷ Parker, S. (2017). *Cross the line: It all starts with a choice.* Give more Media Inc.

²⁴⁸ Berger W. (2014). *A more beautiful question: The power of inquiry to spark breakthrough ideas.* Bloomsbery USA.

²⁴⁹ Manzo, P. (2018, September 23). *Fail faster, succeed sooner (SSIR).* Stanford Social Innovation Review. https://ssir.org/articles/entry/fail_faster_succeed_sooner.

²⁵⁰ Fulghum, R. (1997). *True Love: Stories Told to and by Robert Fulghum.* Harper Collins. p. 98.

²⁵¹ Ellison, S. (Ed.). (2004). *If women ruled the world: How to create the world we want to live in.* Inner Ocean Publishing Inc. p. 90.

²⁵² Villasante, T. R. (1994). *Las ciudades hablan: identidades y movimientos sociales en seis metrópolis latinoamericanas* [Cities speak: identities and social movements in six Latin American metropolises]. Editorial Nueva Sociedad. P. 264.

²⁵³ Medawar, David. Interview. Conducted by Melkart Rouhana, 17 November 2016.

²⁵⁴ *Raise Your Flag english translation.* (n.d.). Abcsonglyrics. https://www.abcsonglyrics.com/man-with-a-mission/raise-your-flag.html.

Lightning Source UK Ltd.
Milton Keynes UK
UKHW020635061121
393477UK00012B/580/J